THE ATLAS OF
LEGENDARY
PLACES

Mont-St-Michel, FRANCE

THE ATLAS OF
LEGENDARY
PLACES

JAMES HARPUR

JENNIFER WESTWOOD

GUILD PUBLISHING
LONDON · NEW YORK · SYDNEY · TORONTO

Editor **James Bremner**   Art Director **David Goodman**
Associate Editor **Anne Kilborn**   Picture Editor **Richard Philpott**
Managing Editor **Ruth Binney**   Production **Barry Baker**
Research **Jazz Wilson**   **Janice Storr**

A Marshall Edition
The Atlas of Legendary Places
was conceived, edited and designed by
Marshall Editions Limited
170 Piccadilly
London W1V 9DD

Copyright © 1989 by Marshall Editions Limited

This edition published 1989 by
Guild Publishing
by arrangement with
Marshall Editions Limited, London
Published in the UK by
Bloomsbury Publishing Limited

Originated by Reprocolor Llovet SA, Barcelona, Spain
Typeset by Servis Filmsetting Limited, Manchester, UK
Printed and bound in Spain by
Printer Industria Gráfica, S.A., Barcelona

1 2 3 4 5 93 92 91 90 89

CN 2529

CONTENTS

INTRODUCTION

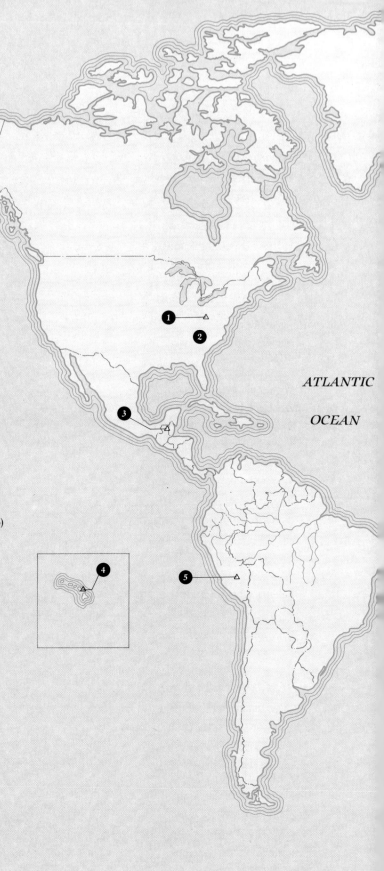

❝*We are the Pilgrims, master; we shall go*
Always a little further: it may be
Beyond that last blue mountain barred with snow,
Across that angry or that glimmering sea,

White on a throne or guarded in a cave
There lives a prophet who can understand
Why men were born: but surely we are brave,
Who make the golden journey to Samarkand.❞

JAMES ELROY FLECKER (1884–1915)

ALL OVER THE WORLD THERE ARE CERTAIN PLACES, CREATED
by nature and man, where beauty and mystique combine
to produce a magical atmosphere. Many of these places
have direct associations with myths and legends, others
have become legendary from some historical circumstance
that has fired the imagination. Some are endowed with a
natural grandeur and, like lodestones, have attracted a
wealth of stories and folk traditions. Others have become
sacred over the centuries from the cumulative attentions of
pilgrims and poets.

A dramatic event or an outstanding individual may have
sown the seed of legend in yet other places. Assisi, for
example, is celebrated as the town of St Francis whose
goodness and mystical communion with nature have
become legendary. Indeed "legend" comes from the Middle
English word *legende*, which meant a story of a saint's life.

This book is a personal selection of sites throughout the
world which have become the stuff of legend. There are
eternal realms, whose fabled existence has inspired poets,
painters and scholars; landscapes imbued with a divine
spirit or numen; sacred ruins ennobled by their settings;
monuments of man, the fruit of his creative imagination;
and shrines which testify to the indomitable human spirit.

In our Brave New World, where rapid change is so often
the keynote, it is refreshing to contemplate places which
have been held sacred for centuries—places whose
resonance continues to draw both pilgrims and dreamers.

ATLANTIC

OCEAN

The map shows *the locations of the places featured in*
this book. Sites are marked by numbers and triangles
which correspond to the list of places (RIGHT).

PACIFIC

OCEAN

INDIAN

OCEAN

1 Serpent Mound (U.S.A)

2 Shenandoah Valley (U.S.A)

3 Tikal (GUATEMALA)

4 Haleakala Crater (HAWAII)

5 Machu Picchu (PERU)

6 The Italian Chapel
(ORKNEY, GREAT BRITAIN)

7 Coventry Cathedral
(GREAT BRITAIN)

8 Tintern Abbey
(GREAT BRITAIN)

9 Glastonbury (Avalon?)
(GREAT BRITAIN)

10 Cadbury Castle (Camelot?)
(GREAT BRITAIN)

11 Altamira (SPAIN)

12 The Alhambra (GRANADA, SPAIN)

13 Stonehenge (GREAT BRITAIN)

14 Mont-St-Michel (FRANCE)

15 Gotland (SWEDEN)

16 Elsinore (HELSINGØR, SWEDEN)

17 Neuschwanstein (WEST GERMANY)

18 Oberammergau (WEST GERMANY)

19 Assisi (ITALY)

20 Delphi (GREECE)

21 Thera (Atlantis?) (GREECE)

22 Arkadi Monastery
(CRETE, GREECE)

23 The Tomb of Tutankhamun
(EGYPT)

24 The Nile (AFRICA)

25 Petra (JORDAN)

26 Cappadocia (TURKEY)

27 Haghia Sophia
(ISTANBUL, TURKEY)

28 Mount Ararat (TURKEY)

29 The Taj Mahal (AGRA, INDIA)

30 The Ganges (INDIA)

31 The Himalayas (ASIA)

32 The Potala (LHASA, TIBET)

33 Shwedagon Pagoda
(RANGOON, BURMA)

34 The Forbidden City
(BEIJING, CHINA)

35 Mount Fuji (JAPAN)

36 Ayers Rock (Uluru)
(AUSTRALIA)

ETERNAL REALMS

*My soul, there is a country
Far beyond the stars....*

HENRY VAUGHAN (1622–1695)

We carry within us all the wonders we seek without us.

SIR THOMAS BROWNE (1605–1682)

According to the Book of Genesis, God created the Garden of Eden, a lush idyllic place where plants and fruit-bearing trees abounded and the first man and woman lived in harmony with animals and birds. Such visions of an earthly paradise, places of wonder and delight, can be found in the myths of other cultures. The Greek philosopher Plato was the first to describe the island of Atlantis, where the inhabitants enjoyed a Golden Age existence of luxury and ease. In the same tradition is Avalon, an island of myth and magic, where enchantresses healed the wounds of those who came to them.

Legends are vague as to the exact locations of these realms—Atlantis lay somewhere beyond the "Pillars of Hercules" (Straits of Gibraltar), Avalon "across the waters to the west"; but explorers and scholars have repeatedly tried to place them. Camelot, King Arthur's capital, has been identified with a hill fort in southern England. Yet, like Atlantis and Avalon, Camelot is as much an *idea* as an actual place, in this case one that symbolized order and harmony. Transcending time and space, eternal realms have inspired writers, poets and artists with a vision of a world more perfect than their own.

THE GARDEN OF EDEN

> ❛ *And the Lord God planted a garden eastward in Eden; and there he put the man whom he had formed.* ❜
>
> GENESIS 2:8.

IN THE SECOND CHAPTER OF GENESIS, THE FIRST book of the Bible, God creates what has become the world's most famous garden—an idyllic, well-watered place, abundant in food and cared for by the first man, Adam. According to Genesis, a river flows through the garden and then, after leaving it, branches into four streams: the Pishon, Gihon, Tigris and Euphrates. For Adam's sake, God creates "every beast of the field, and every fowl of the air" and then a woman, named Eve, to be his partner.

But the peaceful existence of mankind's parents comes to an abrupt end when Eve, tempted by the serpent, disobeys God's order and eats the fruit of the tree of the knowledge of good and evil. Adam is also persuaded to eat the fruit. Because of their disobedience, and to stop them eating from the tree of life, God banishes Adam and Eve from the garden. Now in exile, they can no longer stroll among the shade of trees, pick fruit and watch the sparkling river glide between its banks. Now they must toil for their food from ground bristling with thorns and thistles.

The lost paradise

The garden that Adam and Eve were compelled to leave has fascinated Jews and Christians, theologians, writers and artists down the ages. Yet Genesis gives few details as to what it actually looked like. Its shape, size and exact location are left open to interpretation. The only type of tree that can be inferred from the account in Genesis is the fig, though later tradition identified the tree of life with the palm tree and the tree of knowledge of good and evil with the banana tree.

The garden is often depicted as being enclosed, perhaps because the Greek word *paradeisos*, used to translate the "Garden of Eden", is derived from the Persian for "an enclosed piece of land". Also, the image of an enclosed garden occurs in the Song of Solomon 4:12, where it is applied to the lover addressed in the song: "A garden enclosed is my sister, my spouse; a spring shut up, a fountain sealed."

However, despite the lack of a detailed Biblical description, scholars, commentators, poets and painters have at all times interpreted and amplified the account of the garden in Genesis, often drawing on other traditions of the earthly paradise. One of the oldest accounts of such a place is that of Dilmun, the paradise of the Sumerians of

The Garden of Eden *has for centuries inspired writers and artists to amplify the account of it in the Bible. Although there are few details in Genesis of how the garden looked, it is traditionally depicted as an idyllic, well-watered place, where Adam and Eve lived in harmony with the animals, as depicted (ABOVE) in a painting by the Dutch artist Hieronymus Bosch (?1450–1516).*

The story of Adam and Eve's disobedience and their expulsion from the garden is shown (RIGHT) in a 15th-century French manuscript. Eve eats the forbidden fruit of the tree of the knowledge of good and evil, then persuades Adam to do the same. God rebukes them, and they are expelled from the garden. The wall around the garden is a traditional element not found in Genesis.

An abundance of flowers and fruit-bearing trees characterizes this illustration of the Garden of Eden in Paradisi in sole by John Parkinson, published in 1629. Recognizable among the trees is the palm, traditionally identified with the tree of life.

Most interesting is the depiction of the Scythian lamb (BACKGROUND, CENTRE), which was said to live somewhere in Asia. It was a hybrid creature, composed of a slim, treelike stem on top of which was the body of a lamb. It survived by eating the grass around its stem.

The belief in the lamb's existence came from the need to establish a link between plant and animal life. For at this time there still prevailed the ancient Greek idea of a great chain of being, with all forms of life connected to one another in ascending order from rocks to angels via plants, animals and man.

PARADISI IN SOLE
Paradisus Terrestris.
or
A Garden of all sorts of pleasant flowers which our English ayre will permitt to be noursed vp:
with
A Kitchen garden of all manner of herbes, rootes, & fruites, for meate or sause vsed with vs;
and
An Orchard of all sorte of fruitbearing Trees and shrubbes fit for our Land
together
With the right orderinge planting & preseruing of them. and their vses & vertues
Collected by John Parkinson.
Apothecary of London.
1629

Qui veut parangonner l'artifice a Nature,
Et nos parcs a l'Eden. indiscret il mesure.

Le pas de l'elephant par le pas du ciron,
Et de l'Aigle le vol pareil du moucheron.

Mesopotamia, whose culture flourished during the third millennium B.C. Situated where the sun rises, Dilmun was the abode of the gods, ''where the raven's croak could not be heard'' and where there was no illness, grieving or old age.

There is also a more specific reference to a magical garden in the Sumerian *Epic of Gilgamesh*. In this story, the hero Gilgamesh journeys to a mountaintop ''garden of the gods'', a place where bushes glitter with gems, with fruits of carnelian and leaves of lapis lazuli. Though this garden with its gleaming jewels and mountain setting differs from the Garden of Eden in Genesis, it is reminiscent of ''God's garden'' in the book of Ezekiel. Like the Sumerian garden, Ezekiel's sparkles with gemstones—diamonds, sapphires and emeralds.

The place at the ''world's end''

Of all the non-Biblical sources to influence descriptions of the earthly paradise by later Christian scholars and writers, the most important were the Classical poets. The great Greek epic poet Homer (*c*. eighth century B.C.) described a place called Elysium (or the Elysian Fields) which was said to be ''at the world's end'', where no snow falls, no strong winds blow—only a ''soft refreshing breeze from Ocean''.

Hesiod, probably a contemporary of Homer, introduced in his poem *Works and Days* the notion of a Golden Age—a time in the distant past when men lived happily and peacefully, never growing old, and who were free from toil since, like Adam and Eve, they could live off the fruits of the land. In the same poem, Hesiod mentions the Isles of the Blessed, the abode of the heroes who live a life free from care with their wants supplied by the fertile earth. These isles were, like Homer's Elysium, situated ''at the world's end'', and so the places became identified with each other in the works of later poets.

Homer and Hesiod, and later Classical writers such as the Roman poets Virgil and Ovid, influenced Christian conceptions of the Garden of Eden from the early centuries A.D. to the Renaissance. This was especially true of the great seventeenth-century English poet John Milton (1608–74), in whose epic poem *Paradise Lost* the Garden of Eden is described in vivid detail.

Milton's vision of paradise is a walled plateau on a craggy, wooded mountain. His garden has cascading streams, a steep path

Heracles, the hero of Greek myth, overcomes the dragon guarding the golden apples of the Garden of the Hesperides (BELOW). The garden was situated at ''the world's end'', linking it with Elysium and the Isles of the Blessed. In obtaining the apples, Heracles was fulfilling the penultimate of 12 labours imposed on him by Eurystheus, king of Argos.

The temptation of Eve by the serpent, depicted (LEFT) in a woodcut by the German artist Albrecht Dürer (1471–1528), seems to exhibit motifs similar to those in the Heracles myth (ABOVE). But the two stories differ in their conclusions: for Heracles, the fruit represents the successful goal of a quest; for Adam and Eve the eating of the fruit leads to their expulsion from a state of luxury and ease.

leading up to it, and a guarded gate. There is birdsong in the air which is filled with the perfume of roses and myrtle, myrrh and balm, jasmine, violets, and hyacinths. Shade is provided by palms, cedars and pines. Traditional elements from both Biblical and non-Biblical sources inspire the variety of detail that Milton uses to evoke the garden. Sweet smells, fountains, perpetual springtime, the fertile earth suggest, for example, the Classical Elysium.

The sensual appeal of Milton's garden is also found in the paradise of Islam, which differs from the Garden of Eden in being a

THE GARDEN OF EDEN

heavenly paradise. According to the Koran, god-fearing and steadfast Muslims will be rewarded in the afterlife with gardens with gushing fountains and flowing springs, shade-giving trees (including the palm and the pomegranate) and soft couches to recline on. Dressed in beautiful green silk robes, the blessed will be served food in silver dishes and be attended to by virgins "as fair as rubies and corals".

Actual Islamic gardens, with their limpid pools of water dyed blue by the sky, plashing fountains, scented flowers and shade-giving trees mirror the Koranic paradise. The typical garden, whether in Iran, India, Moorish Spain or elsewhere, was enclosed, rectangular, and divided into four quarters by water channels that met in the centre, symbolizing the four rivers of life.

In search of Eden

While their Muslim counterparts made gardens on earth to re-create paradise above, Christians, up until the sixteenth century, were more concerned with the existence of the earthly paradise of Eden. Interpreting Genesis literally, Churchmen from the first centuries A.D. to the Middle Ages debated whether or not the garden could still be found and, if so, where.

Some thought that Adam and Eve's garden must have been destroyed in the great flood that Noah survived. Others believed it had escaped destruction by being situated on top of a mountain. It was also suggested that the garden lay somewhere in the east, beyond the kingdom of the legendary Christian king Prester John (the location of which was also unknown), or that it lay on an island—Sri Lanka being one of the favourite sites.

During the great age of discovery in the fifteenth and sixteenth centuries, explorers were hopeful of finding the Garden of Eden across the ocean in the east, or to the west in the New World. In fact Christopher Columbus (1451–1506), after his third voyage, came to conceive of the world as being the shape of a rounded pear, or a ball with a nipple-shaped projection on it. He proposed that on top of the pear's stalk or the ball's nipple lay the Garden of Eden "whither no one can go but by God's permission".

Although more and more of the world became charted, no conclusive evidence for either a surviving terrestrial paradise or the site of the destroyed Garden of Eden was found. Since the only specific reference to the garden's location was in Genesis, scholars and writers had to be content to study their Bibles for clues to its whereabouts. The obvious place to start was in Mesopotamia, because Genesis explicitly mentions the rivers Tigris and Euphrates. Mesopotamia, however, was a vast area, and scholars were unable to identify the other two Biblical rivers, the Pishon and Gihon.

Other commentators felt that "eastward, in Eden", meant somewhere to the east of Judea, that is, Syria. Jerusalem itself and Golgotha, the spot where Jesus was crucified,

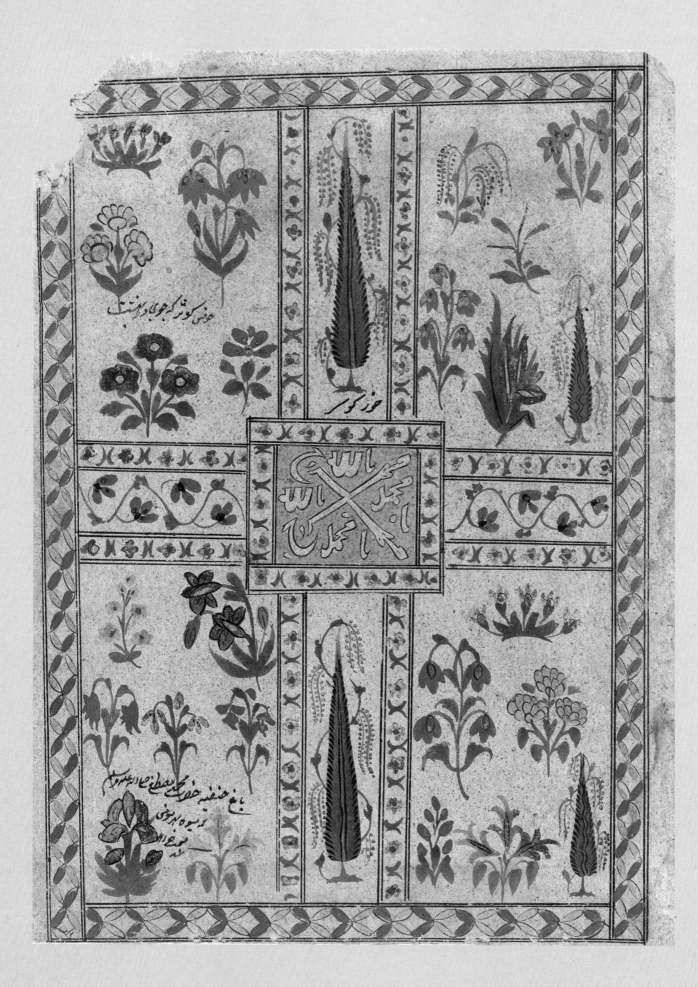

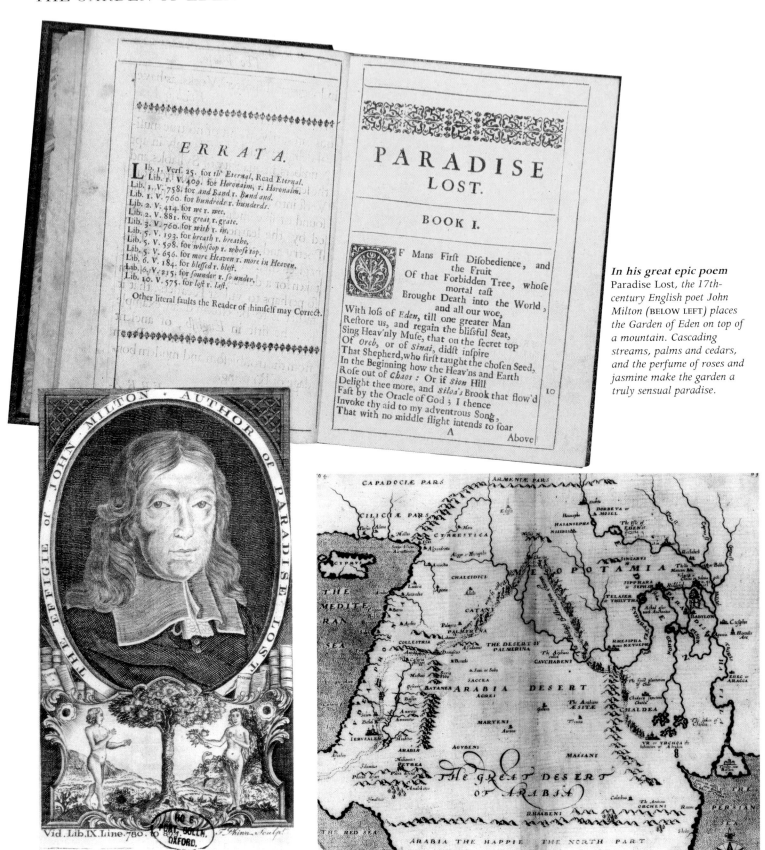

In his great epic poem Paradise Lost, *the 17th-century English poet John Milton (BELOW LEFT) places the Garden of Eden on top of a mountain. Cascading streams, palms and cedars, and the perfume of roses and jasmine make the garden a truly sensual paradise.*

The favourite location *for the Garden of Eden was Mesopotamia, shown in a map (ABOVE) from the* History of the World *by the English explorer Sir Walter Raleigh (?1552–1618). Paradise is marked amid the four rivers stated in Genesis.*

were also identified with the garden. Since Jesus was often typified as the second Adam, it seemed satisfying to link the death of Jesus with the place of Adam's banishment.

Re-creating Eden

The Garden of Eden has never been discovered on this earth; but the archetypal image of Adam and Eve living a Golden Age existence has prompted countless writings and inspired early explorers with the hope of discovering the garden.

Perhaps, as historian John Prest has argued, it was the very failure to find the terrestrial paradise that marked in the west the beginnings of the botanic garden. During the sixteenth and seventeenth centuries, at Padua, Paris, Oxford and elsewhere, such gardens were designed to re-create Eden.

Following the tradition of the enclosed garden of the Song of Songs, these gardens were walled and usually square in shape. Plants, flowers and trees were laid out in symmetrical patterns, often with intricate designs, creating a natural visual harmony.

The botanic garden was usually divided into four equal parts by paths that met in the centre, symbolizing the four corners of the earth, and, now, the four continents of Europe, Asia, Africa and newly discovered America. It was regarded as a place where the far-flung seeds of God's creation could be gathered together as a living encyclopedia. If man could not find the garden that God created, he would create his own garden in the image of God's.

The plan of the botanic garden at Oxford (BELOW), *which was founded in 1621, shows the quadripartite design that symbolizes the four rivers of life and the four continents of Europe, Africa, Asia and America. The botanic gardens were conscious attempts to re-create the Garden of Eden by gathering in one place flowers, shrubs and herbs from all over the world.*

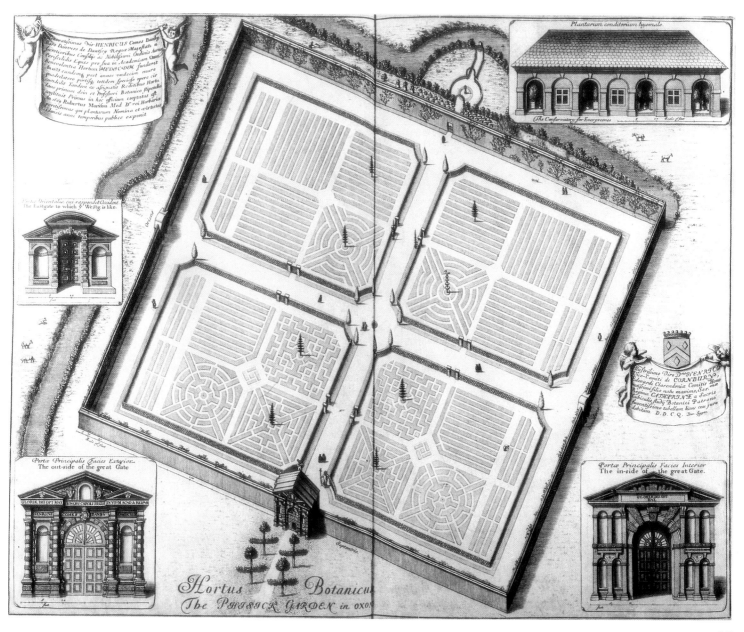

ATLANTIS

AN IDYLLIC GOLDEN AGE, A VAST CONTINENT lost beneath the deeps, a great imperial power swept away overnight by a cataclysmic disaster—the account of the rise and fall of Atlantis by the Greek philosopher Plato has haunted the Western imagination for more than two millennia. In his dialogues *Timaeus* and *Critias*, Plato gives the first written account of this legendary island civilization. He describes Atlantis as a great maritime nation, fabulously wealthy, lying beyond the "Pillars of Heracles" (Straits of Gilbraltar) and dominating the Mediterranean as far as Egypt and Tuscany.

It was a place rich in natural resources: timber, precious metals and stones were as abundant as fruit trees, vegetables and herbs. Magnificent mountains provided shelter from the northern winds, and wild and tame animals, including elephants, roamed among meadows, streams and lakes. Ten kings, all descendants of Poseidon, reigned over the ten regions of this paradisal island, coexisting in perfect accord.

Atlantis, Plato relates, had been given to Poseidon, god of the sea and earthquakes, at the sharing out of the earth. There the god had found a mortal woman named Cleito, living on a hill. He married her and fortified her dwelling place with concentric rings, two of land, three of water. His descendants, the Atlanteans, incorporated these rings into the city they founded on and around Cleito's hill.

On the hill itself they built the royal palace, and in the middle of it, the temple of Poseidon. Surrounded by a golden wall, the temple was faced with silver and adorned with gold pinnacles. Inside it stood a golden statue of the god in his chariot driving six winged horses. Nearby, a hot and a cold spring fed reservoirs and baths. On the two land rings they laid out temples and gardens, exercise grounds for horses and men, and a racecourse. In the harbours, fully equipped triremes lay ready to venture across the seas.

Destruction of the island

But Atlantis and all its splendour was destroyed from within by the corruption of its inhabitants. At first noble and innocent, the Atlanteans in time became power-hungry aggressors, seeking to subjugate neighbouring lands. Eventually, however, they were defeated by the Athenians, and then their island was destroyed by natural forces, earthquake and flood.

The island of Atlantis was, according to legend, destroyed in a great natural disaster. Some scholars identify it with the Greek volcanic island of Thera, destroyed by eruption in about 1500 B.C. The circular rim of Thera's crater is clearly shown in the aerial photograph (ABOVE).

Sheer volcanic cliffs bear witness to the terrible cataclysm that befell Thera. When the island, also known as Santorini, exploded about 3,500 years ago, it was inhabited by people of the Minoan culture. Were they the Atlanteans described by Plato?

The people of Atlantis, which is shown (ABOVE) in a painting by the late Sir Gerald Hargreaves from his book Atalanta *(1949), enjoyed a luxurious Golden Age existence. Plato describes delightful gardens, parks and fountains and buildings adorned with gold and silver. There was also an exercise ground for horses and a racecourse.*

The Greek philosopher Plato, shown with his pupil Aristotle standing to his left, was the first to give an account of Atlantis. Plato claimed his story was true, though Aristotle, for one, did not believe it. Nevertheless, since Plato's time, the Atlantis legend has inspired countless books and theories.

Plato, who died in 347 B.C., claimed that this "true story" had been told about 200 years before his time to the Athenian Solon by the priests of Saïs, the capital of Lower Egypt. Solon passed the story down orally until it reached the ears of Plato, the only ancient source for the tale. He presents it as

fact, but was using it as an allegory to illustrate a point. Aristotle, his most famous pupil, did not believe it. Yet since Plato's day, more than 2,000 books on Atlantis have been published, most accepting Plato's account as true.

The mystery of whether Atlantis actually existed and, if so, where it might have been, has attracted scholars and mystics for centuries. In the sixteenth century, Dr John Dee, Queen Elizabeth I's astrologer, suggested that the newly discovered Americas were Atlantis. In the following century, a Swede named Olof Rudbeck located the great sunken continent in Sweden.

Indeed, over the years, Atlantis has been identified with places ranging from Australia and Brazil to Malta, Britain and Greenland.

In recent times, the American clairvoyant Edgar Cayce (1877–1945) prophesied that temples of Atlantis would be discovered near Bimini in the Bahamas in 1968 or 1969. In 1968, a local Bahamian diver drew attention to what looked like a great stone "pathway" lying on the sea bed off Bimini. The discovery caused great excitement, but whether the Bimini "road" is man-made or natural has not yet been ascertained.

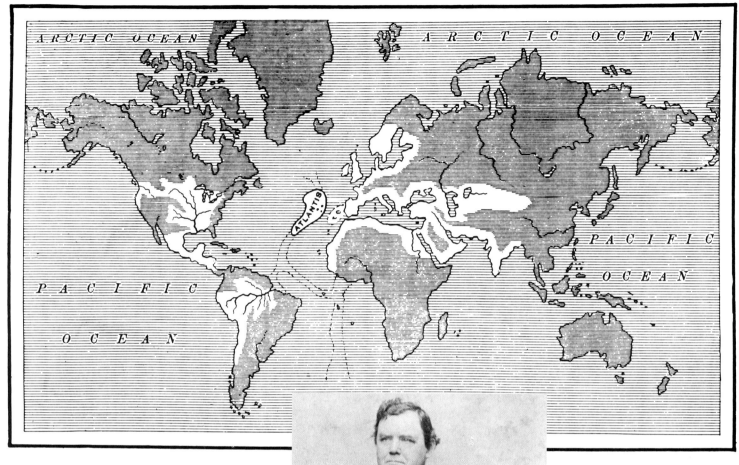

Many Atlantis-hunters still place absolute trust in Plato's statement that the island lay beyond the Straits of Gibraltar. Others think that the description of Atlantis has echoes of the civilization known to have flourished on the Greek island of Thera until it was all but destroyed in a massive volcanic explosion in about 1500 B.C. Excavated Theran pots and frescoes are similar in style to those of the sophisticated Minoan culture of Crete, 75 miles south of Thera.

Atlantis and the Minoans

It is possible that the Thera explosion not only blew the island apart, but precipitated the downfall of Minoan Crete, known to have occurred in about 1450 B.C. Could Plato's story be a garbled tradition of this?

Like the Atlanteans, the Minoans were island-dwellers with shipyards, powerful fleets and a thriving maritime commerce. They had fine houses and superb artefacts, and were skilful builders and engineers— again like the Atlanteans. As in Atlantis, the bull, sacred to Poseidon the earth-shaker, was important in Minoan rituals. Moreover, this rich civilization also seems to have come to a sudden end. If Plato's date for Atlantis,

Ignatius Donnelly (1831–1901), an American scholar and politician, published in 1882 a book on Atlantis which became a classic for those believing in its existence. His map (ABOVE) places the island in the Atlantic Ocean, beyond the Pillars of Hercules, where Plato located it.

9,000 years before Solon, were to lose a zero (a scribal error, perhaps, or storyteller's exaggeration), it would fit neatly into the time-scale of Minoan culture.

But problems remain, not least the fact that Plato explicitly states that Atlantis lay beyond the Pillars of Hercules. Meanwhile, people continue the search for Plato's Utopian island, inspired by its physical beauty and the lives of its Golden Age inhabitants— "for the intents of their hearts were true...."

CAMELOT

IN THE TALES OF MEDIEVAL POETS AND other writers, Camelot was the capital of the realm of King Arthur, the British hero who reigned at the heart of a dazzling court. Here the king lived, surrounded by his Knights of the Round Table—Gawain, Perceval, Lancelot, Galahad and the rest. It is first named as the seat of Arthur's court by the French poet Chrétien de Troyes in the second half of the twelfth century. During the thirteenth, it became prominent in French Romance and from then on was the place where the famous Round Table was housed.

This poets' Camelot lies in a timeless land of enchanted forests and mysterious castles, where marvels and magic abound. Here Arthur, with his queen Guinevere beside him, resides at the head of a chivalric order based on that of early medieval France. Meanwhile, Arthur's knights set out on quests, do battle with monsters, rescue damsels from the clutches of evil wizards, or become embroiled with seductive ladies who turn out to be fairies. They run the gauntlet of physical and supernatural dangers, and at the beginning and end of every adventure stands Camelot, the hub of their universe.

The description of this Camelot of Romance is that of a medieval castle with a town below it, though its location is never quite made clear. Sir Thomas Malory, writing in the fifteenth century, identified it with the town of Winchester in southern England, because this was the capital of the Saxon kings from the time of Alfred the Great (849–99) to the Norman Conquest (1066). But even Malory is inconsistent, and once places it beyond Carlisle, in the north of England.

A symbol of order

Camelot is nowhere and everywhere, less a historical place than an idealized city. It became a symbol from the Middle Ages of order amid chaos, of the ideal state versus anarchy, of civilization versus barbarism. It began and ended with Arthur—no one reigned there before him and some medieval authors say that, after his death, King Mark of Cornwall destroyed it. Yet, like Arthur himself, it is imperishable.

The twelfth-century English writer Geoffrey of Monmouth supplies the first real picture of Arthur's court, and sets it, not at Camelot, but at Caerleon in South Wales. Caerleon was the site of an important Roman legionary fortress and boasts perhaps the finest Roman amphitheatre in Britain. In

Cadbury Castle, *a hill fort at South Cadbury in Somerset, has been identified with Camelot, the legendary capital of King Arthur, since at least the 16th century. According to a later folk tradition, every Christmas and Midsummer Eve, Arthur and his knights rode over the top of the hill and down to water their horses at a spring in the nearby village of Sutton Montis.*

Built by British Celts in the last centuries B.C., Cadbury was refortified toward the end of the 6th century A.D. The elaborate nature of the new structure suggests the presence of a powerful leader or prince. The date coincides with that proposed by scholars for a historical Arthur.

WALES

ENGLAND

Caerleon

Glastonbury

Cadbury Castle
(CAMELOT?)

Winchester

ENGLISH CHANNEL

King Arthur's famous Round Table was, according to medieval writers, housed at Camelot. The 12th-century English poet Layamon suggested the king chose this shape to prevent disputes among his knights over precedence. However, it is unlikely that any table could have seated as many as 1,600 people, as Layamon said, or even 140—the lowest estimate.

Some medieval artists depicted the table as annular, as in this 14th-century manuscript, in which Arthur and his companions see a vision of the Holy Grail. Like Camelot itself, the Round Table became a symbol. It represented the unity of Arthur's knights, necessary to the order of his kingdom. When that unity was broken, anarchy overtook the ideal realm.

Geoffrey's day, the ruins of baths and hypercausts (central heating systems) could still be seen; he probably chose the town for Arthur's court simply because he knew it well, and it looked as if it once had been splendid enough for Arthur's city.

Geoffrey tells how Arthur kept Whitsun at Caerleon in a celebration lasting four days, during which he wore his crown and was attended by his sub-kings, nobles and bishops—like a Norman king of Geoffrey's time. Among the knights present were Bedivere and Kay, and the four days were passed in tournaments and other entertainments.

Caerleon, Geoffrey writes, is situated on the River Usk, which "flowed by it on one side, and up this the kings and princes who were to come from across the sea could be carried in a fleet of ships. On the other side, which was flanked by meadows and wooded groves, they had adorned the city with royal palaces, and by the gold-painted gables of its roofs it was a match for Rome." His account of Caerleon became the basis for descriptions of Camelot and is essentially the one known today through illustrators and film-makers, though now it is generally shown as a pinnacled castle, with pennants flying, of the High Middle Ages.

The hill fort at Cadbury

The name "Camelot", used by medieval writers, led later antiquarians to identify it with locations with similar sounding names. Some said it was Roman *Camulodunum*, Colchester in Essex; others located it near Tintagel in Cornwall, reputedly Arthur's birthplace, in a district through which runs the River Camel. However, the place with the strongest claim to be the "real" Camelot is Cadbury Castle at South Cadbury in Somerset, near the village of Queen Camel and overlooking the little River Cam.

The first person to identify Cadbury with Camelot in print was the King's Antiquary John Leland, who, in 1542, wrote: "At the very south end of the church of South-Cadbyri standeth Camallate, sometime a famous town or castle. . . ." However, the local people seemed to know very little about this, and Leland perhaps jumped to the conclusion that it was Camelot because of the village name Camel. But it is just possible that he had heard a genuine tradition going back centuries.

For if a historical Arthur ever existed behind the one of legend and romance, he

Arthur did not die, according to one tradition, but sleeps beneath the Eildon Hills (OPPOSITE PAGE) in the Scottish Borders. Here an old man, who some say is the magician Merlin, gathers together horses for Arthur for when he wakes. Merlin is portrayed here by the 19th-century British artist Aubrey Beardsley.

A vision of turrets and spires is how the 19th-century French artist Gustave Doré depicted Arthur's castle at Caerleon, South Wales.

would probably have been a British war leader of the fifth century following the Roman period. Cadbury is today recognized as the largest and most formidable of known British strongholds of the period, and is considered to be the headquarters of a king who could marshal resources unequalled in the Britain of his time.

Unlike the castles of the Middle Ages, Cadbury was simply a hill which had been fortified with earthen ramparts and ditches by British Celts during the last centuries B.C. Excavations have shown that the fort remained untouched during the Roman occupation of southern Britain beginning in A.D. 43, but was stormed and captured by the Romans two decades later. They cleared out its inhabitants, and for about 400 years the fort stood more or less empty. When the legions withdrew, a native leader of some wealth reoccupied it. Toward the end of the sixth century, a timber hall was built on the plateau on top of the hill and new defences superimposed on the upper rampart. These were elaborate, clearly needing much labour, and thus raised the question of who at this time had the necessary manpower. Could it have been Arthur?

Certainly, after Leland, there were many traditions connecting Arthur with Cadbury. The most striking of these is that on top of the hill, near the traces of the timber hall, was a spot that, by the end of the sixteenth century, was known as King Arthur's Palace.

The last battle

Many years ago, a farmer digging in a field near the River Cam found skeletons huddled

King Arthur is shown as one of the Nine Worthies in a French tapestry (LEFT) made in about 1385 probably by Nicolas Bataille of Paris. The Worthies were, traditionally, 3 pagan, 3 Jewish and 3 Christian heroes, including Alexander the Great, Julius Caesar, Judas Maccabeus and Charlemagne.

Riding with his knights beside him, Arthur returns to Camelot in this late 15th-century Flemish manuscript. The popular conception of Camelot is of a fairytale castle with pinnacles and pennants flying. Here it is a fortified city of the period, entered through a high-arched gate.

together. Some people think this discovery supports the claim that, besides being Camelot, South Cadbury was the scene of Arthur's last battle. The historical evidence for this battle comes in the tenth-century *Annals of Wales*, in which, under the date A.D. 539, appears the entry: "The strife of Camlann in which Arthur and Medraut perished."

The information was quite possibly derived from earlier annals contemporary with the event, and it is the closest those seeking Arthur ever come to solid ground. The name Camlann is probably derived from the old British word *Camboglanna*, "crooked bank", that is, of a winding river. A strong case has been made therefore for the scene of the last battle having been the Roman fort of *Camboglanna* on Hadrian's Wall, possibly modern Birdoswald above the winding River Irving.

Arthurian landscapes

But when Geoffrey of Monmouth came to tell the story of the battle, he knew that Welsh tradition implied a Camlann in or near Cornwall, and chose the River Camel in that county. By the sixteenth century, a water-meadow near Slaughter Bridge, which crosses the Camel about a mile above Camelford, was believed to be the site. Upstream from Slaughter Bridge on the bank of the Camel can still be seen "King Arthur's Tomb", a flat stone slab which, in the sixteenth century, was thought by locals to bear Arthur's name and mark his grave. Malory, on the other hand, sets the last battle on "a down beside Salisbury", not far from *his* Camelot, Winchester.

The truth is that over the centuries tales of Arthur so captured the national imagination that every region wanted to lay claim to him; and many landscape features were linked with him. This is the Arthur, not of Romance, but of myth and legend, often a titanic figure capable of throwing the many Arthur's Quoits—prehistoric burial chambers, nine of which are found in Wales alone; or of sitting in Arthur's Seat, the great volcanic rock that towers over Edinburgh.

This is the Arthur, too, who is not dead but sleeps in a mysterious underground place surrounded by his knights. Several Arthur's Caves in Wales conceal him; and he is also said to sleep under castles and hills in more than a dozen places in northern England and Scotland. Among these are Sewingshields Castle, which once stood beside Hadrian's Wall, and the Eildon Hills in the Scottish Borders.

In the south he rests under Cadbury Castle, in a cavern closed with iron gates. Here, according to local lore, on one night of the year when they stand open, it is possible to see him inside. The firm conviction that Arthur had never died apparently survived here, within sight of Glastonbury (where, in 1191, Arthur's "official" grave was said to have been found) into the nineteenth century: it is reported that one of the villagers anxiously asked a group of antiquaries, who had come to Cadbury to see "Camelot", if they were going to take out the king. Even if there never was a Camelot, nor an Arthur, nevertheless they have both certainly achieved true immortality.

Arthur's last battle, "the strife at Camlann", is depicted in a 14th-century manuscript (LEFT). Here Arthur, mortally wounded, is being taken away from the fighting in a cart. In front of him rides a knight who appears to be Sir Bedivere, carrying Arthur's legendary sword, Excalibur.

Dozmary Pool on Bodmin Moor in Cornwall (BELOW LEFT) was, according to a late tradition, the lake into which the mortally wounded Arthur asked Sir Bedivere to throw his sword Excalibur.

This 14th-century Dutch manuscript shows the hand of the Lady of the Lake, which rose above the surface, caught the sword and drew it down beneath the water. Arthur sits dolefully on the shore.

A weathered inscription on this flat stone slab near Slaughter Bridge on the banks of the River Camel in Cornwall led to speculation that it marked King Arthur's tomb.

According to a 12th-century tradition, his last battle was fought along this river. In the 16th century a meadow near Slaughter Bridge, just above Camelford, was pinpointed as the battle site. Although in Tudor times the slab was thought to bear Arthur's name, closer examination has revealed that the name is, in fact, Latinus.

AVALON

A PARADISE WHERE IT WAS ALWAYS SPRING
and no one grew old; where there was
everlasting peace; and where no toil was
needed because the land remained ever
fruitful: this was Avalon. As well as resembling other mythical realms, such as Atlantis,
where the inhabitants enjoyed a Golden Age
existence, Avalon became known as the place
to which the British hero King Arthur was
carried to be healed of his wounds after his
last battle of Camlann.

The twelfth-century English writer Geoffrey of Monmouth was the man who popular-
ized the connection of Arthur with Avalon in
his imaginative *History of the Kings of Britain.*
The book became a medieval bestseller,
establishing Avalon as the name of Arthur's
last known destination. In a later book, the
Life of Merlin, Geoffrey describes Avalon as
an island: "It is called the Fortunate Isle. . . .
Grain and grapes are produced without
tending, and apple trees grow in the woods
from the close-clipped grass. The earth of its
own accord brings forth . . . all things in
superabundance. . . ." The island was inhabited by nine sorceresses and ruled by
their leader Morgen (Morgan le Fay), who
undertook to heal Arthur if he stayed there.

In 1191, at a time when the legends of King
Arthur were widely popular, the question of
what had happened to him thereafter took a
new turn. The monks of Glastonbury, a town
in the west of England, announced that they
had exhumed his remains from the graveyard
of their ancient Abbey, together with a
leaden cross which proclaimed in Latin,
"Here lies entombed the renowned King
Arthur with Guinevere his second wife in the
Isle of Avalon."

The grave of King Arthur?
Though the monks had probably exhumed
someone (archeologists have found traces of
their digging), could it have been King
Arthur? What casts doubt on the monks'
"discovery" is that it took place not long
after a disastrous fire had destroyed the
oldest and holiest part of Glastonbury
Abbey. This was a small wattle and daub
church of great antiquity, known simply as
the "Old Church". Lost with the Old Church

The island of Avalon, where the wounded King
Arthur was taken, has been identified with
Glastonbury, Somerset, since the alleged discovery of
Arthur's grave at Glastonbury Abbey in 1191.
Glastonbury Tor (RIGHT), rising above marshy land, in
early times gave the impression of being an island.

30

AVALON

In the Middle Ages, Glastonbury gave rise to a number of legends and fairytales. This was probably because of its mysterious tor, almost certainly a pagan site in earlier times, and its abbey (BELOW), the origins of which were so old they had been forgotten.

Shrouded in mystery, but of palpable sanctity, the abbey acquired Otherworld connotations through its ancient graveyard, which dated back to the beginnings of Christianity in Britain. It contained the remains of several early kings and saints and was a most suitable place for Arthur to be buried.

were the abbey's treasures, including holy relics, which gave it status and a source of income. The need to restore prestige and attract pilgrims was acute.

The discovery was also suspiciously convenient for the Anglo-Norman rulers of England. Two or three years later, the chronicler Gerald of Wales wrote that Henry II had encouraged the Glastonbury monks to make the search for Arthur's grave: "Many tales are told . . . about King Arthur and his mysterious ending. . . . The fairy-tales have been snuffed out. . . ." This would have been precisely Henry's intention.

Early references to Arthur's death all state that his grave was unknown. The historian William of Malmesbury had pinpointed the problem in 1125, when he wrote that "the tomb of Arthur is nowhere seen, whence ancient rhymes fable that he is yet to come". Because there was no proof that he was dead, the Celtic Bretons, Cornish and Welsh expected him to return and free them from the yoke of the Norman kings.

Henry, who ruled on both sides of the English Channel, had experienced trouble with the Bretons and the Welsh, and it was in his interest to demonstrate once and for all that Arthur had died. To have established his grave on English soil would have been a political triumph.

The interests of Church and State coincided. Arthur's "grave" was widely publicized, and to reconcile it with the story of Arthur in Geoffrey's *History*, Glastonbury was identified with Avalon.

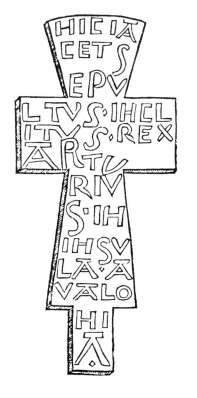

This was made easier by the fact that Glastonbury was—and still is—possessed by what Arthurian expert Geoffrey Ashe has called "a lingering sense of 'otherness'". Imbued with a thousand years of Christian prayer and perhaps with as many years of pagan worship before that, it fitted people's idea of Avalon. Moreover, since it was completely surrounded by marsh, which was often covered with standing water, Glastonbury, with its tor rising high above the landscape, was virtually an island.

Arthur and "Riothamus"

Geoffrey's picture of the magical island of Avalon inhabited by sorceresses seems to merge historical facts with strands of Otherworld lore. He explains its name as being derived from an old British word aval, "apple", and meaning "island of apples". This is disputed by scholars, but if Geoffrey were right, Avalon would be in the tradition of mythical islands connected with apples.

Ashe suggests that behind the figure of Arthur may lie the man known in historical records as "Riothamus", called "King of the Britons". In A.D. 468, Riothamus took his troops to Gaul and campaigned there on behalf of the Roman Empire. In a final battle, he was defeated. With the remnants of his army he escaped to Burgundian territory, and is heard of no more.

"Riothamus" appears to be not a name but a title in British—Rigotamos, "supreme king". His career shows similarities with Arthur's and the date is right for a historical

Arthur, who, if he existed, was probably a British war lord immediately after the Roman period. Also, Riothamus' line of retreat was in the direction of the Burgundian town of Avallon. This Avallon was not an island; and this idea may derive from the tradition of the healing sanctuary said by the Classical geographer Pomponius Mela in the first century A.D. to be on the island of Sein off the coast of Brittany. Here, as on Geoffrey's island, lived nine enchantresses, who cured the ills of all who sought their help.

Paradisal islands

Geoffrey's Avalon follows the tradition of the paradisal islands that in mythology lay somewhere to the west. These include Atlantis; the Garden of the Hesperides with their golden apples and the Fortunate Islands of the Greeks; and St Brendan's Isle, described in the ninth-century *Voyage of St Brendan*, which was covered in apple trees. By calling Avalon the Fortunate Isle, Geoffrey was connecting it with mythical islands associated with apples, probably because they were the fruit of immortality in Celtic and other mythologies.

If Henry II really tried to eradicate the belief in Arthur's survival, he failed. In 1190 the English poet Layamon wrote: ''The Britons believe yet that he [Arthur] is alive, and dwelleth in Avalun with the fairest of all elves.'' The related belief that Arthur slept in a cave or under a hill, surrounded by his knights, is known to have survived in Britain as late as the nineteenth century.

Like Camelot, Avalon is everywhere and nowhere—it is contrary to its spirit to try to pin it down. It lies in the dimension of myth, where truth is manifold. The historical Arthur may have been buried at Glastonbury; but the real Arthur waits in that place where ''healing does not fail''—the place which Geoffrey called Avalon.

*The Death of Arthur (*LEFT*) by the 19th-century British artist James Archer. According to Sir Thomas Malory, writing in the 15th century, Arthur was taken to Avalon in a mysterious boat in which were women in black hoods—among them 3 queens.*

***Avalon belongs to a long tradition** of paradisal islands, ''somewhere to the west''. One of these was St Brendan's Isle, supposedly in the Atlantic near the Azores, which was last seriously searched for in the 18th century. It is described in* The Voyage of St Brendan *(*RIGHT*), probably written in the 9th century.*

Brendan was an Irish monk who went on a sea voyage that lasted from 565 to 573, during which he appears to have visited Iona and the west of Scotland. However, though Brendan certainly existed, much of his Voyage *is legendary. It was a Christian version of an Irish literary genre known as the* immram, *which involved visits to magical Otherworld islands.*

TIMELESS LANDSCAPES

All things are full of gods.

THALES (*c.*636–*c.*546 B.C.)

Golden lie the meadows; golden run the streams; red gold is on the pine-stems. The sun is coming down to earth, and walks the fields and the waters.

GEORGE MEREDITH (1828–1909)

*T*he natural world is a source of wonder and awe, of history and legend. Mountains, rivers and valleys continue to draw travellers and pilgrims to where heroes and gods have walked. The Himalayas, mightiest of the world's mountain ranges, are the abode of the gods in Hindu and Buddhist traditions. Associated with the giant crater of Haleakala is the Polynesian god Maui, who is said to have lassoed the sun's rays as they passed over the rim of the crater. Only when the sun promised to move more slowly through the skies did he release it.

The great rivers of the world run strong with spirit and power. The Ganges, the holiest river in the Hindu religion, is held to be the embodiment of Ganga, the goddess of purification, while the Nile is Egypt's very lifeblood—its waters a source of fertility and sustenance for body and mind.

As the pace of the modern world increases, these precious landscapes, seemingly timeless, refresh the human spirit with their beauty. While palaces, temples and other works of man in time turn to dust, the great monuments of nature endure, landmarks of the past and the future.

MOUNT ARARAT

> *And the ark rested in the seventh month, on the seventeenth day of the month, upon the mountains of Ararat.*
>
> GENESIS 8:4.

IN EASTERN TURKEY, NEAR THE BORDERS WITH Iran and the U.S.S.R., the clouds are pierced by a snow-topped mountain which soars 17,000 feet into the sky. Ağrı Dağı, traditionally known as the Biblical Mount Ararat, rises suddenly from a dusty, rugged plain which emphasizes the mountain's elegant pyramidal form. Crowning this giant is the zone of perpetual snow—"a cap of dazzling silver"—which was, according to tradition, the resting place of Noah's ark.

For centuries, local Armenians and Persians were convinced that Ararat could not be scaled. This was partly due to its height and daunting snowcap, but also because the mountain had taken on an almost mystical aura. For example, when James Morier, a British diplomat and traveller, visited the Ararat region at the start of the nineteenth century, he heard stories that the mountain was inhabited by "snow worms"—small white worms so cold that they could "effectively cool a large bowl of sherbet".

Apart from mythical creatures, there were dangerous wild ones to contend with, including poisonous snakes and spiders, lynxes, leopards, bears and wild boars. There were also reports that a dragon was threatening travelling merchants, who had also to brave brigands and outlaws. But despite these hazards, Morier describes Ararat in terms that capture its time-honoured beauty and mystique: "It is perfect in all its parts, no hard rugged feature . . . every thing is in harmony. . . ."

The cataclysmic flood

Today, despite dangers from avalanches and wild dogs, it is quite possible to climb Ararat and see the same eternal landscape of valleys, plains and distant mountains that existed in Biblical times. The linking of Ararat with Noah's ark is made in Genesis, the first book of the Bible. According to this account, God became so dismayed with the wickedness of the human race that he decided to wipe it out with a cataclysmic flood. Only a man named Noah was to be spared. So God warned Noah to build a boat to house his family and the birds and animals of the earth.

Mount Ararat, the traditional resting place of Noah's ark, has been identified with the Turkish mountain Ağrı Dağı from before the Christian era. Its magnificent snow-capped peak soars 17,000 feet above a rugged plain in eastern Turkey.

Then for 40 days and nights the rains came until the whole earth was flooded. Eventually, the waters began to subside and Noah's ark landed on the mountains of Ararat. Eventually, Noah and his family and the animals emerged, and began to repopulate the earth.

In fact, the Bible does not specify which mountain of the ancient land of Ararat the ark landed on. But it is unsurprising that the towering Ağrı Dağı was identified with Noah in local Armenian tradition before the Christian era.

Morier asserted "no one since the flood seems to have been on the summit, for the rapid ascent of its snowy top would appear to render such an attempt impossible". However, the first man to prove Morier wrong was a 37-year-old German professor named Friedrich Parrot.

In September 1829, accompanied by five others, including a Russian soldier who wore

*"**And it came to pass** at the end of 40 days, that Noah opened the window of the ark which he had made: and . . . sent forth a dove from him, to see if the waters were abated from off the face of the ground." Genesis, the first book of the Bible, describes the sending out of the dove, an episode illustrated (*RIGHT*) by the 19th-century French artist Gustave Doré.*

Genesis relates that the dove returned to the ark because the world was still flooded. Seven days later, it was sent out again, and this time came back with an olive leaf in its beak. After another seven days, Noah sent out the dove once more: the bird did not return, indicating that the land was dry enough for Noah, his family and the animals to set out and begin to repopulate the earth.

his best dress uniform beneath his cloak out of respect for the venture, the German reached the top at his third attempt. It was a marvellous moment. Speculating on the exact spot where the ark might have landed, Parrot surveyed the awe-inspiring view of the valley of the Araxes, with the town of Erivan a dark spot "no bigger than my hand". The occasion was marked by the raising of a wooden cross, and a drink of wine to toast Noah, the father of viticulture.

Searchers for the lost ark

However, such was Ararat's reputation that many people refused to believe Parrot's account of his ascent. In the following years, a handful of other expeditions scaled the heights, including, in 1876, one led by James Bryce, a British historian and statesman. Bryce was one of the first to spot a possible relic of the ark—a piece of wood cut by a tool and found well above the tree line.

Over the years, other visitors to Ararat, including a Nestorian churchman in 1893, a Russian aviator in 1916, and a French indus-

James Bryce (LEFT), *the British historian and statesman, led an expedition in 1876 to scale Ararat, shown* (BELOW LEFT) *in an engraving from the frontispiece of Bryce's book* Transcaucasia and Ararat.

Setting out in the late summer heat with an escort of Cossacks, Bryce was led on by "the sight of the glittering peak above, which was now, like an Eastern beauty, beginning to draw over its face the noonday veil of cloud. . . ." He ended up completing the last stages of the ascent by himself and eventually stood alone on the summit.

Afterward Bryce wrote of his sublime experience: "If it was indeed here that man first set foot again on the unpeopled earth, one could imagine how the great dispersion went as the races spread themselves from these sacred heights along the courses of the great rivers down to the Black and Caspian Seas. . . . No more imposing centre of the world could be imagined."

trialist in 1955, have also either seen something resembling the ark or brought back intriguing bits of wood. But radiocarbon testing of the wood fragments found so far does not indicate the great antiquity that would place them in the time of Noah. Alternatively, it has been suggested that the pieces of wood may have come from medieval relics (perhaps a model ark) left by monks for whom Ararat was a place of pilgrimage.

It seems an impossible task to prove or disprove the historical foundation of the ark story. Nevertheless, if there were some truth in the Biblical account of Noah, then Mount Ararat would certainly be a fitting place for the second beginning of mankind.

THE NILE

❦ *It flows through
old hushed Egypt
and its sands,
Like some grave
mighty thought,
threading a dream....* ❧

BRITISH WRITER JAMES LEIGH HUNT
(1784–1859), IN HIS POEM "THE NILE".

THE NILE, A SYMBOL OF REBIRTH AND ETERNAL life to the ancient Egyptians, has for untold centuries been the lifeblood of their country. The river and its banks appear from the air to be one long green ribbon of fertility snaking through the arid desert. This ribbon *is* Egypt: the Nile's bounty created it, and made possible the rise of one of the world's great civilizations.

From its most remote headstream, the Nile is, at 4,160 miles, the longest river in the world. Its twin sources lie deep in Africa. The White Nile rises from the headwaters of Lake Victoria, and flows north to Khartoum in Sudan, where it merges with the shorter but more powerful Blue Nile. Where the waters meet, it is possible to see the junction between the bluish waters of the Blue Nile and the clear, pale green of the White.

From Khartoum the river flows north to Cairo, where it divides into two main channels, one of which empties itself into the Mediterranean Sea at Damietta, about 40 miles from Port Said; the other proceeds to Rashid (formerly Rosetta). It was here, in 1799, that the famous Rosetta stone was found which helped in the decipherment of Egyptian hieroglyph. Between these two arms stretches the Nile Delta, 14,500 square miles of farmland created by rich alluvial deposits.

The "gift of the Nile"

To the Egyptians, the Nile was, and still is, the hub of their lives. It made the crops grow, it provided fish and the valuable papyrus-reed, and could be used as a river highway. The people's reverence for the river can be heard in *The Hymn to Nile*, which was probably composed during the time of the Middle Kingdom (*c.*2050–1750 B.C.): "Hail O Nile, who issues forth from the earth, who comes to give life to the people of Egypt." The Greek historian Herodotus neatly summed up the relationship between country and river: "Egypt is the gift of the Nile."

Ancient Egypt was originally called by its inhabitants Kemet, meaning "black", because of the contrast between the dark alluvial fields created by the silt of the floods

For centuries the Nile has been the life-giving artery of Egypt. From the land nourished by its waters arose the great civilization of ancient Egypt, with its golden temples and pyramids. Today visitors can cruise between its palm-lined banks on voyages into the past.

THE NILE

The Nile was, and still is, an important means of transport for the people of Egypt. The elegant triangular sails of feluccas (RIGHT) are still as much in evidence as they were when the 19th-century British artist David Roberts painted them (BELOW RIGHT) in a view looking toward the ruins of Luxor. Of the feluccas Roberts recorded in his diary: "Nothing to the painter can exceed in beauty these craft skimming along the river with their white sails spread and shivering in the wind."

and the tawny desert that stretched beyond as far as the eye could see. The Egyptians also seem to have thought of all rivers in terms of the Nile. For example, an inscription on a royal stele of the late sixteenth century B.C. describes the Euphrates, the great Mesopotamian river that flows from north to south, as: "that reversed water that goes downstream in going upstream". In other words, any river that flowed in the opposite direction to the Nile was going the wrong way.

The most vital characteristic of the Nile for Egypt's inhabitants, from remote prehistory up to 1971, was its annual inundation. This gift of the river came about from African rains and the thawing of snow on the Ethiopian highlands which brought tremendous torrents of water north into Egypt: the

river drowned the adjacent fields and left them, as the waters drained away, coated with rich and fertile topsoil. It was this fertility that nourished the ancient Egyptian civilization.

The Roman writer Seneca described how welcome the flooded river was to the Egyptian people: "It is a most beautiful sight when the Nile overflows onto the fields. The plains vanish, the valleys are hidden. Only the towns stick out like islands. The sole means of communicating is by boat; and the more the land is submerged, the greater the people's joy."

In the days of the pharaohs, the Nile supported the lives of millions of people in its passage through the country. There were, of course, bad years, when the inundations failed, as they did during the Seven Lean Years, which traditionally occurred in the reign of Djoser, a king of the Third Dynasty (c. twenty-eighth century B.C.).

But mostly the river provided its dependants with a good life—at least for the upper classes, judging by the verses written to celebrate the new capital of the pharaohs of the Nineteenth Dynasty in the northeast Delta, the Biblical Rameses: "The Residence is pleasant in life; its field is full of everything good; it is (full) of supplies and food every day, its ponds with fish, and its lakes with birds. Its meadows are verdant with grass; its banks bear dates. . . . Its granaries are (so) full of barley and emmer (that) they come near to the sky. Onion and leeks are for food, and lettuce of the garden, pomegranates, apples,

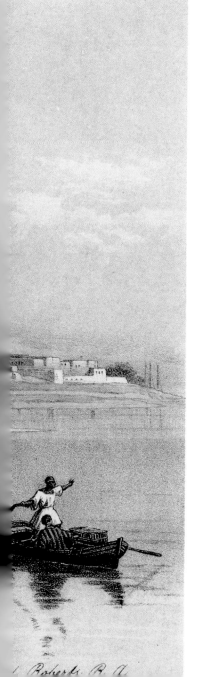

Egypt has been irrigated by the waters of the Nile for thousands of years. Shadufs (LEFT) were introduced during the time of the New Kingdom (c.1567–1085 B.C.). A bucket is dipped into the water and then lifted by means of a counterweight. This primitive machine is still used, especially in Upper Egypt, though it is effective only for light irrigation.

Hapi, the god of the Nile (TOP), was represented as a man with a beard and female breasts, indicative of his fertility. In popular belief he supplied the waters of the annual inundation from his bottomless jar.

An Egyptian nobleman and his wife pay homage to Osiris (ABOVE), a god associated with the Nile. The ornamental pool was an important feature of the rich Egyptian's garden, the water for which was raised by shadufs from canals.

and olives, figs of the orchard, sweet wine of Ka-of-Egypt, surpassing honey. . . .'' (Translation by John A. Wilson.)

Ka-of-Egypt, a well known vineyard of the Delta, and the abundance of vegetables and fruit alluded to here would not have existed but for the Nile.

Agriculture in the region has progressed since that time: seed is no longer trampled into the ground by rams, or, as Herodotus observed in the fifth century B.C., by pigs. Some of the old implements are still in daily use, for example the shaduf, introduced in the New Kingdom (c.1567–1085 B.C.). This simple mechanism enabled a bucket to be dipped into the water and then raised by means of a counterweight. In the years following its invention it significantly increased the amount of land under cultivation, and it is still used by Egyptians today.

But the most dramatic change in recent years has come as a result of the Aswan High Dam, constructed in 1971, and the consequent creation of Lake Nasser, the largest man-made lake in the world. All-year-round irrigation is now possible; however, the great annual inundation is no more, the flow of the river has been dramatically reduced, and the silt, which down the centuries has served Egypt so well, is held back.

In some places the desert is regaining ground: where groves of date palms once cast a cool shade, now only a few parched fronds wave from the top of the encroaching dunes, and green fields are being devoured by the blowing sand.

The gods of life

Everyday life in ancient Egypt was underpinned by a network of religious observances and rituals. The river was associated with a number of gods, its own particular deity being Hapi, Great Lord of Provisions, Lord of Fishes. In popular belief, Hapi was responsible for the floods, supplying the waters of inundation from his bottomless jar as he sat in a cavern below the mountains of Aswan, guarded by serpents. Sacrifices were made yearly at Gebel Silsila to ensure that he tilted his jar at the proper angle: a little too far could mean a deluge, while not far enough would bring drought and famine upon the land.

A statue of Hapi, now in the Vatican Museum in Rome, shows him with 16 children, each 1 cubit tall. This symbolizes the fact that, if the annual flood failed to reach 16 cubits (about 25 feet), then the land would not flourish and the people would go hungry.

Hapi embodies the Nile, but the river was also bound up with the life and death of

Beyond fields made green and fertile by the Nile, the glory of ancient Egypt—the great pyramids of Giza, near Cairo—tower in the distance. The largest of these three colossal structures, which date from the middle of the 3rd millennium B.C., is the Pyramid of Cheops: it is nearly 500 feet high and comprises an estimated $2\frac{1}{2}$ million blocks of limestone.

Osiris the god of the Underworld. Symbolically, the story of Osiris mirrors that of the great river. While King of Egypt he was murdered by his evil brother Set, and the pieces of his body scattered throughout the land. His queen, Isis, after a painstaking search, collected the dismembered limbs and revived him. After his resurrection, a son was born to them—namely Horus, the next King of Egypt and later also a god. Osiris then descended to rule the Underworld.

The life and death of Osiris symbolize the Nile's annual death and rebirth. The evil Set is the hot desert wind that consumes the waters. Osiris is dead when the river is dry, and his body is found by Isis on the day of its annual flood. As Osiris fertilizes Isis, bringing forth new life and hope, so the river overflows its banks to fertilize the fields. Osiris is the Nile, Isis the earth: the marriage of the two is the perennially productive union of water and soil.

Memorials of the past

The prosperity created by the Nile enabled the Egyptians to raise magnificent monuments along its course—temples and memorials to the ancient gods and kings. Inevitably, the demands of modern progress have conflicted with the need to preserve the past. These two considerations were spectacularly reconciled with the building of the Aswan Dam, when the temples of Abu Simbel were saved from the rising waters. The two temples, sculpted from a mountainside on the Nile's west bank, were, in an astonishing feat of engineering completed in 1966, moved bodily 210 feet above their original site.

The temples' builder was Rameses II, the third king of the Nineteenth Dynasty. During his long reign (1290–1224 B.C.) he created nearly half of Egypt's surviving temples, many of them erected to celebrate his deeds in winning back and protecting Egypt's Asiatic empire from the Hittites.

Rameses also left his mark downstream from Abu Simbel, where a staggering array of monuments surrounds the ancient capital of Thebes. For here is Karnak, one of the most awe-inspiring temples on earth. The forest of pillars in its hypostyle hall, towering high overhead and crowding together at their huge bases, seems meant for the passage of great non-corporeal beings.

The huge complex is dedicated to the ram-headed Amun, god of Thebes, later merged with the sun-god Re, to become Amun-Re

and, at Thebes' height, the king of gods. The ruins cover five acres, crowded with the remains of sphinx-lined avenues, huge gateways, shrines and temples, and a sacred lake. Next to Thebes is Luxor, also dedicated to Amun; and across the Nile from Luxor lies the Valley of the Kings, where most of the monarchs of the Eighteenth Dynasty (c.1570–1342 B.C.) were laid to rest.

The most famous of Egypt's monuments are found to the north, almost at the opening of the Delta, where rise the colossal shapes of the great pyramids of Giza, last survivors of the Seven Wonders of the Ancient World.

Along the banks of the Nile, everyday human activities reassert the ancient rhythm of existence. In places this seems scarcely to have changed since Victorian travellers came here to paint the river in all its aspects, and it may not be so very different from the days of the pharaohs.

The two temples of Pharaoh *Rameses II (1290–1224 B.C.)* (OPPOSITE PAGE *and* ABOVE*) at Abu Simbel, on the west bank of the Nile, were saved from destruction in the 1960s. In a magnificent feat of engineering, the temples were lifted more than 200 feet to escape the rising waters created by the building of the Aswan Dam. The monuments were dismantled into 1,060 keyed blocks and hauled away a block at a time. The 4 seated statues of Rameses in the façade of the larger temple, two of which are shown here, rise to 67 feet: they clearly indicate the pharaoh's image of himself.*

AYERS ROCK (ULURU)

> ❛ *Mount Olga is the more wonderful and grotesque; Mount Ayers the more ancient and sublime.* ❜
>
> ERNEST GILES, EXPLORER WHO VISITED THE ROCK IN 1874.

ONE OF THE LARGEST AND MOST FAMOUS monoliths in the world, Ayers Rock is a huge lump of arkose, a sandstone rich in feldspar, lying 200 miles southwest of Alice Springs at the centre of Australia. Its rounded and naturally furrowed cliffs, about 1,100 feet high and 5 miles in girth, are the more startling for rising sheer above the flat desert plain, which is dotted with mulga trees, spinifex grasses and desert oaks. But the revelation of the rock comes at dusk or dawn: the monolith seems to soak up the sunlight and, like a giant chameleon changing its colour, glows with the radiance of myriad rubies.

Ayers Rock was discovered in 1873 by the explorer William Gosse, accompanied by his Afghan camel driver, Khamran. Gosse named the rock after the premier of South Australia, not realizing that it already had an Aborigine name: Uluru. For the Aborigine people, the place had been sacred since the time of their ancestors—an era known as Dreamtime or the Dreaming. This was the period when, according to Aborigine tradition, the ancestors journeyed across the country, creating from their footprints and daily actions various landmarks such as rocks, caves, trees and waterholes.

A potent symbol

Uluru, now associated with the Pitjantjatjara and Yankuntjatjara tribes, is a significant point on the Dreaming trails that traverse the land. But it has also become, in the words of Australian writer Thomas Keneally, "an important, affirmative, national symbol" for Australia's white citizens. Every year, thousands come to this stone omphalos to watch it turn deep Venetian red with the sunset, or, after a storm, stream with silver torrents, like the body of a surfacing whale.

The highlight of a visit is to climb (now with the help of a chain rail) up the rock's western flank, whose smooth surface has in the past claimed several lives. On the wind-swept summit, riven with deep pot-holes and gutters, there are sweeping panoramas all around; none betters the view, through the haze, of the "rounded minarets, giant cupolas, and monstrous domes" of Mount Olga, 20 miles to the west.

At dawn and sunset Ayers Rock, known to the Aborigines as Uluru, is dyed deep red. More than 1,000 feet high and 5 miles in girth, the rock is steeped in Aborigine Dreamtime legends. It has also become an important national symbol for white Australians.

AYERS ROCK (ULURU)

*"**The hill was one immense rock**, rising abruptly from the plain. The holes I had noticed were caused by the water, in some places forming immense caves." So wrote the explorer William Gosse (RIGHT) (1842–81), who discovered Ayers Rock in 1873, and managed to climb to the top with his Afghan camel driver, Khamran.*

***The sheer sides of Ayers Rock** have been scarred with grooves, caves and pot-holes by the forces of erosion. When rainwater penetrates the soft stone surface it loosens the sand grains and causes it to disintegrate. On the north face (BELOW) erosion has carved a shape appropriately known as the Brain.*

The creation of the rock

The geological history of Ayers Rock goes back millions of years. Its vertical layers of rock were once horizontal—part of an ancient ocean floor—until they were upturned by movements of the earth's crust. The forces of erosion that have worn down everything else in the area have weathered and scarred the rock with caves, hollows, ridges and grooves, but have not destroyed it. In fact, through the recurrent process called "spalling", the entire sandstone surface of the rock flakes off evenly so that it "sheds its skin" like a snake but maintains the same shape.

However, Uluru is more than just a giant lump of stone. For the Aborigines, the rock is a living sculpture of ancestral history, and its physical features are accounted for by legends. One of these concerns the battle between two tribes known as the Kunia and the Liru. For example, Maggie Springs waterhole on the rock's southeastern face contains the blood, now turned to water, of a dying Kunia warrior. The marks made by the Liru spears are pot-holes in the rock's southern flank; dark gaping holes in the cliffs are the mouths of shouting Liru; and patches of desert oaks are the transformed bodies of Liru warriors.

The Aborigines keep alive the traditions of their Dreamtime past and celebrate their natural environment in paintings, whose simple but symbolically complex lines and shapes can be seen on different parts of Uluru. Engravings pecked out of the rock are believed by the Aborigines to have been made by their spirit ancestors.

It is unsurprising that this massive rock, with its isolated position, its mysterious deeply grooved walls and uncanny changes of colours, should be steeped in Dreamtime legends. For it is a place where myth meets nature, as the anthropologist Charles Mountford observed: "When I learned the legends of the place. . . . The immense and beautiful surroundings were no longer mere precipices, caves or splashes of colour; they had been vitalized by the stories that the Aborigines had told me. . . ."

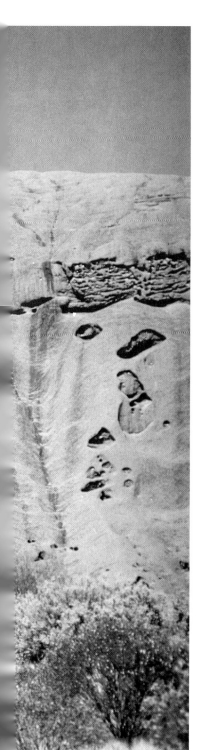

The snake is an important totemic figure in Aboriginal legends and art. The bark painting (RIGHT) shows the spirit of a snake.

The most famous waterhole on Ayers Rock is Maggie Springs (BELOW), known to the Aborigines as Mutijula. Here, according to legend, a warrior of the Kunia, the Carpet Snake people, fought the leader of the Liru, the Poisonous Snake people, during a battle between the two tribes. Maggie Springs is said to contain the blood, now turned to water, of the Kunia warrior.

JAPAN

MOUNT FUJI

> ❝ *O snail, climb Mount Fuji. But slowly. Slowly.* ❞
>
> OLD JAPANESE HAIKU.

"THE MOST BEAUTIFUL SIGHT IN JAPAN . . . IS the distant apparition of Fuji on cloudless days . . . the white cone seeming to hang in heaven. . . ." So wrote the American writer Lafcadio Hearn (1850–1904), who fell in love with Japan when he was 41, and became a Japanese citizen. Mount Fuji, famous for its classical symmetry, is a mountain for all seasons. Many would agree, however, that spring is best, when the summit is topped with snow, and plum and cherry trees blossom among the Fuji Lakes on the mountain's north flank.

Sometimes called by the Japanese "that which is without equal", Fuji is visible on a clear day from more than 50 miles away, and from its summit the views embrace almost the whole of the Japanese mainland. The highest mountain in Japan at nearly 12,500 feet, Fuji is also the holiest. According to the native Japanese religion Shinto, higher spirits, *kami*, exist in all works of nature. This is especially true of Fuji, the mountain Shintoists most revere.

The sleeping volcano

According to Japanese Buddhist tradition, Mount Fuji appeared overnight in 286 B.C., when the ground opened to form Lake Biwa, Japan's largest lake, and the earth from the hole rose up into the mountain. There is some truth in the legend: the landscape of the Japanese archipelago was almost everywhere broken up into mountain ranges and lakes by tectonic faults. Along the biggest of the faults, which runs through the main island of Honshu, cluster the giants among Japan's 265 known volcanoes. Of these Fuji is the colossus.

The mountain has had a long history of volcanic activity. In recent centuries, 18 eruptions have been recorded, including one in 1707 which covered the town of Edo (Tokyo), 65 miles to the east, with a thick layer of ash and cinders. Since that time there has been little sign that the volcano will re-awaken: but it is not dead, only sleeping.

Fuji was first named by the aboriginal Ainu people (who still live on Hokkaido) after their fire goddess Fuchi. The Japanese kept the name and also the tradition of holiness. Buddhists believed the mountain was a gateway to another world; and Shintoists built shrines on it to the goddess Sengen-Sama, also known as Konohana-Sakuyahime (Causing the blossoms to bloom brightly). This goddess, according to

Mount Fuji rises graceful and serene into the moonlit night beyond the glittering lights of the city of Fuji-Yoshida. The highest mountain in Japan at nearly 12,500 feet, Fuji is also the country's most sacred, revered by Buddhists and, especially, Shintoists. Fuji has also been the inspiration for many Japanese poets and painters. The two woodcuts (RIGHT) are from the 36 "Views of Mount Fuji" by Ando Hiroshige, published in 1858.

富士三十六景
駿河三保之松平

富士三十六景
武州七里ヶ濱

tradition, has been glimpsed hovering in a luminous cloud above Fuji's crater.

Journey to the rising sun

Under Shinto, Mount Fuji was officially worshipped as a sacred mountain, and it was the duty of the faithful, up to the end of World War II, to ascend it at least once in a lifetime. In Lafcadio Hearn's day, thousands of pilgrims, clad in white tunics and straw hats and sandals, would climb it every summer. Sometimes the routes to the top were lined with cast-off sandals—they were so flimsy that pilgrims needed several pairs for the trek.

As they toiled toward the summit to watch the celebrated sunrise, the devout would chant the words, ''Be pure. . . . Stay fair, O ye mountain!'' In this century the words have taken on a greater relevance. For though its snows allow access to the top for only two months in the year, Fuji is climbed by more than 300,000 people and suffers accordingly. For many, inspired by the white peak floating above the mist or mirrored in the waters of Lake Ashinoko, the crowds and the mountain's barren volcanic surface can be a disappointment.

Lafcadio Hearn (LEFT), *who wrote lyrically of Fuji's beauty, went to Japan in 1890 and stayed there for the rest of his life. In 1895 he became a Japanese citizen, taking the name of Yakumo Koizimi.*

The shrine on the summit of Fuji (BELOW) is dedicated to Sengen-Sama, the Shinto goddess of the mountain.

An inspiration to artists

Distant views of Fuji, however, have inspired Japan's poets and painters for 12 centuries or more. Even when enveloped in cloud, the mountain's presence moved the famous poet Basho (1644–94) to write: "Though Fuji is hidden,/In the rain and mist of winter,/On such a day, too,/There is joy." Fuji's moods and caprices have also drawn artists to paint it over and over again. Best known in the West are the 36 "Views of Fuji" by Katsushika Hokusai (1769–1849), a series of woodblock prints, every one different.

But if Japan's artists have made Mount Fuji famous, it might also be said that Fuji made them artists. As the British explorer and naturalist Richard Gordon Smith recorded in 1899: "It [Fuji] was enough to fill anyone with awe and to make one reflect that those born within sight of such a mountain must necessarily be born to art and its praises."

Perhaps, like the truth of the rainbow, the truth of Fuji is best recognized from afar, its white cone framed against the blue sky. The mountain is a natural symbol, its apparently simple form belying its multiplicity of meanings. It seems eternal, but was born in fire and may yet perish in fire; it is rock, but its beauty is the fragile beauty of a flower.

*A **fishing boat** glides across the glassy stillness of Lake Shoji, the smallest of the Five Lakes that lie in a wide arc below the north face of Fuji. In spring the area is a riot of colour with the blossoms of cherry trees and azaleas. In the autumn the dense, part primeval forest between the lakes provides a spectacular show of colour. Some of the best views of the mountain can be had in this area.*

CAPPADOCIA

> *We found ourselves suddenly lost in a forest of cones and pillars of rock . . . like the ruins of some great and ancient city.*
>
> BRITISH TRAVELLER W.F. AINSWORTH, WHO VISITED THE REGION IN THE 1840S.

WHEN A FRENCHMAN NAMED PAUL LUCAS published an account of his visit to east central Turkey in the early eighteenth century, his readers found it difficult to believe him. Lucas had described a strange dreamlike landscape where some of the inhabitants lived in caves and hollows carved out of freestanding rocks shaped like cones. But Lucas had not imagined it. He had seen the ancient region of Cappadocia, an astonishing moonscape of rocky pinnacles, covering an area of about 50 square miles, to the southeast of Ankara.

Here, particularly in the area around the towns of Göreme, Ürgüp, Nevşehir and Avanos, the soft volcanic terrain has been gouged out, fashioned and polished by the forces of erosion. The result is a phantasmagorical world where rocks shaped like stepped ziggurats, towers, spires, minarets and cones jut upward into the blue sky.

In some places, the rocks are clustered together like the stone pavilions of an invading army. Others are so smooth and curved they resemble snowdrifts sculpted by the wind, or sandcastles melted by an incoming tide. The stone valleys are imbued with subtle colours, such as creamy yellow, brick red and ash grey, which become vibrant under the pink flush of dawn or dusk. So bizarre are the rock formations that Paul Lucas thought they must have been made by men, not by nature.

A grotesquerie of pinnacles

The geological story of Cappadocia starts millions of years ago when the two great volcanoes of the region—Hasan Dağı and Erciyes Dağı—erupted. Out of their fiery mouths poured lava and clouds of ash and dust which covered the surrounding area, eventually turning into a soft pale rock called tufa. Then, over a period of time, fast-flowing rivers and streams carved out a network of narrow gorges, canyons and valleys. Eventually the eroding forces whittled down areas into the present grotesquerie of pinnacles, their shape being determined by their protective "caps" of weather-resistant basalt.

Since the beginning of history, the inhabitants of Cappadocia have hollowed out the tufa cones and cliffs into honeycombs of rooms for everyday living and for worship. However, it was in the fourth century A.D. that Greek Christians, inspired by Basil the Great, bishop of Caesarea (now Kayseri) and father of eastern monasticism, began to carve

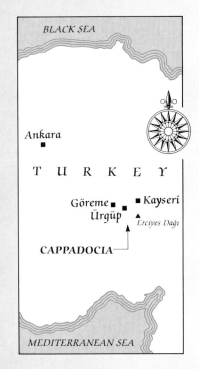

Cappadocia, an area of about 50 square miles southeast of Ankara, is one of the most extraordinary places in the world. Its soft rock, known as tufa, has been naturally eroded into strange conical formations (ABOVE), *which, for centuries, have been hollowed out and used as homes and places of worship by the local inhabitants.*

A few miles northeast of Göreme lies Zelve (FAR RIGHT), *where two valleys converge. Here many Christian churches and monks' cells were carved out of the pinnacled cliffs, parts of which have collapsed, exposing interior chambers. Zelve is also known for its "fairy chimneys"* (RIGHT), *with hard protective caps of rock that produced a different pattern of erosion.*

CAPPADOCIA

out hermitages and small monasteries. From these the now-famous rock-cut churches evolved, and, over the centuries, the Christian communities grew, so that by the thirteenth century there were probably some 300 churches in use.

The rock churches of Göreme

The best known of these lie in the valley of Göreme, a few miles northwest of Ürgüp. Here, at the "open air museum", an amphitheatre of irregular rocks is pitted with the dark holes of doorways and windows. These lead to the mysterious interiors of small churches, and monks' refectories, kitchens and storerooms.

The Christian builders reproduced the internal architecture of freestanding churches and carved out domes, apses, barrel-vaulted ceilings, and columns, arches and even tables and benches from the malleable stone. Sometimes the base of a column has been worn completely away so that instead of "supporting" the structure above, it hangs from it like a stalactite.

The church interiors are covered with a rich variety of Byzantine paintings. Some are simple russet-coloured geometric designs drawn straight onto the rock. Others, especially from the tenth century onward,

are colourful depictions of scenes from the New Testament and portraits of saints, painted on plaster in shades of blue, red, green and white.

Among the most impressive of the churches on view are the Elmalı Kılıse (Church of the Apple), where part of the painted plaster has eroded to reveal simple red monochrome patterns from an earlier era; the Yılanlı Kılıse (Snake Church), famous for its painting of a mounted St George spearing a snake-dragon; and the Karanlık Kılıse (Dark Church), whose frescoes still seem fresh and rich in colour because little sunlight has been able to penetrate the interior.

During the fourteenth century, despite coexisting peacefully with the religiously tolerant Turks, who were then in control of Cappadocia, the Christian communities began to dwindle. However, it was not until 1922, when the Greek minority population was expelled from Turkey, that 16 centuries of Christianity came to an end.

But the cones continue to be used by the local inhabitants. Visitors to the region are still given some idea of what it is like to live in what British traveller W.J. Childs described earlier this century as a "cloudland in green and yellow and soft shadow, but all done in coloured rock".

The French traveller Paul Lucas visited Cappadocia in the early 18th century. His published account of his travels, which included an engraving of inhabited cones (ABOVE), was widely disbelieved in France. Lucas assumed that the rocks must have been the work of man, not of nature.

THE GANGES

> *If only the bone of a person should touch the water of the Ganges, that person shall dwell, honoured, in heaven.*

FROM THE *MAHABHARATA*, ANCIENT HINDU EPIC POEM.

FROM THE "COW'S MOUTH", AN ICE CAVE IN the Himalayas, the sparkling waters of the River Ganges first emerge into sunlight. In its early stages, India's holiest river is known as the Bhagirathi, which dashes through a ravine in the beautiful Garwhal Hills, past pines and deodars and scarlet rhododendrons, down to the town of Devprayag. Here, below towering cliffs, it joins its turbulent waters to those of the River Alaknanda to become the Ganges proper. From there on it flows more sedately and almost constantly east, until it ends its journey in the Bay of Bengal in the many mouths of its delta.

The Ganges, at 1,678 miles, is not one of the world's longest rivers—the Nile and the Amazon, for example, are more than twice as long. But no river is more revered: as a goal of pilgrimage it comes second only to Mecca. The sick are carried to its shores; the dying immersed in its waters. The ashes of the dead, and sometimes their corpses, are committed to it. The many thousands of Hindus who come here are devotees of different gods, but to whichever god he prays, each pilgrim sincerely believes that all his sins will be washed away by the Ganges.

Ganga the "swift-goer"

This most sacred of rivers has excited imaginations far beyond India. It is mentioned by classical and medieval poets, such as Virgil, Ovid and Dante, and Alexander the Great seems to have believed it was the boundary of the universe. The English writer Sir John Mandeville, whose *Travels* were by 1400 known in every major European language, said it flowed out of Paradise and that there was gold in its gravel. In Indian myth it was the earthly continuation of the Milky Way.

For Hindus, the Ganges is none other than Ganga—the "swift-goer"—the goddess of purification. According to legend, King Sagara's 60,000 sons were burnt to ashes by the angry glance of a sage as a punishment for arrogance. When a later king, Bhagirathi, did penance for their offence high in the Himalayas, the Lord Shiva made Ganga descend to earth so that her waters could purify their ashes. To protect the earth from Ganga's fall Shiva caught her in his hair and made her flow through his matted locks in the footsteps of Bhagirathi—out of the mountains, through the foothills, and eastward to Sagar Island, in the Ganges' present mouth. Here the goddess purified the ashes of Sagara's sons and they attained Paradise.

The Ganges *flows more than 1,650 miles from the Himalayas to the Bay of Bengal and is India's most sacred river. The city of Benares (Varanasi) (ABOVE) is famous for its ghats—stone steps from where pilgrims bathe in the river.*

THE GANGES

The tradition of the Ganges' purifying property springs in part from its power to cool. Many Hindu customs are based on the idea that power is heat, and to cool this heat with water nullifies it. Hence water will dispel the power of evil spirits. Also, the waters of the Ganges are reputed to stay fresher than water from other Indian rivers. "No self-respecting germ would live in it," joked the American writer Mark Twain. Yet, at Benares (Varanasi), for example, countless people drink from the Ganges, even near sewer outlets, and appear to be none the worse for it.

For the living and the dead

Every 12 years, when the planet Jupiter enters the house of Aquarius, a great "Kumbh Mela" festival is held at one of the holiest sites along the Ganges, the town of Hardwar in the Himalayan foothills. In 1986 four million pilgrims converged here. Here, too, every spring, more than a hundred thousand arrive to celebrate Ganga's birthday. The pilgrims launch small boats made of leaves bearing marigold petals which have been dipped in ghee and set alight: the tiny flames can be seen bobbing down the river long after nightfall.

The holiest city by the Ganges is probably Benares. Here old and sick pilgrims hope to end their lives; for the river here can so purify the soul that it is released from the weary cycle of rebirth once and for all. Here, too, are the famous "ghats", a four-mile stretch of stone steps leading down to bathing places.

At the Manikarnika Burning Ghat, the bodies of the dead are burnt on pyres of sandalwood or neem, for rich and poor respectively. The very poor simply weight their dead with stones, before placing them in the river. All day and night, the fires of the Burning Ghat are tended by men of a special caste; and, all night long, bards chant ancient Hindu epics on the river banks.

Along with the parakeets, hoopoes and drongos, vultures inevitably haunt the banks of the Ganges. For pious Hindus, however, the sight of decomposing corpses is a natural one; for they know their beloved dead are being borne down in Ganga's arms to Sagar Island, there, with King Sagara's sons, to be granted Paradise.

At the town of Hardwar (LEFT) *pilgrims line the banks of the Ganges during a Kumbh Mela festival, which is held every 12 years. In 1986, 4 million people gathered here to purify themselves in the holy waters.*

By the cliffs of Devprayag (ABOVE) the waters of the River Bhagirathi join with those of the River Alaknanda to form the Ganges proper. The ghats here are provided with sturdy chains which bathers can hang on to as they wash themselves in the fast-moving waters.

The source of the Ganges is in the foothills of the Himalayas. The remote tranquillity of its upper reaches (RIGHT) contrasts sharply with the animated scenes along its banks as it flows through towns on its journey east.

65

HALEAKALA CRATER

Haleakala, the giant crater on the Hawaiian island of Maui, rises into a white sea of sun-gilt clouds. According to Polynesian legend, the god Maui tied up the sun as its rays broke over the crater's rim, freeing it only when it had promised to move more slowly through the skies.

The volcanic landscape inside the crater is studded with huge cinder cones (FAR RIGHT), and bejewelled by the rare silversword plant (RIGHT).

> ❛ *Haleakala has a message of beauty and wonder for the human soul that cannot be delivered by proxy.* ❜
> AMERICAN ADVENTURER JACK LONDON
> WHO VISITED THE CRATER IN 1907.

"A GROWING WARMTH SUFFUSED THE horizon, and soon the sun emerged and looked out over the cloud-waste, flinging bars of ruddy light across its folds and billow-caps with blushes. . . ." When Mark Twain (1835–1910) witnessed this sunrise, he was standing 10,000 feet above sea level on the rim of Haleakala, the giant volcanic crater that dominates Maui, the second largest of the Hawaiian islands. The 31-year-old writer had taken two days to climb what the British explorer James Cook had, in 1778, dismissed as "an elevated hill . . . whose summit rose above the clouds".

Twain and his companions reached the top by nightfall, made a fire and waited for the dawn. When the sun eventually burst forth, setting the clouds on fire, it was, in Twain's words, "the sublimest spectacle I ever witnessed, and I think the memory of it will remain with me always".

House of the Sun

Watching the sun rise over Haleakala—the Polynesian name meaning "House of the Sun"—is a primal experience and one which is linked in Polynesian mythology with the trickster god Maui. According to legend, there was once a time when the island received only a few hours of daylight because the sun would race across the sky so that it could go back to sleep. Because of this, Maui's mother, Hina, was unable to dry her *tapa* cloth, made from pounded tree bark.

So Maui decided to trap the sun. He wove a rope out of coconut fibre, climbed up to the top of Haleakala at night, and lay in wait. At dawn, as the sun's rays broke over the crater's rim, Maui lassoed each one, tied up the sun, and released it only when it had promised to move more slowly through the sky. From that moment on, the island received its full quota of light, and Hina could dry her cloth.

Haleakala, now a national park, has not erupted since 1790, but its 19-square-mile crater—Manhattan island could fit into it—is not extinct. The road up to it winds peacefully through groves of eucalyptus trees and green meadows. On a clear day there are panoramic views over the sugarcane fields and the island-flecked sea to the mountains of Hawaii island, some 80 miles away. On approaching the top, the surprise is to find, instead of a mountain peak, an enormous hollowed-out crater whose precipitous walls enclose a unique landscape.

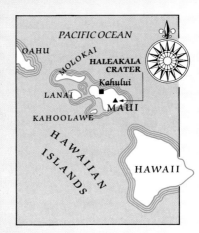

PACIFIC OCEAN

OAHU
MOLOKAI
HALEAKALA CRATER
Kahului
LANAI
MAUI
KAHOOLAWE
HAWAIIAN ISLANDS
HAWAII

The American writer Mark Twain (BELOW LEFT) *came to Hawaii in 1866, and climbed to the top of Haleakala to watch the sunrise. At the edge of the crater, Twain and his companions, depicted in an engraving (LEFT) from Twain's book* Roughing It, *tumbled rocks into the crater and watched them leap into the air: "It was magnificent sport," Twain wrote, "we wore ourselves out at it."*

"We gazed down upon a place of fire and earthquake. The tie-ribs of earth lay bare before us." Jack London, an American writer and adventurer, visited Haleakala in 1907. His description evokes the primordial grandeur of the crater, whose size and shape can be appreciated from the map (RIGHT).

The map shows the two huge gaps, known as Koolau and Kaupo, in Haleakala's walls. Formed by erosion, the gaps allow swirling white clouds to billow into the crater.

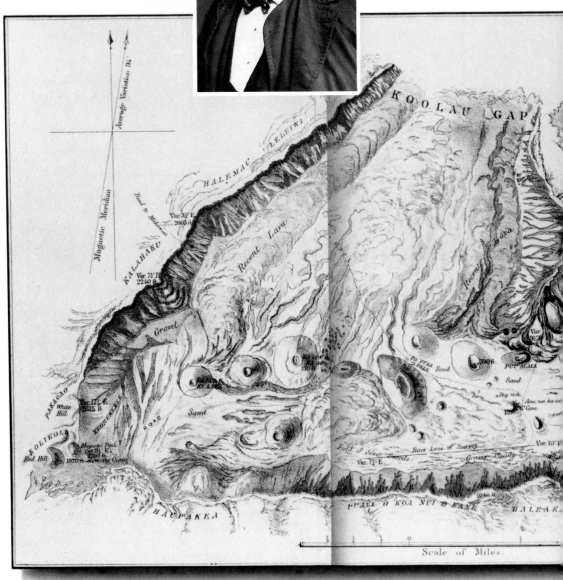

From Kalahuku or Red Hill Overlook on the west side of the crater, the view down 3,000 feet into its plunging depths is breathtaking. Sometimes, especially during the first hours of the day, the great basin may be swirling with clouds billowing in from two huge gaps in the northwest and southeast walls of the crater.

As the heat of day disperses the layers of white mist, the bottom of Haleakala is revealed in all its glory: the House of the Sun looks like the surface of the moon. A multicoloured lunar landscape of ash grey, russet, brick red and purple, streaked by black lava flows, stretches away for miles. From the ash and dust of the crater floor rise symmetrical cone-shaped hills or mounds that can tower to heights of 900 feet.

The crater's floor is crisscrossed by 30 miles of trails, some of which lead to simple cabins, where travellers can stay overnight. One of these, Sliding Sands trail, descends into the crater from the west over a slippery surface of cinders and ash. With every step the sides of the crater loom higher all around. At the bottom, brick-red or terracotta cones rise up like miniature volcanoes out of the gaunt terrain, silent except for the crunch of footsteps on the dark sands. After a while, the trail arrives at Pele's Paint Pot, a cone of subtle greys, reds and purples, named after the Polynesian fire goddess.

A highlight of such a trek is spotting a silversword, a plant unique to Hawaii, if not to Haleakala. Scattered like glittering stars in a universe of dark dust, silverswords are clusters of gleaming spikes, packed tightly like the quills of a porcupine. The plant grows for several years and then sends out a tall, sturdy stem of purplish flowers, sometimes nine feet high. Once it has blossomed, it dies. Over the years, souvenir hunters and hungry goats have turned the silversword into a protected species.

Haleakala has always been a special place for Hawaiians, who once used to place in the crater propitiatory offerings of food wrapped up in leaves. There is also evidence to suggest that it was once a burial place for Hawaiian chiefs. But for modern visitors, what makes the crater unforgettable are its dark cliffs, shifting cloud formations and solitude. Mark Twain was stunned by its grandeur, and felt like ''the Last Man, neglected of the judgment, and left pinnacled in mid-heaven, a forgotten relic of a vanished world''.

MAP OF THE CRATER
— O F —
HALEAKALA

W. D. ALEXANDER, SURVEYOR,
1869.

Visitors to Haleakala in the 19th century included a group of Catholic fathers (BOTTOM), who came equipped with warm clothing and guns to hunt the wild goats.

The intrepid British traveller Isabella Bird (BELOW) climbed up Haleakala in 1873 and, like Jack London, was awed by its grandeur: ''Was it nearer God,'' she asked, ''because so far from man and his little ways?''

SHENANDOAH VALLEY

> **❝** *Equal to the promised land in fertility, and far superior to it for beauty.* **❞**
>
> AMERICAN WRITER WASHINGTON IRVING
> (1783–1859).

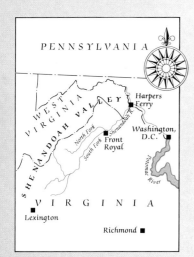

THE RIVER WHICH THE AMERICAN INDIANS called Shenandoah (Daughter of the Stars) is not one of the largest in the world; but the valley through which its waters flow has been endowed with great natural beauty and a rich historic past.

Part of the great Appalachian Valley, the Shenandoah Valley is about 150 miles long and lies between the Allegheny and Shenandoah Mountains to the west, and the Blue Ridge Mountains to the east, along the western border of Virginia. The Shenandoah is really two rivers, North Fork and South Fork, which run northeast along the valley, passing one on either side of the great canoe-shaped ridge of Massanutten Mountain. At the town of Front Royal, their waters unite and briefly flow as one over the boundary into West Virginia to join the Potomac at Harpers Ferry.

Here, from a bluff now known as Jefferson's Rock, Thomas Jefferson, future president of the United States, viewed the spot where the rivers joined forces to battle their way through the Blue Ridge Mountains. He pronounced the prospect of riven cliffs and hills and rushing water "worth a voyage across the Atlantic".

The view has changed little. Farther south, from the misty heights of the Blue Ridge, there are breathtaking vistas over the lazy loops of the Shenandoah South Fork through what is sometimes known as the Luray or Page Valley. South of Front Royal, where the trees of George Washington National Forest come down to the water's edge, the river and its setting are idyllic. Yet it is the North Fork, twisting like a serpent as it approaches Front Royal, that is traditionally regarded as *the* Shenandoah, the "rolling river" of the famous sea shanty.

Settlers and the sound of guns

Before the arrival of white settlers in the early eighteenth century, Tuscarora and Shawnee Indians travelled along a trail that followed the valley bottom, now an interstate highway, the Valley Pike. In 1716 Governor Alexander Spotswood of Virginia, partly from a desire to make his own fortune, led a party of adventurous gentlemen westward. Climbing to the crest of the Blue Ridge, they gazed down on the Shenandoah, and toasted their achievement with wine.

This began the occupation of the Virginia back country beyond the mountains. The land was not, of course, uninhabited: up at

The waters of the Shenandoah River *meet with those of the Potomac at Harpers Ferry, West Virginia* (ABOVE). *It was from a bluff near here that Thomas Jefferson gazed upon the confluence of the two rivers and declared the scene to be "worth a voyage across the Atlantic".*

The singular beauty of the valley is reflected in its name—Shenandoah is an American Indian name meaning Daughter of the Stars. During the Civil War the valley was devastated; but now.its pastures and orchards once more exude an air of timeless tranquillity.

PHILIP SHERIDAN, U.S.A.

STONEWALL JACKSON, C.S.A.

Harpers Ferry, Robert Harper was to lose a house in the great "pumpkin flood", so called because it brought pumpkins bobbing down from Indian gardens upstream. But now white settlers, mainly of Scotch-Irish and Pennsylvania German stock, began to arrive, the Germans as early as 1727. The latter were particularly good farmers, and, under their care, the rich, fertile land gradually blossomed with orchards, pastures and cornfields.

But the tranquillity of the valley was shattered in 1862 by the sound of guns and marching soldiers: the Civil War had begun. In later years, the valley would be associated with two great Civil War generals, Philip Sheridan of the North, and, especially, the legendary Stonewall Jackson of the South.

Devastation and recovery

For the Confederates, the valley was their "breadbasket", a crucial source of wheat, livestock, vegetables and fruit. It was also strategically important—providing a naturally protected route for troops moving north or south. Here, in spring 1862, Stonewall Jackson gained immortality for his Valley Campaign, in which he and his fast-moving "foot cavalry" outfought the Federals with victories at McDowell, Front Royal, Winchester, Cross Keys and Port Republic.

The Shenandoah Valley was the scene of fierce fighting during the Civil War. In 1862 the great Southern general Stonewall Jackson won everlasting fame for his Valley Campaign. He and his troops—nicknamed "foot cavalry" because of the speed at which they marched—inflicted 5 defeats in quick succession upon the Federals.

In 1864, however, the Northern general Philip Sheridan devastated the valley, which had been the South's "breadbasket", and won a decisive victory at Cedar Creek. The engraving (LEFT) shows the havoc caused in the valley by a Federal raiding party under George Armstrong Custer.

Two years later, the valley once again echoed with gunshots, but this time the Southerners would be defeated and the valley devastated. In spring 1864, the Federals were beaten at New Market, in which teenaged cadets from the South's Virginia Military Institute fought heroically. But later in the year, Philip Sheridan and his men laid waste to the valley and won a decisive victory at Cedar Creek. The Federals burned crops, mills, granaries, farms, residences, so that "a crow flying over the country would need to carry his rations".

The 80 miles from Harpers Ferry to New Market was described by a farmer as "almost a desert. We had no cattle, hogs, sheep, or horses. . . . The barns were all burned; chimneys standing without houses, and houses standing without roofs, or doors, or

windows." The prosperous valley had been transformed into a smouldering ruin.

It must have seemed to the survivors of the war that the valley would never bloom again. But, as with the battlefields of northern France after the two World Wars, the healing forces of nature, combined with hard work and perseverance, in time re-created a new landscape. Now the vineyards, pastures and orchards, bordered by the woodlands and open meadows of Shenandoah National Park, flourish once more. It is a place for lovers of nature, and for those wishing to see poignant reminders of the Civil War. Here the past merges with the present; and both blur into timelessness with the view from the Blue Ridge across the valley, when the light of a winter's day falls on the silver coils of the Daughter of the Stars.

The battlefield at New Market (BELOW) *was the scene for a stirring Southern victory against a superior Federal force. At a crucial point in the battle, a gap was blown in the Confederate battle line that seemed to beckon disaster. However, the Confederate general John C. Breckinridge ordered forward teenaged cadets from the V.M.I. to plug the gap with the words: "Put the boys in, and God forgive me the order."*

The cadets charged under fierce enemy fire and closed the gap, paving the way for a Confederate victory.

THE HIMALAYAS

> ❛ *The sight of the snows wipes out the sins of the world.* ❜
>
> HINDU PROVERB.

"THE SUN HAD BURNT DOWN FROM AN ENDLESS blue sky, and the sea of snow summits was etched sharply in the crystal clear air. . . . Pristine, untouchable. Lofting into the sky, perfectly beautiful." The words of British climber Joe Simpson evoke both the grandeur and sense of purity that make the Himalayas ("the abode of the snow") one of the most majestic places on earth. To enter the Himalayan region is to pass into a world conceived on a giant scale, where colossal peaks, such as Everest, Nanga Parbat and Kanchenjunga tower into the sky.

This is a land steeped in religion and myth—the abode of the gods in Hindu and Buddhist traditions. These were the mountains that were the great barrier to fabled cities that lay along the Silk Road—Samarkand and Bukhara, Kashgar and Kotan; and the Himalayas still evoke the image of a lost world, untouched by human progress, home of solitary ascetics and the yeti—the abominable snowman said to inhabit their innermost reaches.

Nowhere on the surface of the earth are there mountains like those at the heart of Asia. Lying in a broad curving belt along the neck of the Indian subcontinent, six great mountain systems interlock. The greatest of these is the Himalayas, which extend west from the cold white pyramid of Namche Barwa in the northern forests of Assam, along the edge of the Tibetan plateau, through Bhutan and Sikkim, Nepal and Ladakh, to end triumphantly in their great western bastion, Nanga Parbat.

The Himalayas themselves comprise three roughly parallel ranges, the highest of which is the Great Himalaya (pronounced to rhyme with "Somalia"), and includes the giants Everest and Kanchenjunga. But "Himalayas" is also loosely used to refer to other ranges in the region, for example the Gangdise Shan or Kailas Range which lies immediately behind the Great Himalaya.

The country of the gods

The names of the Great Himalaya speak of the awe in which they have been held since human eyes first saw them: Chomo Lhari, "Goddess of the Holy Mountain"; Nanda

The Himalayas, meaning the "abode of the gods" in Sanskrit, stretch about 1,500 miles between the rivers Brahmaputra and Indus. The Annapurna massif, part of which is shown (RIGHT), has the name of a goddess, testifying to the awe in which it is held by Hindus and Buddhists.

Devi, "the goddess Nanda"; and Annapurna—the goddess of food. Even Everest, named by the British after a Surveyor-General of India, has also as its Tibetan name Chomo Lungma, "Mother goddess of the land".

For, according to the most ancient Hindu writings, this is Devabhumi, the country of the gods. Here, on Gaurishankar, lived Shankar and his wife Gauri, who are better known

 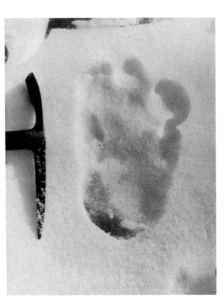

Are these the tracks of the so-called Abominable Snowman, the elusive yeti said to haunt the slopes of the Himalayas? The line of footprints (LEFT) could be those of a mountain goat enlarged by the melting of snow in the sunshine. But the single print (RIGHT) has yet to be explained satisfactorily. The photograph was taken by Eric Shipton in 1951 and remains one of the best pieces of evidence for the existence of the creature called by the Tibetans "the demon of the snow".

as the great god Shiva and his consort Durga or Mahadevi. Shiva, one of the supreme triad of Hindu gods, was the lord of agriculture in early Hindu mythology; his home was in the Himalayas, from which flowed the great life-giving rivers of India—the Indus, the Brahmaputra and the Ganges.

Mount Meru

Nor were Shiva and his consort the only deities who lived in the Himalayas. According to Buddhist and Hindu myth, at the centre of the earth stood the mountain of Meru. It was inhabited by the gods, and around it revolved the sun, moon and stars. Hindus identified Meru with Mount Kailas or Kailasa in Tibet, and here Kubera, king of the Yaksas and god of riches, was said to live. Kubera was lord of the treasures of the earth, and he and the Yaksas—supernatural beings associated with mountains—controlled the fertility of the earth as well as its underground metals.

Mount Meru was also associated with Indra, the god of the atmosphere and supreme god of the Vedic (early Hindu)

pantheon. It was to Indra's heaven on the mountain that the warrior heroes, the Pandarvas, retired after winning a great battle involving gods and men. The Pandarvas are now little worshipped, except in south India, where five stones representing the five Pandarva princes are sometimes seen in a field guarding the crops; but they are still closely associated with the Himalayas, where many spots associated with the wanderings of the princes are venerated.

The conquest of the peaks

If the Himalayas are home of Indra's heaven, they are also the paradise of climbers who, especially this century, have been drawn to the colossal ranges. In 1852, Peak XV was discovered to be the highest in the world. To Indians this giant is Sagarmatha, "Summit of Heaven"; to westerners, Mount Everest, at 29,028 feet above sea level, the ultimate challenge. On 29 May 1953, the dream of conquest was made reality by the New Zealand climber Edmund Hillary and Sherpa Tenzing Norkay, members of a British team.

At the western end of the Himalayas, one of the great climbing challenges is Nanga Parbat, a massif that rises almost sheer from the bed of the River Indus to 26,658 feet above sea level. From its rocky summit fall three vast faces, one of them, the Rupal Flank, plunging for 14,800 feet, perhaps the highest precipice in the world.

Nanga Parbat means in Sanskrit "naked mountain", but those who live on its western slopes call it Diamir, King of the Mountains. A first sight of it takes the breath away. Nothing in the approaches through the wooded valleys of Kashmir, with their steep hillsides and waterfalls, prepares the traveller for the moment when suddenly the view opens out and the sky is filled with that astonishing bulk hung about with glittering ice fields.

Fairies and yetis

But the mountain has a reputation for malevolence. In less than a hundred years, as many as 36 men, 17 of whom were experienced sherpas, have perished in attempts to climb it. This same malevolence is found in a local Kafir fairytale, which relates how a man lost in the mountains chanced to stumble upon a palace that belonged to the fairies of Nanga Parbat.

Made of sparkling crystal, the palace stood in a garden, in the midst of which grew a tree with pearls hanging from its branches. The man picked them and was making off when he noticed snakes pursuing him. Terrified, he threw down the pearls; but though he managed to reach home safely, he died four days later. For the fairies do not forgive those who discover their secrets.

Another secret the Himalayas still carefully guard is that of the yeti, long reputed to haunt their innermost reaches. No reliable photograph of this creature has been taken, though many have claimed to have seen either it or its footprints. The British climber Don Whillans, for example, is reported to have glimpsed by moonlight a creature crossing the snow with an "ape-like gait". Indeed, local belief in the yeti is so powerful that some sherpas take the precaution of carrying special "yeti wood" with a smell supposedly repellent to the creature.

Known to Indians as Sagarmatha, "Summit of Heaven", Mount Everest, the peak on the left of the photograph, is the highest in the world. Its summit, 29,028 feet high, was conquered by Edmund Hillary and Tenszing Norkay in 1953; but could George Mallory and Andrew Irvine, who disappeared on Everest in 1924, have been there before them?

THE HIMALAYAS

In the 1950s, the Nepalese government went so far as to make it a crime to kill a yeti or smuggle one out of the country. So far, no one has succeeded in breaking this law; perhaps, after all, the yeti is a demon spirit, as the Tibetans believe it to be ("abominable snowman" is a mistranslation of the Tibetan for "demon of the snow").

The great peaks keep their mysteries to themselves. The gods of ice rear their glittering crowns against the sky, and remain a splendid, numinous world, known to but a few. For, as an ancient Hindu text says: "As the dew before the sun, so does everything base vanish away at the sight of the eternally pure Home of the Snow."

Mount Meru or Kailas, home of the gods, is shown (BELOW) inhabited by Shiva and Parvati and their children. Parvati, "Daughter of the mountain", who was also known as Mahadevi, was the child of Himavat, the personification of the Himalayas.

Everywhere in the Himalayas can be seen signs of faith. Prayer flags (RIGHT) flutter in Nepal against a vista of the snow-clad mountains.

SACRED WONDERS

‘*And thorns shall come up in her palaces, nettles and brambles in the fortresses thereof: and it shall be an habitation of dragons, and a court for owls.*’

ISAIAH, 34:13

‘*There is nothing hidden by the earth, but time shall bring forth into sunlight.*’

HORACE (65–8 B.C.)

*I*n the Stone Age, humans were moved for the first time to represent their world in pictures. They chose as their canvas the walls of caves—magnificent art galleries shaped by the forces of nature. Over the following millennia, the natural world has continued to provide similarly inspiring and sacred contexts for the creations of artists and visionaries. The Greek shrine of Delphi, home of Apollo's oracle, is set below towering cliffs and overlooks a sea of shimmering olive groves stretching to the Gulf of Corinth. The prehistoric North American people chose a site on the top of a steep bluff, next to a river, to construct their sacred Serpent Mound.

The beauty of the natural landscape is incorporated in the spirit of Stonehenge, the circle of gaunt standing stones on Salisbury Plain in southern England; in the ship graves found in secluded groves on the Swedish island of Gotland; and in Petra, the lost city of the Nabataeans, carved out of pink sandstone cliffs in the heart of the Jordanian desert.

All these sites derive their beauty and magic from the interaction of nature and the works of man, and are imbued with a *spiritus loci*, a spirit of place. Simply to see them is a sacred experience.

ALTAMIRA

> 6 Papa, mira toros
> pintados!
> (Papa, look at the
> painted bulls!) 9

MARIA DE SAUTUOLA ON SEEING THE
PAINTED BISON OF ALTAMIRA IN 1879.

DURING A HOT SUMMER IN THE NORTH OF Spain in 1879, Don Marcelino Sanz de Sautuola, a Spanish nobleman and amateur archeologist, was looking for evidence of prehistoric remains at a cave known as Altamira. A hunter had discovered the cave by chance in 1868, and Sautuola had visited it seven years later, when he had found some interesting flints and animal bones.

But this time, accompanied by his 12-year-old daughter Maria, he was to see something so extraordinary that it would be some 20 years before experts would agree upon the authenticity of the discovery. For, as he dug away near the cave's entrance, he heard a sudden cry out of the darkness. Maria had wandered into the cave and was calling him to come and see the "toros!" ("bulls!").

Sautuola rushed in and found his daughter in a pocket of the cave where the roof was so low he had to bend double. Then, in the light of their flickering lanterns, he saw to his astonishment the painted form of a bison looming over him on the roof of the cave. As he looked around at the strange undulating rock canopy, more and more animals emerged in shades of red, brown, yellow and black, roused, as it were, from thousands of years of stony sleep.

Creations from the Stone Age

Sautuola was looking at stylish, colourful paintings that had been drawn by Stone Age artists some 13,000 years before. But when Sautuola's discovery was made public, most scholars were dismissive of his claim that the paintings were thousands of years old. Nothing like them had been seen before, and it seemed scarcely credible that Stone Age man could have created anything so sophisticated. It was only in the first years of this century, after the discovery of cave paintings in southwest France and the Pyrenees, that academics changed their minds, and Altamira became recognized as one of the most important of the Stone Age painted caves.

The cave of Altamira, a prehistoric gallery of Stone Age art, was discovered by chance in 1868. The floor of the Painted Hall (ABOVE) was later lowered so that its magnificent undulating ceiling, painted with animals, could be properly studied.

The polychrome bison (RIGHT) is one of the 25 animals depicted on the ceiling of the Painted Hall. The Stone Age artist used paint made from natural pigments, such as ochre. A copy of the bison (TOP RIGHT) was made by the French scholar Abbé Breuil earlier this century.

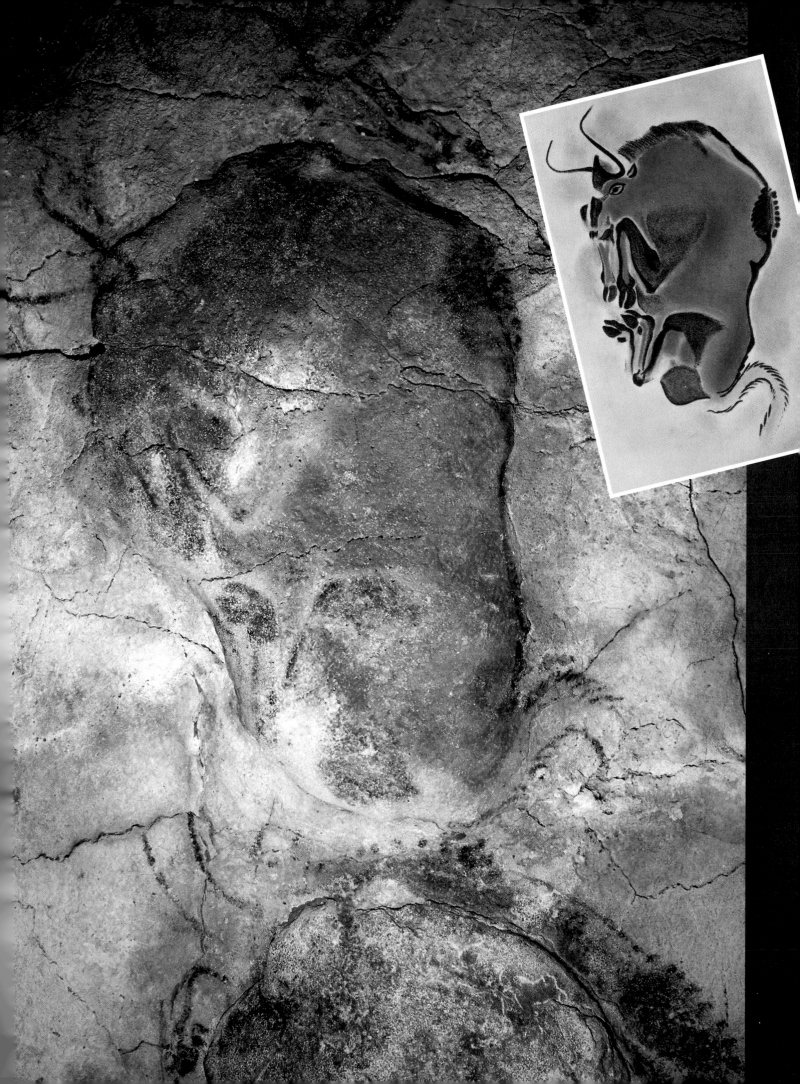

ALTAMIRA

Don Marcelino Sanz de Sautuola (ABOVE) *discovered the paintings of Altamira in 1879 after his daughter had wandered into the cave and alerted him to their presence. When Sautuola made his discovery public, he was generally disbelieved by the academic establishment. The importance of Altamira became apparent only at the start of this century, after the discovery of cave paintings in southwest France and the Pyrenees. Abbé Breuil, shown standing by the entrance of the Painted Hall* (BELOW), *pioneered the study of the cave.*

The cave of Altamira, which is now open to small parties of visitors, is a long twisting cavern that penetrates 300 yards into the hillside and tapers into a low, narrow "tail", where it is necessary to crawl on all fours. From entrance to tail, the walls are decorated with numerous engravings and drawings of animals, especially bison, deer, wild boar, and ibex, as well as various enigmatic abstract symbols and images created by blowing paint through a tube around a human hand pressed to the wall.

But the highlight of a visit to Altamira is the Painted Hall (where Maria first saw the *toros*). In this chamber, which lies to the left just beyond the entrance, the floor has been lowered so that the paintings can be seen in all their glory. Measuring 60 feet long and 30 feet wide, the ceiling is alive with the shapes of 25 animals, mostly bison, with three wild boar, three deer, two horses and a wolf. Some scholars believe that the ceiling was composed as a single work of art, and that it depicts a bison hunt.

Many of the creatures were painted on top of earlier black and red images, which were used as a base to give the later additions a richer texture. The animals' power and vitality are brilliantly enhanced by the ingenuity of the original artists, who utilized the natural undulations of their stone canvas to give their creations a third dimension. Bumps and hollows were painted to represent heads and bodies, with natural fissures in the rock often worked into the picture.

Paint was made from natural pigments, such as ochre, haematite and manganese, which gave the artist different shades of red, brown, yellow and black, but not, it seems, blue or green. The pigments were ground into a powder and probably mixed with a binding agent, such as animal grease, to form a paste. This would then be applied to the cave walls and ceilings with the fingers, or perhaps with a brush consisting of hair, clumps of moss, feathers or sticks.

"Hunting magic"

It is now thought that the paintings at Altamira and elsewhere played an important part—perhaps ritual or ceremonial—in the life of Stone Age people. The great French scholar Abbé Breuil championed the theory that the animal paintings were examples of "hunting magic", designed to ensnare certain animals by casting a pictorial spell on them. If this were the case it is strange that reindeer, which were an important source of food, do not frequently appear in Stone Age paintings.

But whatever Altamira's paintings meant for their creators, it is their haunting beauty (which inspired Pablo Picasso) and great antiquity that now attract visitors. If the mind can be emptied of its speculations and theories, it is possible to see why Maria de Sautuola was so startled when she suddenly saw the bison stampeding over her head.

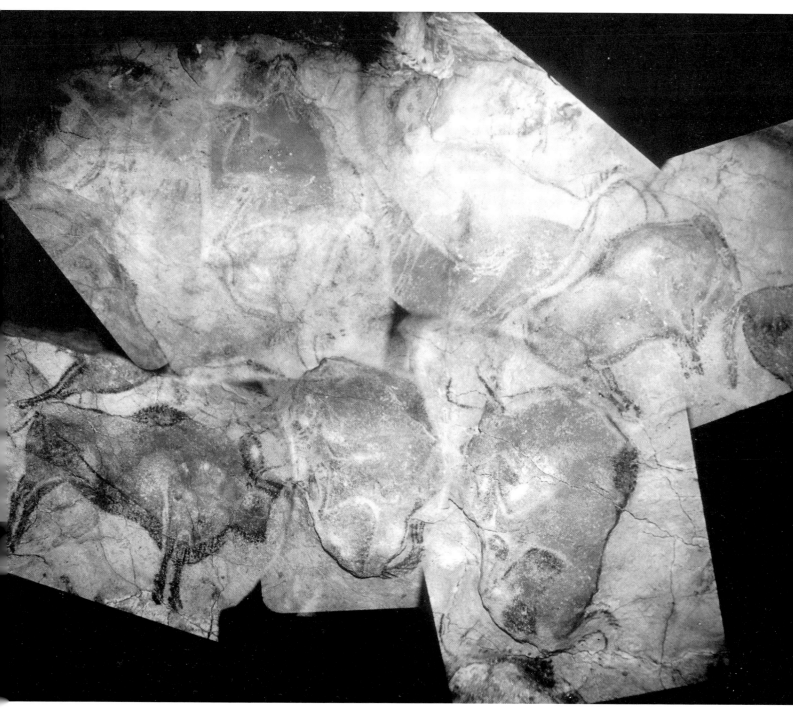

The superb style and technique used by the artists is shown in the photomontage (ABOVE) of part of the ceiling of the Painted Hall. Some scholars believe that the ceiling's images (LEFT) should be regarded as a single composition, perhaps depicting a bison hunt.

STONEHENGE

SURROUNDED BY THE OPEN CHALK DOWNS OF Salisbury Plain, the gaunt, grey circle of standing stones named by the Saxons Stonehenge ("the stone gallows") reaches back into the mists of British history. This enigmatic monument was as ancient to the Romans as Roman remains are to the twentieth century. The stones were raised about 4,000 years ago, though the site was in use a thousand years before that time.

Stonehenge has fascinated archeologists, writers, artists and mystics, and draws thousands of curious visitors each year. Its massive trilithons, carefully cut, dressed and fitted, are dramatically set in an area peppered with ancient burial mounds and farms. For the British people, the stones have become part of the national psyche, and conjure up images of groups gathered to watch the midsummer sunrise, white-robed Druids, and ancient astronomy.

The first written record of Stonehenge is found in the works of Geoffrey of Monmouth (c. A.D. 1100–54). He refers to the stones as the "Giants' Dance", a name that could mean either a ring built by giants, or a ring *of* giants. For in folklore traditions, many stone circles are said to be petrified dancers, and Stonehenge's great trilithons might well have suggested the image of giants dancing, hands on shoulders.

The origins of Stonehenge

Geoffrey also tells the tale that the stones were brought by the magician Merlin from Ireland with the help of "Engines" to mark a mass grave of Britons. There may be a grain of truth in this, for of the monument's two types of stones—bluestones and sarsens—the former were brought from the Preseli Hills in southwest Wales. All 80 stones, each weighing about 4 tons, were hauled on sledges and rollers to the Welsh coast. Lifted onto rafts, they were taken up the mouth of the River Severn and then inland via other rivers to a point where they were dragged overland to the site. The same route was also used by traders travelling to and from Ireland, which may well account for the story of the stones' Irish origins.

Storm clouds and a rainbow provide a dramatic backdrop for Stonehenge's awesome power. Gaunt and solitary in its bleak setting on Salisbury Plain, this ancient stone circle, older than Egypt's great pyramids, was not always so aloof. It once stood at the centre of a thriving community.

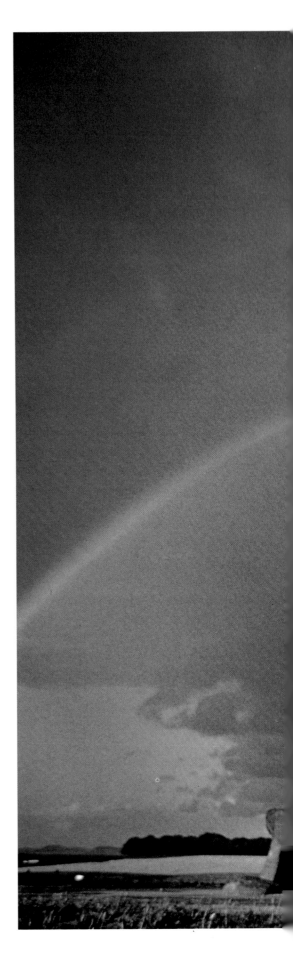

A. *Saxa que vocantur Corselones pondere 12 tonnay:*
  altitudine 24 pedes, latitudine pedes 7. ambitu 10;
B. *Saxa que vocantur Cronete, 6. vel 7. tonnarum;*
C. *Locus vbi ossa humana effodiuntur*

The magician Merlin
transported Stonehenge to Salisbury Plain according to the medieval writer Geoffrey of Monmouth. A 14th-century manuscript shows him (ABOVE LEFT) effortlessly positioning a massive stone lintel, watched by two awestruck admirers.

Another common folk tradition proposed that stone circles were petrified giants. This belief may have inspired the engraving (ABOVE RIGHT) of semi-humanized stones, reproduced in the 1660 edition of William Camden's Britannia.

Stonehenge is now thought to have been the focal point of a vast cemetery of burial mounds or barrows in the area. There were three main phases in the site's development. In about 3100 B.C., the ditch and bank were built, enclosing a circle of small pits—known as the Aubrey holes—whose function is unknown. After some 500 years, the site was abandoned until about 2100 B.C., when the bluestones were raised in two incomplete circles around the centre of the site. Finally, about 100 years later, the bluestones were rearranged and sarsen stones brought from the Marlborough Downs, 20 miles to the north.

During Stonehenge's last phase of construction, Salisbury Plain was probably populated by a people of a Bronze Age culture, who exported bronze tools and gold ornaments to Europe. They buried their dead in round burial mounds and probably financed the building of Stonehenge.

This ancient people may have spoken a language ancestral to the Celtic tongue, but there is no concrete evidence to connect them with the later Celtic priesthood known to Roman authors as the Druids. These mysterious figures, who performed animal and, it is said, human sacrifices, were linked with Stonehenge only in the mid-seventeenth century, when the antiquary John Aubrey first suggested that Britain's stone circles were Druidical temples. This idea dominated the Romantic Age, when Stonehenge was painted against a backdrop of tempestuous skies, and poems evoked scenes of human sacrifice: "the Druids long of yore/Purpled thy circles with unhallowed gore. . . ."

Although the monument predates by about 2,000 years the time when the Druids were known to have lived, their alleged connection with the stones persisted. For example, the so called "Slaughter Stone" was proposed in 1799 as being "designed for the

John Aubrey (1626–97), an antiquarian and writer, was the first to connect Stonehenge with the Druids.

slaying or preparing of victims'', but is now thought to be a fallen standing stone.

"The Druid's groves are gone—so much the better. Stonehenge is not—but what the devil is it?'' wrote Lord Byron. Byron's question still stands. In recent times, Stonehenge has been described as a sophisticated astronomical observatory. Certainly in its most developed phase it was laid out so that midsummer sunrise and midwinter moonrise could be observed from within the horseshoe of sarsen stones, but its astronomical function was part of a greater whole.

Stonehenge was probably built, like the great medieval cathedrals, as a ritual space, to the glory of God and as a symbol of the prestige of the community and its ruler. It may have been a temple, a tomb, a meeting place for rituals or festivals. Certainly it was the biggest of the 900 or more stone circles of Britain, and, in its day, the architectural wonder of western Europe.

In the mid-17th century, John Aubrey first suggested that Britain's stone circles were Druidical temples. Though a contemporary described him as "a shiftless person, roving, magotie-headed and sometimes little better than crased'', Aubrey's ideas later appealed to Romantic poets and artists. At this time paintings of Stonehenge, such as that by John Constable (ABOVE), often used wild weather to heighten the impact of the stones.

THE TOMB OF TUTANKHAMUN

> *At last have made wonderful discovery in Valley; a magnificent tomb with seals intact; re-covered same for your arrival; congratulations.*
>
> CABLE SENT BY HOWARD CARTER TO LORD CARNARVON, 5 NOVEMBER 1922.

FOR 33 CENTURIES A DARK PASSAGEWAY CUT out of the Valley of the Kings, a burial ground for Egyptian pharaohs, had been undisturbed by human voices and footsteps. But on 26 November 1922 the British Egyptologist Howard Carter and his patron Lord Carnarvon stood there in the darkness, face to face with a sealed doorway. Behind it they hoped to discover the tomb of the shadowy young pharaoh Tutankhamun, with all its attendant treasures and artefacts. Their one fear was that they would find instead an empty chamber—the legacy of ancient Egyptian robbers who had despoiled all the other tombs in the valley.

In one of the great moments of archeology, Carter, his hands trembling, made a small hole in the top left-hand corner of the door and poked an iron rod through to check for any obstructions. He then tested for noxious gases with a candle, enlarged the hole, inserted the candle, and peered in. At first he could discern nothing in the murky gloom. But as his eyes grew accustomed to the light, he was "struck dumb with amazement". For Lord Carnarvon, the suspense was almost unbearable; and, according to Carter, Carnarvon "inquired anxiously, 'Can you see any-thing?'" It was all Carter "could do to get out the words, 'Yes, wonderful things.'"

What Carter and Carnarvon saw when they flashed an electric lamp around the dark interior was a cornucopia of strange magical objects—some of the burial equipment of, they were now sure, Tutankhamun. Heads of carved animals reared up at them in the lamplight; gilded couches, golden chariot wheels, alabaster vases, inlaid caskets, a gold throne—all were heaped together in a jumble of staggering opulence. Over to the right, two lifesize human statues stood guard on either side of another sealed doorway: the prospect of still more exciting revelations beckoned.

Searching for the lost pharaoh

Tutankhamun's name is now linked in the popular imagination with golden treasures and coffins containing mummies and inscribed with magical texts. Yet, in his own day, he was a relatively unimportant king, who came to the Egyptian throne in about 1361 B.C. Now his fame is such that thousands come to the Valley of the Kings each year to see his tomb.

Howard Carter had been hired in 1907 by a wealthy British aristocrat named Lord

The Valley of the Kings, burial ground of the Egyptian pharaohs, lies by Thebes on the west bank of the Nile. Here, in 1922, the tomb of Tutankhamun was unearthed by Howard Carter.

The boy-king Tutankhamun gazes from the darkness, 33 centuries after his burial. This gold mask was placed over the head of the king's mummy, and is thought to resemble him closely.

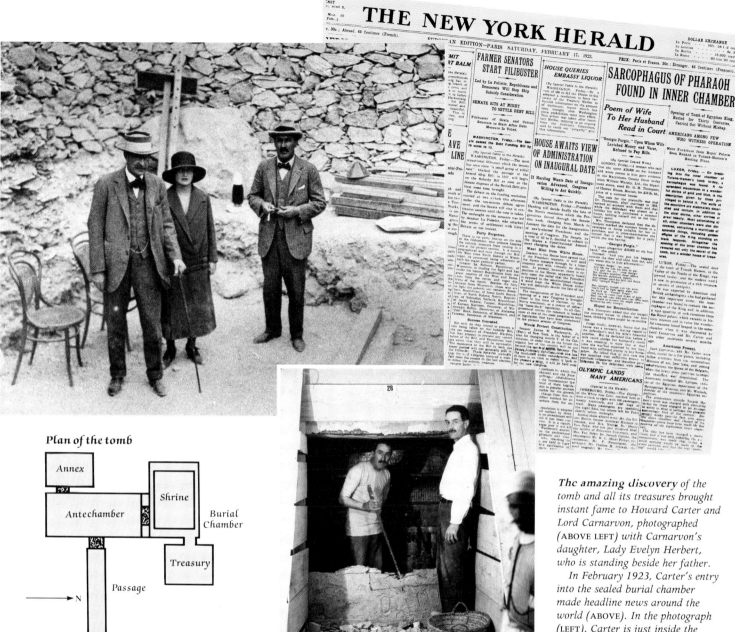

FARMER SENATORS START FILIBUSTER

SARCOPHAGUS OF PHARAOH FOUND IN INNER CHAMBER

Poem of Wife To Her Husband Read in Court

Plan of the tomb

Annex

Shrine

Antechamber

Burial Chamber

Treasury

Passage

Entrance

N

Sealed Doors

The amazing discovery of the tomb and all its treasures brought instant fame to Howard Carter and Lord Carnarvon, photographed (ABOVE LEFT) with Carnarvon's daughter, Lady Evelyn Herbert, who is standing beside her father.

In February 1923, Carter's entry into the sealed burial chamber made headline news around the world (ABOVE). In the photograph (LEFT), Carter is just inside the chamber with the massive golden shrine behind him. His colleague A.C. Mace stands among bits of chipped-off plaster.

Carnarvon, a keen amateur Egyptologist, to excavate for him. For five years, Carter dug an area near the Valley of the Kings without spectacular success. In 1914, the Egyptian authorities granted him the crucial concession to dig in the valley, but it was three more years before excavations could really begin in earnest.

After several seasons of largely fruitless digging, Carnarvon almost decided to close down the operation. But Carter, who knew that almost all of the tombs of the pharaohs of the 18th Dynasty (c.1570–1320 B.C.) had been found in the valley, was convinced that

Tutankhamun's tomb lay waiting to be unearthed. He therefore persuaded Carnarvon to let him dig for one more season beneath the huts of ancient Egyptian workmen discovered near the tomb of Rameses VI.

On 4 November 1922 Carter was vindicated. Under the first hut excavated a step cut into the valley floor was uncovered. Excitement grew as more steps were revealed—leading down to the upper part of a doorway, which had been plastered and sealed. Next day, Carter rushed off a cable to Carnarvon, who was in England, telling him the momentous news.

Steps leading to the tomb of Tutankhamun (OPPOSITE PAGE) lie to the left of the packing cases (RIGHT FOREGROUND), in a photograph taken soon after the discovery. The yawning entrance to the tomb of Rameses VI is directly above the steps.

THE TOMB OF TUTANKHAMUN

On the north wall of the burial chamber, Tutankhamun (BELOW) is represented as Osiris, god of the dead. The king is about to undergo the Opening of the Mouth ceremony, part of his funeral ritual.

The gold-plated throne (BOTTOM) was found in the antechamber. The backrest shows the young pharaoh sitting in a relaxed pose with his queen Ankhesenamun leaning toward him.

Carnarvon reached Luxor on 23 November with his daughter Lady Evelyn Herbert. They went to the site the following day. The whole staircase was then cleared—16 steps in all—and the entire door was revealed. It bore seals with a royal name: Tutankhamun. However, their delight was short-lived, for close examination of some of the seals and the plasterwork showed that the tomb had been entered twice after it had been originally sealed. The heartbreaking possibility existed that the tomb had been plundered.

There was only one way to find out. The door was taken down, revealing a passageway filled with rubble and stone—an attempt to deter robbers. The passage was then cleared out, enabling Carter, on 26 November, to peer through the second sealed door and see those "wonderful things".

This first room was opened up the next day. It turned out to be the tomb's antechamber. Just under 12 feet wide and over 26 feet long, with bare walls, it was filled with the pharaoh's funerary equipment—objects which it was believed he would need in the afterlife. Fortunately, it looked as if the thieves had disturbed, but had not had time to carry off, the numerous treasures, any one of which, Carter reckoned, would have rewarded a season's digging.

The priceless objects in the antechamber and the annex—a smaller room leading off the antechamber to the southwest—had to be dutifully recorded, photographed, and preserved before being shipped to Cairo for safekeeping. Only then could Carter turn his attention to the third sealed door and what lay behind it. Meanwhile, news of the discovery spread like wildfire and gripped the public imagination all over the world. The excavators were inundated with telegrams, letters, offers of assistance, and besieged by reporters, friends and other visitors—so much so that valuable work time was inevitably lost.

Opening the burial chamber

By February 1923, however, the antechamber had been cleared. Now was the moment of truth: would they find the king's mummy behind the sealed door? Disconcertingly, this door too showed signs of intrusion. On 17 February Carter began to chip away the door's plaster, watched by a small group of guests. After ten minutes, he had made a hole big enough to insert a lamp. What he saw was extraordinary: not more

With arms outstretched, a gold statue of the goddess Serket (LEFT) keeps guard over a gilded wooden shrine containing the viscera of Tutankhamun. Three other goddesses, Isis, Nephthys, and Neith, protect the other sides of the shrine.

The head of a lionlike creature (ABOVE), made of gilded wood with crystal eyes, formed part of a bed found in the antechamber. Two similar beds, bearing the heads of cows and hippopotamuses, were also found in the chamber. All three are the wrong shape and size for practical use, and were part of the pharaoh's funerary equipment.

than a yard from the door was a solid wall of
gold stretching as far as the eye could see.
With help he quickly dismantled the rest of
the doorway and saw that the wall, glittering
with gold and inlaid with blue faience, was a
magnificent rectangular shrine. It was so
huge that there was barely space to move
between it and the walls of the room, which
was slightly smaller than the antechamber.
This shrine, Carter hoped, would contain the
royal sarcophagus.

As he and Carnarvon edged their way
around the burial chamber, they could see
that its walls had been painted. Furthermore,
the excavators were amazed to discover in
the eastern wall an entrance to yet another
chamber, guarded by a forbidding black
statue of the jackal-headed god Anubis.

Dubbed the "treasury" by Carter, this
room was full of more beautiful objects:
miniature boats, statuettes, the gilded head of
a cow representing the goddess Hathor, a
model granary, vases, chests containing
bracelets, rings, pendants, earrings, made of
gold, amethyst, turquoise, cornelian and
other precious materials.

Gilded shrines and nested coffins

The next crucial phase was the opening of the
gilded shrine, though it would be several
years (mainly due to protracted negotiations
with the Eyptian government to extend the
concession) before work got under way.
When it did, they found a second golden
shrine fitted within the first. And still the
suspense continued as two more nested
shrines, both glittering with gold, were
revealed. Finally, with "suppressed excitement" Carter opened the last shrine and saw a
magnificent yellow quartzite sarcophagus,
rectangular in shape, with a rose granite lid.
They were nearing the end of their trail.

The four shrines had to be carefully
dismantled—a long and painstaking operation—before Carter could concentrate on
the sarcophagus. The granite lid was eventually lifted with a hoist. At first they saw
only linen shrouds within. But when these
were peeled back, a gasp went up when a
golden effigy of the boy king—the lid of a
human-shaped coffin—stared up at them.
Nor did the seemingly endless drama end
there. For tightly nested within this coffin
were two more, the second of which, to their
amazement, was made of solid gold.

Finally, in late October 1926, the last
coffin lid was raised and the king's mummy

exposed for the first time in 33 centuries. There, in contrast to the dark sticky mass of anointing unguents that had been poured over the body (and had destroyed most of it) the sad but serene face of Tutankhamun gazed up at them from a beaten gold mask. Of consummate beauty, the mask had prevented the corrosion of the pharaoh's actual face, which, according to Carter, looked "refined and cultured", when the mask was eventually separated from it. For Howard Carter, whose work on the tomb continued into the 1930s, and Lord Carnarvon, who died from pneumonia in 1923, the discovery of the tomb was the find of a lifetime.

Today most of Tutankhamun's treasures can be seen in the Cairo Museum. The tomb itself is empty except for the sarcophagus containing one of the golden coffins in which the king's body rests in peace. The tomb may seem stark and bare, but its sacredness has not diminished. It can still convey to the visitor the sense of magic that Carter and his colleagues felt after they had gazed on the first golden coffin. That night, leaving the tomb, they "beheld the blue vault of the heavens, where the Sun is Lord, but our inner thoughts still lingered over the splendour of that vanished Pharaoh. . . ."

The jackal-headed god Anubis (ABOVE) *guards the entrance to the "treasury", which leads off from the burial chamber. Here Carter found a number of wooden shrines containing ritual statuettes. Three of these (*LEFT*), depicting Tutankhamun, are carved in wood, coated in gesso and gilded. The first shows the king stepping forward, holding the crook and flail, symbols of royal office. The statuettes inside the shrine represent the king harpooning from a boat made of papyrus.*

Howard Carter brushes dust off the second of the nested coffins. Inside this coffin was a third, made of solid gold, which contained the mummy of the king.*

DELPHI

> ❝ I know the number
> of the sands,
> and the measure
> of the sea;
> I understand the
> dumb and hear
> him who does
> not speak. ❞
>
> THE DELPHIC ORACLE IN REPLY TO
> QUESTIONERS SENT BY KING CROESUS.

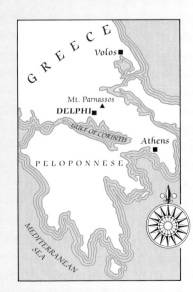

MORE THAN 2,500 YEARS AGO, PILGRIMS FROM all over Greece and farther abroad used to make their way to the sacred site of Delphi in central Greece. They came to consult the most famous oracle of the ancient world. Some travelled by foot along the road that led from Athens to the southwest. Others came by ship, disembarking at a port, now known as Itea, on the north coast of the Gulf of Corinth. From here, a journey of about three hours took them through a broad plain and into full view of Mount Parnassus, which towered above a sprawling glitter of white buildings and monuments.

As they approached, they would have gained a clearer view of the Sacred Way as it skirted the mountainside and snaked up through the Sanctuary of Apollo, crowned by its magnificent temple. Other buildings would have come into view: the white marble theatre; the 7,000-seater stadium at the top of the town; the gymnasium with its open-air and covered race tracks; and the elegant circle of Doric columns that formed the outside of the *tholos*, or rotunda, in the sanctuary of Athena Pronaia.

Little now remains of the buildings of Delphi. But its dramatic setting—rocky crags, crevices, gushing springs, imposing cliffs—is still awesome. Below the sanctuary is a precipitous drop down to the gorge of Pleistos, which dissolves into the broad expanse of olive trees leading to the blue waters of the gulf. Above it rise great barren cliffs which, because they reflected light and glowed at sunset, were known as the Phaedriades, the "Shining Ones". A chasm cuts into these cliffs and at its base flows the Castalian spring, whose waters were used for ritual purification.

The coming of Apollo

Delphi's wild mountain scenery, 2,000 feet above sea level, naturally lent itself to the veneration of Gē, the Earth goddess, to whom the site was originally sacred. The Greeks considered Delphi to be the centre of the world. According to legend, Zeus, father of the gods, released two eagles from the opposite ends of the earth. The spot below the point where they met—Delphi—was deemed to be the centre, and was marked by a stone known as the *omphalos* ("navel").

Another legend relates that a monstrous serpent guarded the place, which was then known as Pytho, and Gē's oracle there. However, Apollo, son of Zeus and god of

The ruins of Delphi, home of the most famous oracle in the ancient world, are set among rugged cliffs in central Greece. Just east of the main sanctuary is the tholos (RIGHT), a circular building of the early 4th century B.C., the function of which is unknown.

The waters of the Castalian spring were used for ritual purification by questioners before they consulted the oracle.

The spring was later conceived by Roman poets to be the source of poetic inspiration. Ovid (43 B.C.–A.D. 18), for example, wrote in his Amores: "May golden Apollo minister me with cups brimming with Castalian water."

DELPHI

King Aegeus of Athens consults the oracle (RIGHT) in the stylized decoration of a 5th-century vase. The Pythia is sitting on her tripod and holds a sprig of laurel and a bowl, possibly filled with holy water.

The god Apollo and his sister Artemis (BELOW) stand either side of the omphalos, a stone at Delphi which the Greeks believed marked the centre of the world.

light, came to Pytho and slew the serpent or "Python". He then set up his own oracle, with a priestess, known as the Pythia, acting as the medium through which the god replied to questioners.

At the height of its popularity, the shrine needed up to three Pythias to cope with the questioners' demands. According to the Roman historian Diodorus Siculus, the Pythias were at first young virgins. However, when one of them was abducted and raped by a Thessalian rogue, it was decided that they should be chaste matrons of at least 50 years of age.

The legends relate that the Pythia sat on a three-legged bowl or tripod placed over a deep crack in the earth. From this fissure intoxicating vapours would rise, inducing the Pythia to utter a stream of frenzied and incoherent sounds. Other evidence suggests that she entered a state of trance by chewing laurel leaves.

The Pythia was consulted on all manner of things—matters of religion, money, marriage, and especially colonial enterprises. Questioners were required to purify themselves beforehand in the waters of the Castalian spring. There then followed a ritual in which a goat was sprinkled with cold water: if it trembled all over, the signs were right for the goat to be sacrificed and for the god to be petitioned. The questioner duly paid a fee and waited his turn. Questions were written down on tablets and handed to the Pythia, who then entered a trance and babbled out an answer. This, in turn, was interpreted by a priest, who wrote it down in verse and gave it to the questioner.

The ambiguous oracle

The answers given by the oracle must have been found consistently accurate or helpful enough down the ages for the Greek historian Strabo to state that it had the reputation for being the most truthful in the world. Yet the oracle was also notorious for the ambiguity of its pronouncements.

It is said that Croesus, King of Lydia (560–546 B.C.) in Asia Minor, decided to test the truthfulness of the Delphic and other oracles by asking them simultaneously through proxies what he, Croesus, was doing at the time of questioning. Only the Delphic oracle answered correctly: Croesus was boiling up a tortoise and a lamb in a brass pot. The king was so impressed by this that he showered Delphi with expensive gifts.

Apollo, son of Zeus, is said to have established his oracle at Delphi after killing a serpent known as the Python. Apollo's priestess, the Pythia, operated within the god's temple, whose few remaining columns can be seen below the well-preserved 4th-century theatre.

However, the oracle hardly repaid this lavishness when it was asked by Croesus what would happen if he attacked the Persians. The cryptic reply was that if he did, he would destroy a great empire. The oracle was correct. But it was Croesus' own empire that was destroyed.

With similar ambiguity the oracle warned the Spartan Phalanthos, who was leading a colonial expedition to Italy, that he would capture the town of Tarentum as soon as he felt rain falling from a clear sky. Impossible though this seemed, the oracle was vindicated when Phalanthos felt the tears on his neck (''rain'') of his weeping wife Aithra (whose name means ''clear sky''): he then went on to capture the town.

The oracle also warned the Roman emperor Nero to beware of the 73rd year. This turned out to be not his own, but a veiled reference to his successor, the 73-year-old Galba. It was more straightforward when it declared that the Greek philosopher Socrates was the wisest man in Greece, and told Alexander the Great: ''My son, none can resist you.''

The historical origins of Delphi go back more than 3,000 years. But it was only from the eighth to the sixth century B.C. that the place began to grow and flourish. Today, the splendour of the sanctuary of Apollo, enclosed within a roughly rectangular area measuring 200 by 140 yards, has to be reconstructed in the mind from the ruins of its buildings, monuments and statues. Flanking the Sacred Way that twists uphill to the temple of Apollo were numerous small temple-like buildings known as ''treasuries''. These were erected by city states to house valuable gifts dedicated to the god in appreciation of the oracle, and also to show off their opulence and prestige.

The head of the famous Bronze Charioteer of Delphi is part of a lifesize statue in the site's museum. Excavated in 1896, the figure would originally have stood in a chariot drawn by graceful horses. The whole piece was probably dedicated in 475 B.C. by the Sicilian prince Polyzelos to commemorate his victory at the Pythian Games, which had been established at Delphi in 590 B.C.

Small temple-like buildings, known as ''treasuries'', were built by city states to house gifts presented to Apollo in appreciation of the oracle. The Treasury of the Athenians (LEFT), restored earlier this century, was erected soon after the Battle of Marathon in 490 B.C., in which the Athenians defeated the Persians.

DELPHI

The treasury of the Siphnians, with two caryatids—columns in the form of female figures—supporting the porch, was built with money obtained from the gold mines of Siphnos. The Athenians' treasury—the only one to be restored—was a marble building of the Doric order. Its outside walls were covered with inscriptions, including two hymns to Apollo, complete with ancient musical notation.

Among other sights visitors would have seen were the circular *halos*, or threshing floor, where theatrical enactments of Apollo slaying the Python were periodically staged; the elegant colonnade erected by Athens; and the striking monument of three bronze intertwined snakes rising up and supporting a tripod, raised by the Greeks after their victory against the Persians at Plataia in 479 B.C. Dominating the sanctuary was the temple of Apollo, rebuilt twice, in 546 and 373 B.C., after destruction by fire and earthquake respectively. Although the Pythia operated from within the temple, it is difficult to determine exactly where. Nor has the vapour-exuding chasm ever been found.

Decline and fall

Delphi's importance and prestige survived the oracle's unpatriotic advice to the Greeks not to withstand the invading Persians in the early fifth century B.C. The Greeks even showered the place with statues, monuments and trophies in celebration of their victory. But during the following centuries, the oracle's reputation for impartiality declined with its allegiance to different powerful states, including Athens and Sparta.

In the second century B.C., the Romans took over Delphi, and its influence and prestige sank further. The emperor Nero (A.D. 54–68) plundered more than 500 statues from the site. By the time the emperor Julian (A.D. 360–66) sent a questioner to Delphi, it was a ghost of its former self. The answer the oracle is said to have given Julian evokes a poignant image of its sad lapse into decay: "Tell the king this: the glorious temple has fallen into ruin; Apollo has no roof over his head; the bay leaves are silent, the prophetic springs and fountains are dead."

With its spirit already broken, the oracle was officially closed down in about 385 by the Christian emperor Theodosius. The Apollonian cult, which had usurped that of the Earth goddess, had been ousted by a brave new religion.

The oracle at Delphi was notorious for the ambiguity of its pronouncements. It told King Croesus of Lydia, for example, that if he attacked the Persians, he would destroy a great empire. Croesus did attack them, but destroyed his own empire.

However, the oracle could also be straightforward. Alexander the Great (356–323 B.C.) (LEFT), one of the most brilliant generals of all time, was told: "My son, none can resist you."

The oracle also informed the Greek philosopher Socrates (469–399 B.C.) (BELOW) that he was the wisest man in Greece. Socrates is said to have construed this to mean that, unlike others, his wisdom lay in being aware of his ignorance.

French archeologists gather around a newly unearthed statue of a youth or kouros (OPPOSITE PAGE) in 1894. Serious excavation of Delphi had begun the year before under the direction of Théophile Homolle, head of the French School of Archeology at Athens. Greek villagers who were living on the ancient site had to be rehoused so that digging could start.

GOTLAND

> 6 *The Gotlanders have so much gold they cannot weigh it. Their pigs eat from silver troughs. Their women spin with golden distaffs.* 9
>
> HANS STRELOW, *CHRONICLES OF THE GOTLANDERS*, 1633.

THE LARGEST ISLAND IN THE BALTIC SEA, Gotland is sometimes called the "island of roses", since its climate is temperate enough for roses to bloom in December. Gotland has also been proposed as the site of legendary Atlantis, perhaps because it has been fabulously rich in the past, and still is idyllic. Few places so small—about 80 miles long and half as wide—have such a range of landscape: dense forests and rolling fields, rugged cliffs and sandy beaches. And in few places can be found such an array of historical remains.

The island has about 400 Bronze Age stone mounds or cairns and 350 ship graves; 70 Iron Age forts; and 100 or more Romanesque and Early Gothic churches, some of them the finest in northern Europe. It also boasts Scandinavia's best known stone maze, Trojeborg, as well as unique "picture stones"— memorial stones of the first millennium A.D.

According to the second-century historian Jordanes, Gotland was the home of the Goths, foremost of the barbarians who carved Europe into kingdoms at the fall of the Roman Empire. Legend relates that the first person to set foot on Gotland was a man named Tjelvar. In those days the island was controlled by evil spirits who made it sink by day and rise by night. But Tjelvar lit a fire that broke the spell, and the island thereafter remained above the water.

Traders and ships

Behind the legend is the fact that during the Stone Age, about 7,000 years ago, men certainly lived where Tjelvar landed—in the northeast around Gothem. They exported stone axeheads across the Baltic to south Sweden and Denmark, so beginning what would become a dominant theme in Gotland's history: trade. From its position in the Baltic, Gotland commanded routes south, east and west. From the Iron Age (beginning *c.*500 B.C.) through the Viking Age (A.D. 800–*c.*1050) to medieval times commerce was the island's lifeblood.

But if one *leitmotiv* of Gotland's history has been trade, another is ships. Ships were part of daily life: they were also part of death. Of all the island's ancient monuments the most evocative are its Bronze Age (*c.*1500–

The outline of a ship in stones at Klintehamn on the west coast of Gotland is one of many ship graves on this Baltic island. Dating from the Bronze Age and later, they are poignant memorials of an ancient faith— symbolic soul ships carrying the dead on their voyage to the Underworld.

GOTLAND

Visby, capital of Gotland, looks much the same today as it did in the Middle Ages, when for a time it was the trading centre of Europe, its only rival London. Its massive walls, built in the mid-13th century and bastioned by more than 30 towers, still enclose the tall warehouses which once held furs from Russia, Rhenish wine, English cloth and Byzantine gold.

The elegant picture stone (RIGHT) found at Sanda Church, Gotland, is a memorial stone dating from about A.D. 500. Originally painted in bright colours, its symbols may represent the cosmos, dominated by a great whirling disc. This has been interpreted as an image of the passing of time and therefore of fate.

In the middle is a tree, perhaps the World Tree, Yggdrasill, which stood at the centre of the Norse cosmos. The monster below it may be the World Serpent, Midgardsormr, who lay coiled around the world. Below him is a ship, probably signifying the Underworld, to which time and fate inexorably lead.

The picture stone (FAR RIGHT) of the Viking Age from Larbro St Hammers shows, at the top, a death in battle, and, at the bottom, a ship symbolizing the dead man's journey to the Underworld. The third panel down possibly depicts a ritual hanging connected with the cult of the war god Odin. An eagle, his emblem, appears above the victim, as does the valknut, *the three intertwined triangles, symbol of his power to bind and loose.*

500 B.C.) ship graves. These were symbolic memorials in which standing stones were set in the outline of elegant ships with high prows and raking lines.

In Bronze Age art, ships, wagons and the sun-disc (symbol of the Scandinavian sky god), were common motifs. The wagon is thought to symbolize the sun's journey across the sky by day, the ship its journey by night, when the sun seemed to sink into the sea. By association, the ship came to represent the soul's journey to the land of the dead.

The island is littered with these ship graves, which are often found in peaceful glades. Some are huge, such as the one at Gnisvard, south of Visby, which is 140 feet long and 23 feet wide. Big or small, the graves are among the most poignant of all the works of ancient man—soul ships, voyaging hopefully on, bearing their precious cargo.

Ships also adorn Gotland's unique picture stones. These memorial stones, as much as 10 feet high, date from the fifth century A.D. to the end of the Viking Age. The earlier stones bear abstract symbols, originally painted in bright colours. The later ones carry mythological scenes, some identifiable from Viking literature.

Underworld symbolism may also lie behind Gotland's famous stone maze, Trojeborg (Troy Castle), near Visby. Like the turf mazes of Great Britain, the stone mazes of Scandinavia are hard to date. They may be medieval or later, but the ritual use of the maze is very ancient. The labyrinth, sometimes depicted on megalithic tombs, may represent the path of the dead to the Underworld; and actual mazes may have been used for a type of funerary ritual. Most stone mazes lie by the sea, and it has been suggested that sailors used them to perform magic rituals: by symbolically entering the realm of the dead, they protected themselves against the dangers of the coming voyage.

Whether heaped in a cairn, painted, or marking out a ship grave or a maze, the stones of Gotland are eloquent of the past. Their rich, subtle symbolism speaks of a different cosmic order, a world in which the sky god was supreme, and ships carried the dead to their final resting place.

109

SERPENT MOUND

> *Probably the most extraordinary earthwork thus far discovered in the West, is the Great Serpent. . . .*
>
> EPHRAIM SQUIER AND EDWIN DAVIS, WHO SURVEYED THE MOUND IN 1846.

IN ADAMS COUNTY, OHIO, A SPUR OF LAND, 150 feet high, rises sheer over a bend in a small river named Brush Creek. Seen from below, the tree-covered slopes seem unexceptional. But on the plateau on top of the hill is one of the strangest sights in North America. For here, rising a yard from the ground, a gigantic earthen serpent, its back covered with a skin of emerald grass, uncoils across the summit.

Serpent Mound, now preserved by the Ohio Historical Society, is one of the most dramatic of North America's ancient earthworks. From the observation tower near its tail, its twisting body seems to bulge out of the ground, with seven deep coils unravelling from the tightly wound tail, then straightening into the neck. Its mouth is stretched wide open as if about to swallow what looks like an egg—a separate oval mound, 100 feet long. The shape of the snake is so crisply defined that it looks as if a giant serpentine mould has just been lifted from it.

In fact the mound was made hundreds of years ago from basketloads of earth deposited between an outline marked by stones or a mixture of ashes and clay. Measuring 20 feet wide and more than 1,000 feet long, the Great Serpent is one of thousands of earthworks, varying in shape and size, built by the prehistoric ancestors of the North American Indians. From the Great Lakes to the Gulf of Mexico, but especially in the Mississippi and Ohio River valleys, these mounds were usually the domed or conical coverings of graves or platforms for wooden temples. Some, however, known as "effigy mounds", and mostly found in Wisconsin, were shaped like animals—birds, bears, elks, buffaloes, and serpents.

The mystery of the mound builders

Serpent Mound was first surveyed in 1846 by Ephraim Squier, a journalist, and Edwin Davis, a physician. The two men took precise measurements of the site, but were unable to say who had built it, or when.

In fact, these enigmatic mounds had puzzled white settlers ever since they first came across them in the eighteenth century. The typical view was that they were too sophisti-

A massive serpent, more than 1,000 feet long, endows a grassy ridge overlooking Brush Creek in Ohio with a special quality of mystery and primitive magic. Serpent Mound was one of many earthworks constructed in North America by the ancestors of the American Indians.

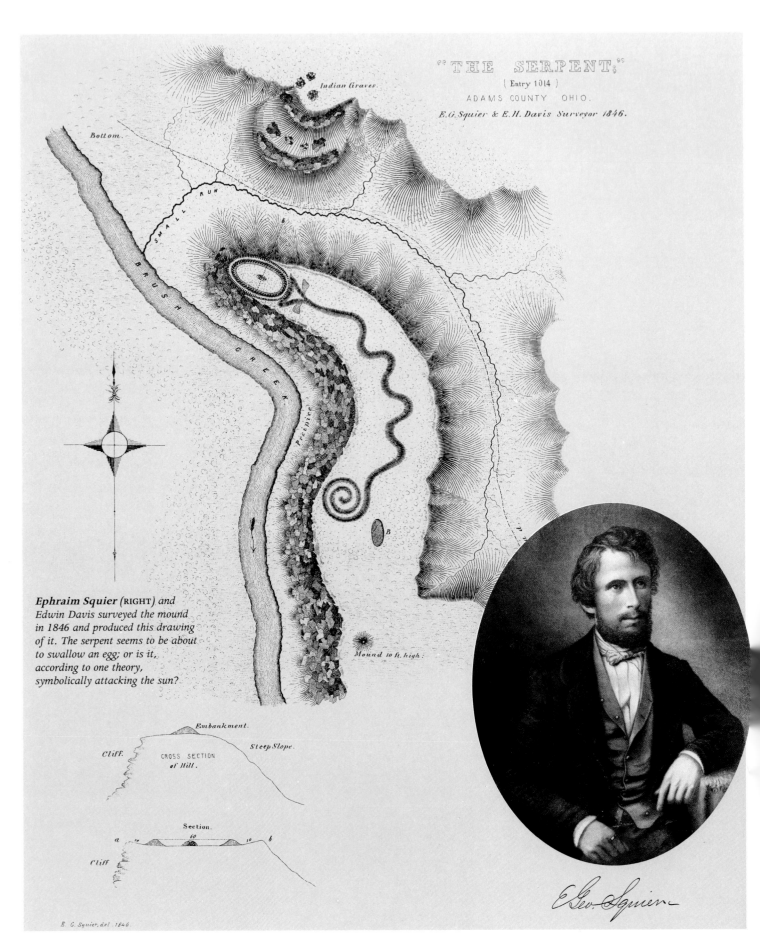

"THE SERPENT,"
(Entry 1014)
ADAMS COUNTY OHIO.
E. G. Squier & E. H. Davis Surveyor 1846.

Indian Graves.

Bottom.

SMALL RUN

BRUSH CREEK

Precipice

B

Mound 10 ft. high.

Ephraim Squier (RIGHT) and
Edwin Davis surveyed the mound
in 1846 and produced this drawing
of it. The serpent seems to be about
to swallow an egg; or is it,
according to one theory,
symbolically attacking the sun?

Embankment.

Cliff.   CROSS SECTION   Steep Slope.
of Hill.

Section.

Cliff

E. G. Squier, del. 1846.

112

cated to have been the work of contemporary Indians, whom most then considered to be mere "savages". This assumption was also strengthened by the sophistication and beauty of the grave goods unearthed in some of the burial mounds: freshwater pearls, obsidian spearheads, mica mirrors, engraved stones, carved smoking pipes and conch drinking cups.

A number of fanciful theories arose attempting to explain the mounds. Some suggested, for example, that the Egyptians or Vikings, or even the lost tribes of Israel, must have emigrated to the New World at some time in the past. Only gradually, toward the end of the nineteenth century, was it generally accepted that these ancient earthworks were created by American Indians.

Many scholars now believe that the Great Serpent was the work of the prehistoric Adena people, who flourished from about 1000 to 100 B.C. in the Ohio River Valley and adjacent areas. The Adenas were hunters and foragers, lived in small communities of a few simple houses, and were the earliest growers of maize in North America. Others think that Serpent Mound shows a scale of execution more compatible with the Hopewell people, mound builders whose more developed culture superseded that of the Adenas after about 100 B.C. But why exactly the Adenas, or the Hopewells, built this great snake remains a mystery.

The symbolic snake

From the ancient Greeks to the Australian aborigines, the snake has appeared prominently in the myths and religions of people all over the world. For the North American Indians, the snake was a powerful symbol: the rattlesnake, for example, was revered by the Cherokees, and thought to be a god-sent guardian spirit by the Mohicans and Delawares.

Perhaps the key to the meaning of Serpent Mound lies in the traditions of the Indians. Recently, an authority on the mound, William F. Romain, has argued that its builders were symbolically depicting a solar eclipse, in which the sun (the oval mound) is being attacked or eaten by a serpent. The image of the sun being swallowed by a monster occurs in a number of legends. The Iroquois, for example, believed that eclipses of the moon and the sun were caused by "fire dragons" eating them. In Cherokee tradition, the sun was afflicting their people with sickness so

they sent a huge serpent named Uktena to devour it. Romain points out that it may be significant that both the Iroquois and the Cherokees inhabited territories close to Serpent Mound.

Whatever its meaning, Ohio's great snake is a work of consummate beauty. For the thousands of people who visit it each year, its huge but graceful undulating body, fusing stillness with the dynamism of its uncoiling tail, remains an indelible memory.

An Adena stone effigy pipe dating from 1000 B.C. Carved pipes, such as this one, were used for smoking tobacco, and are among the most ancient stone sculptures found in eastern North America. Serpent Mound was thought to have been built by either the Adena (c. 1000–100 B.C.) or Hopewell (c. 100 B.C.–A.D. 400) peoples.

PETRA

> *The longer we staid, and the more mountain temples we climbed to, the more I felt that the inhabitants, among their other peculiarities, must have been winged.*
>
> BRITISH TRAVELLER HARRIET MARTINEAU
> AFTER VISITING PETRA IN 1847.

DURING HIS JOURNEY FROM SYRIA TO EGYPT IN late August 1812, the young Swiss explorer Johann Burckhardt met local Arab tribesmen just south of the Dead Sea who told him about "antiquities" in a nearby secluded valley known as Wadi Mousa—the Valley of Moses. Burckhardt's curiosity was aroused and so he went to the valley.

What he found there was a revelation. In the midst of the desert was an ancient city carved out of dramatic sandstone cliffs coloured different shades of pink and red. In every direction the dark entrances to hundreds upon hundreds of tombs, temples and houses—some small and simple, others with magnificent columned façades—had been cut into the natural mountain walls.

Burckhardt had found Petra (meaning "rock"), the city of the Nabataeans, an Arab tribe who had inhabited the site from the fourth century B.C. until the city's demise some 700 years later. Although the place had been known to Europeans from ancient writers, details of its location had been lost since the Crusaders had briefly occupied it in the twelfth century.

When news of Burckhardt's discovery filtered through to the western world, Petra became the exotic and romantic stopping-place for intrepid Europeans travelling in the Near East. In 1818 two British Naval commanders, Captains Irby and Mangles, were entranced by the surreal quality of the place, which they thought had "more the air of a fantastical scene in a theatre than an architectural work in stone".

Later travellers included the French aristocrat Léon de Laborde; the American Biblical scholar Edward Robinson; the British artist David Roberts; and the British writer Edward Lear, whose cook, Giorgio, described Petra as "a world where everything is made of chocolate, ham, curry-powder and salmon". Now visitors from all over the world come to see, in the immortal words of Dean John Burgon, a British Victorian, this "rose-red city half as old as Time".

An infidel in disguise

Burckhardt, disguised as an Arab for protection against tribesmen hostile to "infidel" Europeans, made his discovery during a journey from the Syrian town of Aleppo to Cairo. When he heard of the Wadi Mousa ruins, he hired a guide for the price of a pair of old horseshoes to take him there. Burckhardt needed a plausible excuse for this

The Anglo-Swiss explorer Johann Ludwig Burckhardt (1784–1817) rediscovered the city of Petra by chance on a journey from Syria to Cairo. Disguised as an Arab, he was the first European to enter the city for seven centuries.

The dazzling rock-cut façade of the Khasneh al Faroun, the "Pharaoh's Treasury", lies at the end of the narrow gorge that gives access to Petra. The Khasneh is so called because local Bedouins believed that the urn on top of the pavilion on the second storey contained treasure. The urn, which is made of solid rock, was regularly shot at by Bedouins, who hoped to liberate the gold they thought lay inside.

Petra's magnificent theatre, carved from the hillside, lies just beyond the Khasneh, toward the centre of the city. First built by the Nabataeans, the theatre was renovated by the Romans after Petra came under their jurisdiction in A.D. 106. An estimated 4,000 spectators would have sat on its tiers of stone seats.

The approach to the theatre (RIGHT) is lined with a series of tombs, cut out of the cliff at different heights. Their relatively simple façades may indicate that they are among the oldest of Petra's tombs.

excursion because a mere curiosity in the ruins would have convinced the local Bedouins—volatile at the best of times—that he was a "magician in search of treasures". He therefore told his guide that he had vowed to sacrifice a goat at the tomb of Aaron, which was situated near the valley.

Carrying the goat and a water-skin, the explorer and his guide made their way to Wadi Mousa until they came to a point where their advance seemed to be blocked by a solid wall of rock. Then they noticed a great cleft in the rockface, the entrance to a mysterious winding gorge, known locally as the Siq, which is still used by modern visitors for access to the city.

As they entered the Siq, precipices towered above them and the sky became a thin, jagged ribbon of light. After walking in the twilit gloom for 25 minutes, Burckhardt came to a point where the sides of the Siq suddenly framed, like a giant irregular keyhole, the glittering reddish-pink façade of a building, 90 feet high, which had evidently been carved out of the cliff face.

At this point, now famous, the Siq opens up and the magnificent temple-like front of the Khasneh al Faroun, the "Pharaoh's Treasury", can be seen in all its glory. Sunlight casts shadows from the crisp lines of stately Corinthian columns, friezes and scrollwork that seem freshly cut from the rock. The function of the building is unknown, but its position at the end of the Inner Siq seems designed to create a dazzling impression on travellers emerging from the dark confines of the gorge.

Entering the rose-red city

Burckhardt was on the threshold of the ancient city. As he continued along what is now called the Outer Siq, he saw dark openings to what he supposed were tombs cut out of the cliffs at different heights. The valley began to widen and he came to a semicircular theatre, hewn from the hillside, before emerging onto a broad open area of the valley, enclosed by cliffs, and dominated from the west by the great rock of Umm el Biyara. Here he found "heaps of hewn stones, foundations of buildings, fragments of columns, and vestiges of paved streets". The young Swiss explorer was standing in the heart of Petra.

The cliffs that enclose the central city area are cut by chasms and peppered with hundreds of empty chambers of Nabataean tombs, temples and dwellings. Some of the façades are simple and austere. Others are magnificently fashioned with imposing doorways, columns and pediments sculpted from the cliffs in a hybrid architectural style that quite clearly shows both Hellenistic and Roman influences.

117

PETRA

The 19th-century British artist David Roberts (RIGHT), disguised as a Muslim, came to Petra in March 1839. Accompanied by guides and 21 camels, Roberts and his party had to bribe the local Arabs to let them pitch their tents there.

The visit to Petra was part of Roberts's journey through Egypt and the Holy Land, of which he painted a number of Romantic, yet largely accurate, views. His painting (BELOW) shows the collection of tombs to the east of the city's central area, now known as the Royal Tombs. The façade on the far left is that of the Palace Tomb, so called because it was thought to resemble a Roman Palace. Scholars are not sure when, or for whom, the tomb was constructed.

The Nabataeans and Petra's growth

Petra owed its prosperity to its position at the crossroads of two major trade routes: one linked the Persian Gulf with the Mediterranean, the other linked Syria with the Red Sea. Merchants came with their camel trains to rest, buy food and water, and sell their wares. The Nabataeans grew rich from the taxes they imposed on these caravaners and the services they supplied to them. Eventually they became involved in trade themselves and Petra flourished. It was only in the third century A.D., with the opening up of new trade routes which benefited the city of Palmyra, northeast of Damascus, that Petra began to lose its influence and fell into an irreversible decline.

The most potent symbols of Petra's wealth are the grandiose rock-cut façades of its tombs. Among the most impressive of these are the four Royal Tombs grouped together in the cliffs to the east of the city's central area. The first is the large Urn Tomb whose front is carved with four weather-worn columns. These flank the entrance to an enormous chamber which extends 56 feet into the rock. In front of the tomb is a broad courtyard bordered on either side by an elegant five-column colonnade.

Just to the north lies the exquisite Silk Tomb whose name comes from the colours—shades of red, pink, white, and grey—that streak its sandstone façade. Farther along, the Corinthian Tomb has been so battered by the elements that its once crisply cut columns, similar to those of the Khasneh, seem to be reverting to their natural state. Finally, there is the Palace Tomb whose broad pilastered façade once rose three storeys high, and was said to resemble a Roman palace. Scholars are not sure for whom the tomb was built.

A city of elegance and colourful temples

Petra was more than a city of monumental tombs. The narrow streets of the city's central area were once lined with hundreds of small, flat-roofed shops and houses. Although these have long since been reduced to dust, archeologists have been able to locate some of the more important municipal buildings (though debate still continues over their construction dates and functions).

The people of Petra would have strolled in the shade cast by the roofed columns of the grand Colonnade Street, which ran parallel with the river bed of the Wadi Mousa and led to the *temenos* or holy precinct. If they felt thirsty, there was the Nymphaeum—a large ornate drinking fountain, dedicated to water nymphs, at which they could refresh themselves. Water was brought in from springs outside the city along superbly constructed channels and pipelines.

Petra's citizens worshipped in temples which could be magnificent and colourful. The one just north of the Colonnade Street, probably dedicated to the goddess Atargatis, was reached by a bridge across the wadi and then by terraces which rose to the paved porch and marble-floored interior. The inside was plastered and brightly painted with dolphins, floral garlands and other motifs,

The extraordinary Silk Tomb lies just to the south of the Palace and Corinthian Tombs, set back from the main path. Its name comes from the exquisite colours that streak the sandstone façade, and which have been likened to watered silk.

119

and, at a later period, with single colours. The most important religious building, dominating the *temenos* with its imposing arched entrance, was the grand Kasr el Bint, of which little now remains. Broad marble stairs led to the four giant sandy-coloured columns of the portico and the entrance to the interior. The latter was decorated with painted plaster and naturally illuminated by sunlight filtering through two high windows on the side walls.

The largest temple is known as the Deir, the "Monastery". Its lofty isolated position on the heights to the northwest of the central valley area lends an air of serenity to this colossal building: its façade, 130 feet high, is again carved out of the rock.

Burckhardt did not get as far as the Deir, nor did he see most of the other rock-cut façades. His guide became aggressively suspicious of his curiosity, prompting him to cut short his investigations and hurry on to complete the sacrifice of the goat. The explorer's excursion back into 2,000 years of history was over. He left the valley, making the correct guess that "the ruins in Wadi Mousa are those of the ancient Petra. . . ."

The city of Petra is still as extraordinary a spectacle as when Burckhardt rediscovered it almost 200 years ago. For some, the countless empty chambers hollowed out of the hillsides evoke only an eerie city of the dead. But it must be remembered that, during the height of its prosperity, the central valley and the surrounding cliffs would have echoed with the sound of thousands of people going about their daily lives.

Battered for centuries by the elements, the once-elegant columns of the Corinthian Tomb (LEFT), one of the Royal Tombs, seem to be reverting to their natural state.

The largest tomb in Petra is the Deir or "Monastery" (RIGHT), which stands on heights northwest of the city centre. Superficially, the Deir resembles the Khasneh; but its vast size—it rises to 130 feet— and isolated position give it a greater sense of grandeur.

The British traveller Harriet Martineau (ABOVE RIGHT) came to Petra in 1847 and visited the Deir. She also saw the city filled with local Arabs, who had gathered there to see the effects of a violent thunderstorm: "Row beyond row of the caves gave out yellow gleams; and in the moonlight rose little pillars of white smoke. . . . I had seen Petra populous once more."

TIKAL

> ' *Suddenly we glimpsed an awe-inspiring sight. Four of the great pyramids of Tikal ... like green volcanoes with summits wreathed in white cloud.* '
>
> SIR ERIC THOMPSON ON SEEING TIKAL EARLIER THIS CENTURY.

THE VAST STRETCHES OF RAW JUNGLE AND marshlands that cover more than 14,000 square miles of the Peten District of Guatemala seem an unlikely place for a sophisticated and colourful civilization to have flourished. Jaguars, ocelots, pumas and wild pigs, though depleted in numbers, still patrol the tangled pathways of the forest. Giant trees—ceiba, mahogany, sapote, Spanish cedar, palm—soar up to a height of 130 feet, spreading their branches into a dense emerald canopy. During the day, iridescent hummingbirds and gaudily painted parrots and motmots provide flashes of brilliance amid the welter of green foliage. But as night closes in, the jungle world returns to a primordial darkness punctuated by the unearthly roars of howler monkeys.

Yet during the nineteenth century, explorers began to discover within this rich, ungovernable terrain the extraordinary jungle-covered monuments and buildings of a highly developed civilization. In 1848 Colonel Modesto Mendez and Ambrosio Tut, respectively chief magistrate and governor of Flores in northern Guatemala, found dramatic ruins just to the northwest of the town. It was an astonishing sight: beneath the green of trees, lianas, moss, lichen and fern lay towering pyramids, one more than 200 feet high, multi-levelled palace complexes, temples, plazas and stelae—upright slabs of limestone carved and painted with grotesque figures and enigmatic hieroglyphs.

The two men had discovered Tikal, the largest and grandest city of the Maya people, which had flourished between 100 B.C. and the end of the ninth century A.D. At a time when the Dark Ages had descended on the western world, this huge urban centre rose from the depths of the jungle, as did the other great Maya cities, such as Copan and Palenque. Tikal became the hub of life for tens of thousands of people. Theirs was a highly organized and cultured society where painting, sculpture, writing, and astronomy flourished, and their architecture was the wonder of ancient America.

Stairways to the heavens

For modern visitors, as for the first explorers of Tikal, the city is a place of haunting

Giant pyramids of the Maya city of Tikal break through the green canopy of the Guatemalan jungle. Rising to heights of 200 feet or more, the pyramids supported small austere temples which were topped by "roof combs"—richly carved decorative crests.

In 1848, almost 1,000 years after its demise, Tikal was rediscovered north of Flores in northern Guatemala. Beneath the dense growth of jungle, great stone buildings, such as those of the North Acropolis (RIGHT), showed Maya architecture to be the wonder of ancient America.

mystery and crumbling splendour. From an aircraft, the site reveals itself as five pale islands of limestone floating like the tops of icebergs in a tropical green sea. Down below, the "islands" turn out to be the pinnacles of massive pyramids in the city's central area.

Breaking through the jungle canopy with heights of up to 200 feet or more, the pyramids were built as a series of solid chunky terraces receding to a flat roof, like a giant stone wedge. On the roof stood a relatively small temple with simple lines and elaborately carved lintels of sapote wood over the doorways. The temple walls were often enormously thick—sometimes up to 40 feet—in order to support the "roof comb", a richly carved and brightly painted slab of stone that served as a sort of decorative crest, and added extra height and elegance to the powerful frame of the main building.

Fronting the pyramid was a long protruding staircase, set at a steep angle, which gave priests access to the temple platform. From here, with towering headdresses cascading

The British Mayanist Alfred Maudslay (LEFT) *first came to Tikal in 1881. He found that his native guides were too frightened to sleep in the ruined city because of the "Spirits of the House". According to Teobert Maler, who surveyed Tikal 20 years after Maudslay, the Maya believed that their ancestors haunted "the forsaken temples and palaces" of their former cities. In fact the name "Tikal" means in the Maya language "the place where the spirit voices are heard".*

Maudslay's historic photographs are of the Temple of the Giant Jaguar (RIGHT) *and the view from it looking west* (BELOW).

rainbow plumes like "feathered fire-works", the priests would address the crowds thronging the plaza; or, amid the smell of burning copal incense, they would perform a sacrifice to propitiate the gods.

A Maya city revealed

When Tikal was first rediscovered it had been in the clutches of the jungle for some 900 years. Mendez and Tut left the place more or less as they found it; and later visitors, such as the Swiss botanist Dr Gustave Bernouilli in 1877, Alfred Maudslay in 1881 and 1882, and Teobert Maler in 1904, made little impression on the overgrown monuments. It was only in 1956 that the University of Pennsylvania Museum began a 14-year project to excavate and restore six square miles of the city.

In fact the actual area occupied by Tikal was 25 square miles or more. Until recently, the city was thought to have been merely a vast religious centre, but scholars now believe it was a densely populated metropolis embracing the various aspects of a developed culture. The population at the city's peak may have reached 50,000; and to support these numbers Maya farmers worked hard to produce enough food, including maize, tomatoes, gourds, beans and pumpkins.

Tikal's ruling class lived in homes and offices, now termed "palaces", clustered

The magnificent Temple of the Giant Jaguar, cleared of its jungle covering, dominates the Great Plaza from the east. Rising to more than 140 feet, the temple is named after a carving of a jaguar on the lintel of its door. The eroded roof comb once depicted the painted figure of a ruler.

Wearing elaborate headdresses, necklaces and stylish robes and loincloths, Maya nobles take part in a colourful ritual procession. The scene is a reproduction of a fresco from the Maya site of Bonampak in Chiapas, Mexico.

around the central Great Plaza. These were long stone buildings, sometimes three storeys high, which overlooked courtyards linked by stairways and passages. Dressed in dyed woven robes or simple loincloths, wearing headdresses and jade jewellery, the nobles relaxed and worked in relatively luxurious surroundings. Rooms were plastered and painted, and perhaps embellished with a multicoloured mask hung on the wall. Curtains were used, and jaguar pelts probably covered the floor and were draped over the carved stone seats.

The Great Plaza and its temples

The busiest and most colourful scenes at Tikal would have been in the Great Plaza and at the public market, where pottery, cloth, animal skins, herbs, feathers, knife blades made from obsidian, jade, shells, and food-stuffs were bought and sold with the currency of cacao beans. The plaza was the focal point for large ceremonial gatherings. An open area covering two and a half acres, it was built on four superimposed levels and surfaced with a smooth white plaster, now carpeted with grass, and enclosed by pyramids and other buildings.

Still dominating the plaza to the east and west are, respectively, the Temple of the Giant Jaguar, Tikal's most famous monument, and the Temple of the Masks. The first, named after a carving of a jaguar on the lintel of its temple door, rises more than 140 feet into the air on nine terraces. At the top, the temple supports an eroded roof comb which once depicted the huge figure of a seated ruler, probably painted in red, cream, green and blue. In fact, the whole temple façade, like others at Tikal, may have glowed with

127

The forbidding 10-foot mask of a Maya god,
wearing what have been described as earplugs,
embellishes the façade of a temple in the North
Acropolis, just north of the Great Plaza. The sculpture
shows the square chunky style typical of Maya art.

red paint, like a beacon high above the tropical green wilderness.

The pyramid-temples were the supreme architectural achievement of the Maya, who worked without the help of metal knives, axes, the wheel or beasts of burden. Gangs of workers had to drag enormous quantities of rubble and rock for each pyramid's construction. Tiers were raised by packing the rectangular space between four stone walls with a rough filling of stones which were then plastered to create a smooth, flat finish. Work on the next tier could then begin. As the structure rose, masons used finely cut limestone to face the outside walls. Others heated up stone in kilns to obtain lime to make plaster, mortar and stucco, which was spread on the pyramid's exterior.

The British Mayanist Sir Eric Thompson saw the craft of the Maya plasterer to stunning effect preserved in a pyramid excavated under the shell of one built over it—a common Maya practice: "The whole surface of the pyramid is covered with a thick layer of light cream stucco, dazzlingly bright. . . . One of the most impressive and touching sights I have ever seen was this pyramid, bathed in the light of a full moon. . . ."

A mountain made of stone

Away from the Great Plaza other civic and religious complexes were reached by broad causeways which were plastered and bordered by walls. At the junction of two of these to the west looms probably the highest pyramid in the Maya world—a veritable mountain made of stone, prosaically known as Temple IV. The 212 feet up to the top of this still unexcavated giant is a hard climb since the original stairway has succumbed to the forces of erosion, though nature has provided roots as footholds up the overgrown façade.

At the top, the crowning temple comprises three bare rooms whose walls support the massive roof comb. From the temple platform the panorama is breathtaking: for miles around a rich green treescape unfolds into the distance, holding the secrets of the hundreds of dwellings and farms of the Maya peasants that once covered the area.

The great city of Tikal flourished for about 1,000 years before mysteriously collapsing at the end of the ninth century A.D., along with the other great Maya cities. Suddenly, for reasons scholars still do not fully understand, these urban centres were deserted by their inhabitants.

There may have been severe crop failures owing to soil exhaustion, a dramatic climatic change, an epidemic, or a popular uprising by the peasants against an increasingly oppressive ruling class. Whatever the reason, or reasons, thousands of Maya returned to the forests.

Within a short period of time, the brightly coloured temples and white pyramids began to crumble, and the jungle spread its green tentacles over the limestone ruins. Echoing with the screeches of parrots and the roars of jaguars, Tikal became a lost city, haunted by peccaries and spider monkeys, and the spirits of Maya ancestors.

*The so-called Altar 5 (*BELOW*) is one of the finest to be found at Tikal. The stone has been carved with two priests set within a circular band of numbers known as a "calendar round". The Maya were brilliant mathematicians and developed a sophisticated system of interlocking calendars. From these their astrologers were able to predict solar and lunar eclipses.*

*Of all Tikal's numerous stelae— upright slabs of limestone which were carved and painted with figures and hieroglyphs—Stela 4 (*LEFT*) is one of the most interesting. From its glyphs, scholars have been able to decipher the name of the nobleman whom the stela commemorates—a certain "Curl Nose", who lived at the end of the 4th century A.D.*

MACHU PICCHU

> ❛ *It seemed like an unbelievable dream. . . . What could this place be?* ❜
>
> AMERICAN EXPLORER HIRAM BINGHAM
> ON SETTING FOOT IN MACHU PICCHU.

ONE DAY IN JULY 1911 THE MULE TRAIN OF AN expedition led by the American explorer Hiram Bingham filed out of the old Inca city of Cuzco in Peru. Bingham was hoping to discover Vilcabamba, the last Inca stronghold to fall to the Spanish Conquistadores. Here, in 1572, the Spanish completed their conquest of an empire which, at its height, had stretched 2,500 miles from Ecuador to Chile.

Bingham's party headed northwest along the valley of the River Urabamba and eventually came into a deep, winding canyon. Snow-topped mountains rose above the clouds; sheer granite cliffs echoed with the roar of the foaming rapids.

During a camp stop, Bingham met a local farmer who claimed there were ruins on a nearby mountain called Huayna Picchu. Next day, 24 July, the farmer led the sceptical American up a steep, tree-tangled, snake-infested slope. Near the top, Bingham was amazed to see a flight of stone-faced terraces, hundreds of feet long. Then, suddenly, he came upon the stone walls of Inca houses, overgrown and green with moss and vegetation.

Revelation followed revelation: white granite buildings made of blocks higher than a man, ruined temples, plazas, baths and courtyards left the explorer feeling stunned and asking himself: "Would anyone believe what I had found?"

A city on top of the world

In later years Bingham revisited and excavated the site and became convinced that he had indeed found the city of Vilcabamba. However, recent scholarship indicates that he was mistaken, and that the latter city was at Espiritu Pampa, a jungle-covered area to the northwest. Nevertheless, Bingham's ruins—now known as Machu Picchu—have become the most famous in South America.

Unlike Bingham's trek of several days from Cuzco, some 60 miles away, the modern traveller can now reach Machu Picchu in a matter of hours by taking a train and then a bus, which zigzags up the mountainside to this most spectacular of sites.

A centuries-old silence shrouds the enigmatic Inca city of Machu Picchu, which lies suspended between peaks high in the Peruvian Andes. Built in the 15th century, the city is without any doubt one of the most spectacular archeological sites in the world.

MACHU PICCHU

Machu Picchu lies on a saddle between the peaks of Huayna Picchu and Machu Picchu, some 2,000 feet above the valley floor. Built some time in the fifteenth century, it was probably a small fortified Inca city of around 1,000 inhabitants, linked by a road network to other Andean towns, and abandoned before Vilcabamba fell in 1572. The miracle of

Hiram Bingham (1875–1956), an American historian and archeologist, rediscovered Machu Picchu in 1911. Bingham had in fact set out to find Vilcabamba, the last city of the Incas to fall to the Spanish Conquistadores. To this end he had organized the Yale Peruvian Expedition, which set out from Cuzco in July 1911.

After 5 days, Bingham came upon the jungle-covered ruins of Machu Picchu, and was sure he had found Vilcabamba. Subsequent research, however, suggests that Machu Picchu was not the last Inca stronghold but a small fortified city of around 1,000 inhabitants.

Machu Picchu is that it was never found and destroyed by the Spanish, and so remains in an excellent state of preservation.

With its multi-levelled complex of palaces, temples, houses, stairways, water channels, fountains and agricultural terraces, Machu Picchu is a masterpiece of planning and construction. Inca architects probably built the city from a clay or stone model. Workmen, without the help of draught animals or iron tools, shifted huge lumps of granite to the site with rollers and levers. The blocks were then shaped and polished, and fitted into position without mortar.

Inca society was highly organized and hierarchical, and Machu Picchu would have reflected this. Nobles, priests, craftsmen and common people lived in specific areas of the city, and all knew their appropriate rights, duties, privileges—and even dress.

The hub of city life was the Great Plaza, where festivals and markets took place. The homes and offices of the nobles rose on terraces around the plaza, while the peasants' rough stone houses were situated on lower levels. The latter were thatched with grass and grouped around a courtyard where Inca women carried out their domestic tasks.

Children of the Sun

There are no obviously spectacular buildings at Machu Picchu. Instead of competing with the surrounding peaks, the city's buildings harness them. For example, the huge trapezoidal windows of the Temple of the Three Windows were designed to frame awe-inspiring views over the Andes. This temple, and the Principal Temple next to it, were simple U-shaped structures, probably open to the skies so that the priests could observe the Inca deities of the Sun, Moon and Stars.

The Sun, the divine ancestor of the Inca rulers, was worshipped for the warmth and light he gave to the crops. On the peak of a small hill just beyond the two temples is the sacred Intihuatana, the "Hitching Post of the Sun". This low, irregular-stepped stone platform topped by a short squarish pillar was where the Sun was symbolically tied during the winter solstice to ensure his return next year.

Machu Picchu is one of those rare historic places which exude an air of serenity from having escaped fire and destruction. But its uniqueness lies in its position among the misty peaks of the Andes, a stone eyrie halfway to heaven.

Dense undergrowth *engulfed Machu Picchu when Bingham first came across it. Only after much back-breaking work was the splendid Inca architecture revealed, as shown here in Bingham's photographs.*

Local granite was fashioned into irregular blocks for ordinary dwellings, and into rectangular shapes for more important buildings. Such was the consummate skill of Inca masons that no mortar was needed to hold the stones, so precisely did they fit—a knifeblade will not fit between them.

TINTERN ABBEY

> **❛** *A more pleasing retreat could not easily be found.* **❜**
>
> THE REVD WILLIAM GILPIN, 1782.

ABOUT 200 YEARS AGO, SMALL LUXURY CRUISE boats, rowed by up to six oarsmen and stocked with picnic hampers for their passengers, used to glide regularly along the waters of the River Wye, where it winds through meadows and woods by the southern border of Wales and England. The Wye Tour, as it became known, began at Ross or Monmouth and finished at Chepstow near the river's mouth. The crowning glory of the trip came five miles before the end, when the magnificent shell of Tintern Abbey rose into view, soaring above green pastures and framed by the steep wooded slopes of the valley.

In the late eighteenth and early nineteenth centuries what is now known as the Romantic Movement flourished in Europe. Reacting against the preceding era of rationalism, classical architecture and formal gardens, the Romantics sought out and savoured wild rugged scenery, turreted castles, crumbling ruins—anything which seemed ''natural'' and free from artificiality. With travel to continental Europe hampered by the French Revolution (1789–99), the Wye Tour attracted countless travellers, writers, poets, and painters. And Tintern Abbey, with its pale sandstone picturesquely adorned with hanging ivy, moss and lichen, became for these free-spirited Britons the enchanted place *par excellence.*

Romantic ruins

Once they had disembarked, the tourists would stroll among the sacred stones, broken pillars and pointed Gothic arches. On the soft pelt of grass covering the floor of the nave, they would spread out a sumptuous luncheon and enjoy the harmony of mellow stone blending with the blue sky and the panoramic sweep of rich green firs, beeches, oaks and elms.

To heighten their sense of the sublime, the picnickers could hire a Welsh harper from Chepstow to serenade them. Or, staying overnight at the Beaufort Arms, the incurable Romantic could wander among the ruins silvered by a full moon; or let his imagination run wild at the sight of flaming torches casting silhouettes on the bare walls.

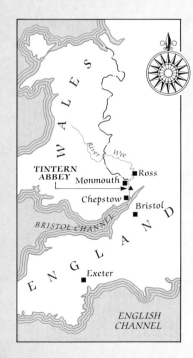

Tintern Abbey, built in the 12th century by Cistercian monks, lies in a wooded valley on the River Wye. Its picturesque ruins, rising above green meadows, made it, about 200 years ago, the high point of the Wye Tour, a delightful river journey which started at Monmouth or Ross and ended at Chepstow.

TINTERN ABBEY

A place for poetry

The most popular guidebook for the Wye Tour at this time had been written by the Revd William Gilpin and published in 1782. Gilpin was enraptured by the abbey's setting—the winding course of the river, the woods and glades, and the pervasive tranquillity. However, sensitive aesthete that he was, Gilpin was more critical of the abbey's interior—in particular the "vulgarity" of "a number of gabel-ends". His remedy for these was radical and simple: "A mallet judiciously used (but who durst use it?) might be of service in fracturing some of them. . . ."

More reverential to Tintern was the great British poet William Wordsworth (1770–1850), who visited the abbey for the second time on 10 July 1798. He was inspired to write one of his great meditative poems, "Lines on Tintern Abbey", of which he said:

"No poem of mine was composed under circumstances more pleasant for me to remember than this."

Artists, too, were attracted to the abbey and its idyllic setting. Most famous of these was J. M. W. Turner (1775–1851), who visited Tintern several times during the 1790s and made sketches of the interior. From these he produced finished watercolours showing sunlight gilding the elegant arches, festooned with green foliage and supporting nothing but the blue sky.

The coming of the white monks

Tintern is still a majestic sight. Although the ivy which so enhanced the walls for Gilpin and for later visitors has been cut away to preserve the stone-work, nevertheless the church and the adjoining complex of dilapi-

During the late 18th and early 19th centuries Tintern Abbey, with its arches festooned with ivy and foliage (LEFT *and* BELOW RIGHT), *attracted numerous Romantic writers and artists. Two of its most famous visitors were the landscape painter J. M. W. Turner and the poet William Wordsworth* (ABOVE RIGHT).

Wordsworth, who had first visited this "very beautiful ruin of the Wye" in 1793, returned 5 years later. He was then inspired to write his famous poem Lines on Tintern Abbey, *in which he captures the tranquillity of the abbey's setting, with the "soft inland murmur" of mountain springs filling the air, the wooded cliffs, cottages, groves, copses and farms.*

Turner, shown in a self-portrait (ABOVE LEFT), *probably completed in 1798, went to Tintern several times. From his sketches he produced delicate watercolours of the abbey's interior.*

dated buildings are much the same as they were 200 years ago.

Tintern was founded by the lord of Chepstow in 1131 for monks of the Cistercian order, known as the "white monks" from their undyed habits. There were probably never more than about 25 of them residing there at any one time in its 400 years of existence. However, to help with farming—in which the Cistercians were great innovators—and with other manual work, lay brothers, or *conversi*, were recruited. These men were bound by less severe rules and swelled the community by up to five times.

During the thirteenth century, Tintern was rebuilt and added to, especially under the patronage of Roger Bigod, Earl of Norfolk. In 1270 Bigod began the erection of a magnificent new Gothic church, the shell of which is seen today. Cruciform in shape and 236 feet long, the church fell into chronic disrepair after Tintern was "dissolved" or closed in 1536, along with a number of other monasteries, by Henry VIII. Today, there is no roof to prevent sunlight flooding through onto the grass carpet of the nave and transepts, which echo with the wingbeat and song of pigeons. But clustered columns and arches, fountains of stone, still soar to the heavens in typical Gothic exuberance.

At the east end of the church, the great window, 64 feet high, has lost all its tracery except one central mullion, as elegant as a slender sapling. Although the Cistercian order forbade the use of colour in their windows, the east window was filled with stained glass, including the emblazoned arms of Roger Bigod. As the sun rose high, it would

have cast rich peacock tails of light over the plastered walls, the tiled floor and carved oak stalls of the monks' choir.

Away from the church sprawl the ruins of the other buildings that cover the 27 acres of the abbey complex. Joining the church to the north is the cloister, an open grass court enclosed by what were once covered alleys where the white monks could stroll or sit and study spiritual texts. The alleys provided covered walkways to other buildings, such as the Chapter House, where matters of discipline were discussed daily, the Parlour, where conversation was permitted, a grand dining hall, 85 feet long, and the inviting Warming House, the only place apart from the Infirmary where a fire was kept burning in winter.

The end of an era

By the end of the thirteenth century, Tintern Abbey owned more than 3,000 acres of farmland, and its possessions were valued at about £150, making it one of the richest monasteries in Wales. But 400 years of spiritual history were cut short in 1536. During this year, an Act was passed in which monasteries whose incomes fell below £200 per year were to be dissolved. Tintern fell £8 short. The monks were pensioned off. The church bells were taken away and valuable lead was stripped from the roof. The abbey soon fell into disrepair, and remained a picturesque ruin until, at the beginning of this century, the ruin was restored.

The wooded slopes which once echoed with church bells summoning the white monks to prayer still provide a backdrop of green or, in autumn, golden brown to the bare walls and arches. The River Wye, flowing smoothly past, contributes to the air of peacefulness. The church roof and stained glass may be gone, but the natural surroundings still enhance the ruins, as one British visitor, A. G. Bradley, noted at the beginning of this century: "It is indeed wonderfully preserved, and who shall say but the sun and moon, the stars and clouds are not as noble a canopy as its vanished roof, or as effective a background for the rich tracery . . . as wood or glass or lead."

This 19th-century view of Tintern by F. W. Watts shows the abbey about 300 years after it had been closed down. The Revd William Gilpin wrote in 1782 that Tintern was "screened on all sides by woody hills . . . and the hills closing on its entrance and its exit, leave no room for inclement blasts to enter".

139

THE CREATIVE VISION

"*Where there is no vision, the people perish.*"

"*Ships, towers, domes, theatres, and temples lie*
Open unto the fields, and to the sky;
All bright and glittering in the smokeless air.
Never did the sun more beautifully steep
In his first splendour valley, rock, or hill. . . ."

WILLIAM WORDSWORTH (1770–1850)

*P*eople's spiritual aspirations and artistic vision have found expression in magnificent buildings throughout the world. Some have a beauty and perfection in their construction, some are sanctified by history and legend; others have been built simply for the glory of God. The Taj Mahal is essentially the vision of one man, who raised this exquisite model of symmetry and proportion to the memory of his beloved wife. Neuschwanstein, the fairytale castle in Bavaria, was the creation of another man's explosive imagination.

The magic of some places rests not so much in a single building as in a collection of structures that combine to create a glorious whole, more than the sum of its parts. The Forbidden City's palaces and halls, aligned on mystic principles, were a harmonious ensemble at the centre of which the Chinese emperor ruled from his Dragon Throne. In the west, the medieval shrines and churches of Assisi, and the shady courtyards of the Alhambra are eloquent examples of the vision of Christian and Islamic architects.

Buildings reflect the culture, time and place in which they were raised, and are among the most telling indicators of man's creative impulse.

SHWEDAGON PAGODA

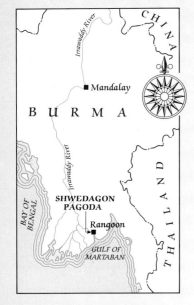

ON TOP OF A HILL IN THE NORTH PART OF Rangoon, capital of Burma, what looks like a giant inverted handbell gleams with pure gold, like sunlight that has been frozen and shaped. Burma has been called a land of pagodas, but the Shwedagon, its giant stupa rising like a gold mountain above a forest of spires of smaller pagodas and pavilions, is the most magnificent of them all. Covering an area of 14 acres, the pagoda is a complex of glittering structures and strange and familiar creatures: leogryphs, sphinxes, dragons, lions and elephants gleam with red and gold, while slender green palms provide relief from this Midas-like setting.

The splendour of the Shwedagon was known to Europeans as far back as the sixteenth century, when the Elizabethan English traveller Ralph Fitch reported that it was: ". . . of a woonderfull bignesse, and all gilded from the foot to the toppe . . . it standeth very high, and there are foure wayes to it, which all along are set with trees of fruit. . . ." Three hundred years later, the British writer Rudyard Kipling was also struck by the pagoda's size and richness. At this time, in the 1890s, the Burmese capital was under British control and had been rebuilt on a grid system of broad tree-lined avenues. It was a city of elegant colonial houses, artificial lakes and brilliant colours seen everywhere in the silk clothing of the Burmese—"lilac, pink, vermillion, lapis lazuli, and blistering blood red under fierce sunlight that mellows and modifies all".

Dominating Rangoon, as indeed it still does, was the Shwedagon. As Kipling wrote: "Then, a golden mystery upheaved itself on the horizon—a beautiful winking wonder that blazed in the sun, of a shape that was neither Muslim dome nor Hindu temple spire."

Relics of the Buddhas

The Shwedagon is one of the most sacred Buddhist sites in the world. Enshrined at the heart of the golden, solid stupa are, it is said, relics from the four Buddhas who have so far appeared on earth. These include eight hairs from the head of the last Buddha, Gautama, who lived during the early sixth century B.C.

The golden stupa of the Shwedagon Pagoda in Rangoon tapers elegantly above the ornate pinnacles of other structures in the 14-acre complex. The pagoda is the most magnificent Buddhist shrine in Burma.

SHWEDAGON PAGODA

The British writer Rudyard Kipling (1865–1936) (RIGHT) visited Rangoon in the 1890s. He found Burma's capital, shown (BELOW) in a contemporary photograph, a city of elegance and colour.

The British writer Rudyard Kipling (1865–1936) (RIGHT) visited Rangoon in the 1890s. He found Burma's capital, shown (BELOW) in a contemporary photograph, a city of elegance and colour.

Although Kipling never actually set foot in the pagoda precincts, he was ever aware of its presence: "The pagoda was always close at hand—as brilliant a mystery as when first sighted far down the river; but it changed its shape as we came nearer, and showed in the middle of a nest of hundreds of smaller pagodas."

According to legend, two Burmese brothers, who were travelling merchants, met the young Gautama in northern India just after he had achieved Enlightenment. The Buddha gave the brothers eight hairs to take home, but on the return journey four

were stolen. However, when they arrived home, in the region of what is now Rangoon, and opened the casket, they found the four missing hairs had been miraculously restored. Not only that but amazing portents occurred—a stream of brilliant light irradiated from the hairs; the blind could see again, the deaf hear and the dumb speak; the earth shook, lightning flashed and jewels fell from the skies.

The hairs were duly enshrined on top of Singuttara Hill along with the other three relics (a staff, a water cup, and an article of clothing) and a gold slab placed on top. A series of pagodas of different materials, fitting one over the other, was raised on top of the relics.

Another legend relates that fabulous treasure was buried with the relics. When reports of this treasure reached the ears of the King of China, he decided he wanted it. So he

sent a magic spirit, disguised as a human being, on a mission to plunder the pagoda. However, when the spirit creature arrived, it was overcome by the Shwedagon's magnificence. While it gazed at it in awe, the pagoda's guardian spirits seized the chance to attack and kill it.

The historical background to the Shwedagon begins with certainty around the eleventh century A.D., when it is known to have been an important Buddhist centre. During the following centuries, various rulers of the region added to and enriched the site. Queen Shinsawbu (1453–72) built walls and terraces and ordered that the stupa should be plated with her weight—90 pounds—in gold leaf. In 1485, King Dhammazedi went one better by giving four times his own weight in gold for the stupa; he also raised three stones inscribed with the history of the pagoda in Burmese, Pali, and Mons, which can still be seen on the site today.

The saga of the bells

It was Dhammazedi who also presented the pagoda with a massive bell weighing 20 tons. In 1608 the bell was plundered by a Portuguese mercenary who wanted to melt it down to make cannons. However, he misjudged the bell's weight and, as he was ferrying it across the River Pegu, it fell into the water, and was lost for ever.

In 1768, the stupa was rebuilt by King Hsibyushin after an earthquake; this is the one that is seen today. The king's son, Singu, gave another bronze bell to the Shwedagon in 1779. About 45 years later, it was plundered by the British during their first occupation of Rangoon from 1824 to 1826. Known as the Maha Gandha bell and weighing 23 tons, it was to be shipped to Calcutta via the River Rangoon; but, as its predecessor had done, it fell into the river. The British could not recover it, but the Burmese succeeded by tying to it a great number of bamboo poles which caused it to float to the surface. The bell was then brought back to the pagoda, where it can be seen today on the northwest side of the main terrace.

The British returned to Rangoon in 1852 with a force of warships and steamers carrying 6,000 troops, and took control of the city. The strategically important pagoda was occupied and fortified and, for 77 years until 1929, it was for the Burmese both a place of great holiness and a reminder of the military might of their oppressors.

A jungle of shrines and pagodas

The Shwedagon is not a single sacred monument nor a place for regular organized worship. It is a focal point for Buddhist pilgrims and monks who wish to meditate and pray in holy surroundings; it is also a meeting place for lay people—students, businessmen, and travellers, who come to lay an offering of flowers, perform the ritual of pressing gold leaf onto the stupa, or simply to converse and watch the world go by.

The usual approach to the site is by one of the four enclosed stairways which throng with people buying incense, Buddha images, gold leaf, and bunches of fragrant flowers from the shops that line the way. Emerging from the semi-gloom of the stairway, visitors are confronted by an extravaganza of pillars,

A reclining Buddha statue serenely smiles at pilgrims inside one of the many tazoungs—richly decorated pavilions which surround the central stupa. The Shwedagon is not a place for regular organized worship, but somewhere for visitors and pilgrims to come to meditate, or place an offering of flowers by one of the Buddha statues, altars or planetary posts.

spires and roofs, rising in spiky tiers, strange statues and the deep saffron robes of the Buddhist monks. "All about," as British writer W. Somerset Maugham recounted, "shrines and pagodas were jumbled pell-mell with the confusion with which trees grow in the jungle. . . . And then, emerging from among them like a great ship surrounded by lighters, rose dim, severe and splendid, the Shwe Dagon."

The central stupa is indeed magnificent— "a pyramid of fire", standing on a series of rectangular and octagonal terraces which soften the transition from its square platform to its circular body. This rises in different tapering sections, typical of traditional pagoda architecture. From the swollen bulb-shaped base, a golden stem reaches upward, narrowing to the elegant *hti*, a gilt iron "umbrella" from which hang gold and silver bells that tinkle gently in the wind. From the *hti* rises a gem-encrusted vane, topped by a golden orb which is studded with more than 4,000 diamonds, including one of 76 carats on the tip.

The stupa's elegant curved lines and uninterrupted expanse of pure gold contrast with the profusion of other structures that cluster around it. Among these are the ornate prayer pavilions or *tazoungs*, with gold and mosaic pillars, their shady interiors housing Buddha images illumined by the flickering light of candles. Elsewhere are shrines and pagodas, golden figures of the Buddha, to

Gleaming pinnacles *of smaller pagodas (*LEFT*) clustering around the main stupa contribute to the opulence of the Shwedagon. The pagodas are topped by umbrella-like htis, from which rise elegant vanes.*

*"**The Shwedagon rose superb,** glistening with its gold, like a sudden hope in the dark night of the soul," recalled British writer W. Somerset Maugham (1874– 1965). The colossal bell-shaped stupa (*ABOVE*) is plated with gold slabs and rises more than 300 feet high, dwarfing the structures around it.*

which offerings of flowers and small flags are made, and eight "planetary posts". These posts mark the compass bearing, the day of the week and the animal or bird associated with a particular planet. The post due east of the central stupa, for example, is where people who were born on Monday lay offerings. The moon is their planet and the tiger their animal. (To gain the extra week-day, Wednesday is divided into two parts, from midnight to noon, and from noon to midnight.)

The same symbolism can be found at the eight-sided Pagoda of the Eight Weekdays, on the northwest side of the terrace, which has niches in each of its sides containing a Buddha image. Above the niches are carved creatures, again representing the compass direction and the associated day of the week and planet. Wednesday morning is connected with the south side; the relevant animal is the elephant, and Venus the planet.

"The fairest place . . . in the world"

To the east of this pagoda is the Shin Itzagone pavilion, named after a legendary alchemist who poked his eyes out in anger after his experiment to produce a magical stone that would turn base metal into gold had seemingly failed. In fact he had been successful, and with the help of the stone he replaced his eyes with two taken from a goat and a bull.

This explains why the Buddha image inside the pavilion has large eyes of different sizes.

With its pavilions, pagodas and shrines glittering with colour and gold, the opulence of the Shwedagon would be oppressive if the site were under cover, like a church or mosque. As it is, exposed to the blue sky and the sun, or, at night, the moon and the stars, the monument seems to be part of a greater and natural whole. Its sharply defined lines and gleaming surfaces are offset by the cut flowers, the trees, and the silk robes of pilgrims, many of whom would agree with the Elizabethan traveller Ralph Fitch that the pagoda is "the fairest place, as I suppose, that is in the world".

*A **procession** of young saffron-robed pilgrims (LEFT) files across the hot paving stones of the pagoda's terrace. With colourful silk sarongs glowing in the sunlight, the fragrance of flowers wafting in the air, and the tinkling of bells delighting the ear, the Shwedagon is a sensual paradise.*

British soldiers march away from the pagoda (ABOVE) in an aquatint of a scene from the First Anglo-Burmese War in 1824. During their 2-year occupation of Rangoon, the British ransacked the pagoda and attempted to carry off the giant Maha Gandha bell (RIGHT) to Calcutta.

The bell, which can now be seen on the northwest side of the terrace, fell into the River Rangoon on its journey to India. The British failed to raise its 23 tons, but the Burmese succeeded by attaching to it countless bamboo poles, which made it float to the surface.

HAGHIA SOPHIA

6 *O Solomon, I have surpassed thee!* 9

THE BYZANTINE EMPEROR JUSTINIAN
ON ENTERING THE NEW CHURCH.

ETCHED AGAINST A PURE BLUE SKY, THE heat-shimmered dome of the church of Haghia Sophia rises above the street cries and hubbub of modern Istanbul. The outside of this great Byzantine church, built in the sixth century A.D., is a sprawl of semi-domes, buttresses, and outbuildings. Offsetting its massive structure, are four elegant minarets, standing guard at the church's four corners.

The real beauty of Haghia Sophia (Holy Wisdom), the greatest church of what was Constantinople, capital of the Byzantine empire, lies within its vast interior. Here, the relentless glare of day gives way to the subtle grandeur of dark space, in which can be discerned the soft edges of vaulted aisles, galleries and avenues of marble columns.

On closer inspection, the exquisite work of the Byzantine craftsman can be seen in the glittering colour of the restored mosaics; and in the deeply cut marble of the nave's column capitals, in which intricate acanthus leaves surround the monogram of Justinian and his wife Theodora. Resplendent above the smooth marble floor, laced with a filigree of shadows spun from hanging chandeliers, is the great dome. From the centre, 40 ribs curve down to its base, which is pierced by 40 windows, like a crown studded by diamonds of light. Although the church has lost most of its original gold and silver decoration, mosaics, and frescoes, there is natural beauty in its spatial magnificence and in the play of darkness and light—a striking chiaroscuro as beams of sunlight ignite the shady interior.

The marvel of Constantinople

The church is the third to be built on this site, and was begun by Justinian in A.D. 532 on one of the hills of Constantinople. This great cosmopolitan city, standing at the crossroads of Europe and Asia, was formerly known as Byzantium, after its legendary founder

The Byzantine church of Haghia Sophia, built by the emperor Justinian in the 6th century, is one of the great monuments of Christianity. The four minarets were added after the church was converted to a mosque in 1453, when the Ottoman Turks captured what was then Constantinople.

The glory of Haghia Sophia lies within its vast interior that covers an area of 9,800 square yards. Its magnificent dome, which is more than 100 feet in diameter, was rebuilt in 558 after the collapse of the previous one.

The monogram of the emperor Justinian and his wife Theodora can be seen amid acanthus leaves on richly carved column capitals (ABOVE). Some of the church's 107 columns were reputedly brought from ancient temples in other parts of the Byzantine Empire.

Under Justinian (A.D. 527–65) (BELOW), the Byzantine Empire entered a golden age of artistic endeavour and military expansion. Justinian's greatest achievement was the codification of Roman law, which influenced the course of legal history.

Byzas. In A.D. 330, Emperor Constantine the Great renamed the city and made it the capital of the Roman Empire. The city became a great religious, commercial and artistic centre, and reached its zenith under Justinian in the sixth century. With its gilded domes, towers, and palaces, and its commanding position on the Bosporus, it is no wonder that the Irish poet W.B. Yeats said he would rather have spent a month here than in any other place in antiquity.

To build the church, Justinian imported beautiful building materials from all over the empire. Red porphyry, verd antique, white and yellow marble were shipped in; and sculptors, carpenters, bricklayers, and mosaicists set to work to create this jewel of Christendom in only five years.

When completed, the dome and the entire ceiling were covered with gold the brilliance of which was mirrored in every polished surface. The marble columns were of such exquisite hues that a contemporary historian named Procopius likened them to a meadow full of flowers in bloom. At night the church was transformed into a firmament ablaze with tiny golden stars from hanging concentric circles of light.

The church's magnificence gradually diminished during its chequered history. With its structure always under threat from fire and earthquake, the building's interior was stripped of its treasures in 1204 by Crusaders, hostile to the Eastern Orthodox Church, on their way to Jerusalem. In 1453 Constantinople fell to the Ottoman Turks. Haghia Sophia was converted into a mosque, and the mosaics were plastered over. Finally, in 1934, Kemal Ataturk, president of Turkey, turned the church into a museum.

The last Communion

Restoration and repair continue. Meanwhile visitors can still enjoy the dimly lit, mysterious interior, substantially the same as when it was last used as a church. This was on the evening of 28 May 1453, when Emperor Constantine XI, with tears in his eyes, received Holy Communion for the last time. For he knew that in a few hours thousands of Turks under Mehmet II would storm the city's walls and slaughter the defenders: the emperor's worst fears were realized.

But the conqueror showed due reverence toward Haghia Sophia. It is said that before Mehmet first entered the church, he poured a handful of earth over his head as an act of

humility. Once inside, he gazed in silence at the church's magnificence, and then seeing a Turkish soldier hacking at the marble floor struck him with his sword.

Now, stripped of any religious function, this great church is still a spiritual oasis in a bustling metropolis. Every year visitors are drawn to its marble floors, its cool columns, and its dome, rising toward the heavens.

*"**Whoever enters there** to worship perceives at once that it is not by any human strength or skill, but by the favour of God, that this work has been perfected." So wrote the 6th-century historian Procopius of Haghia Sophia, shown (ABOVE) in a mid-19th-century engraving.*

THE POTALA

> *No one can remain unmoved by the sheer power and beauty of the structure, with its thousand windows like a thousand eyes. . . .*

CHINESE-BORN ENGLISH NOVELIST HAN SUYIN (B.1917) DESCRIBING THE POTALA.

RISING ABOVE THE HOLY CITY OF LHASA IN Tibet, 12,000 feet above sea level, the white walls and golden roofs of the Potala seem to grow out of the hill on which they stand. From the seventeenth century A.D. for more than 300 years, this great fortress palace was the residence of the Dalai Lamas, the spiritual leaders and rulers of Tibet. Now a museum, the palace is a labyrinth of rooms, interconnected with countless doors, corridors and stairways, and galleries painted or draped with richly coloured silks, and is filled with around 200,000 statues. The Potala served as palace, monastery and government office, and revolved around the Dalai Lama.

Even today few western eyes have seen the Potala, or even the remote and mysterious plateau of Tibet. Before the nineteenth century, Tibet's mountain ramparts deterred all but the most ardent travellers; then, after 1904, it closed its borders to foreigners. When, in 1951, it was annexed by Communist China, yet another barrier was erected. But the difficulties involved in reaching the Potala are also part of its enchantment. The lure of the secret, the hidden, the hardship along the way, and, finally, the reward—the sudden view of the palace from afar—this is its special magic.

A mirage of golden roofs

The French explorer Alexandra David-Neel, who, in 1923, was the first white woman to set foot in Lhasa, later described how after months of walking she first caught sight of the great palace. Its golden roofs, outlined against a clear blue sky, seemed to give off sparks of light, as if the whole structure had been "crowned with flames".

More than 20 years later, Heinrich Harrer, an Austrian mountaineer, escaped to Lhasa from India, where he had been interned by the British during World War II. After 70 days of marching, Harrer and his companion Peter Aufschnaiter, suffering from cold and hunger, rounded a bend and suddenly saw the Potala's roofs gleaming far away in the distance. It was an emotional moment and Harrer had an impulse to touch the ground with his forehead—as a pilgrim would.

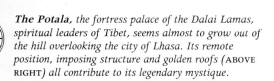

The Potala, the fortress palace of the Dalai Lamas, spiritual leaders of Tibet, seems almost to grow out of the hill overlooking the city of Lhasa. Its remote position, imposing structure and golden roofs (ABOVE RIGHT) all contribute to its legendary mystique.

According to popular Tibetan belief, the Potala, named after a holy mountain in South India, was raised supernaturally in the course of a single night. Harrer, who stayed in Lhasa for five years, once asked a local stonemason why it was that such buildings were no longer put up; the man replied indignantly that the Potala was the handiwork of the gods and beyond the work of mere mortals.

In fact its history began in the seventh century A.D., when Songtsen Gampo, warrior king of Tibet, built himself a palace on what was called Red Hill. However, this structure was later destroyed and rebuilt more than once. Construction of the palace seen today began during the reign of the great Fifth Dalai Lama, Lobsang Gyatso (1617–82). It was an enormous undertaking, involving many thousands of men. So much material for its construction was dug from behind Red Hill that the pit was later turned into a lake, the Dragon King Pool.

By 1648 the outer White Palace—so called because of its whitewashed walls—was complete. The Red Palace, finally completed in 1694, 12 years after Gyatso's death, was the religious centre of the complex. It contained the monks' assembly hall, a multitude of chapels and shrines, libraries of Buddhist scripture, and golden funerary pagodas or stupas, housing the embalmed corpses of some of the Dalai Lamas.

Palace of the god-kings

The greatest of these stupas, that of the Fifth Dalai Lama, can still be visited in the Great West Hall. Made of sandalwood and standing nearly 50 feet high, it is coated with four tons of gold, which glows in the soft light of silver ''butter lamps''. Its golden surface is studded with jewels, including diamonds, sapphires and rubies.

The White Palace contained living quarters, offices, a seminary and the printing house. The printing press was, like all others in the country, under the control of the monks. The traditional process used hand-carved wooden blocks impressed on paper made from the crushed bark of daphne. These printed sheets were then wrapped in silk and kept in wooden covers.

Above all, the Potala was the residence of the Dalai Lamas, the god-kings who ruled Tibet for more than 500 years, each one believed to be the reincarnation of Avalokitshvara, the Buddhist embodiment of compassion. The Fourteenth Dalai Lama was aged only 16 when Tibet was occupied by the Chinese, under whom he ruled in a limited capacity until 1959. He then fled to India with 80,000 followers. Although the god-king has departed, the Potala's magic remains. It seems to possess some transcendent quality quite unconnected with mere bricks and mortar: a mysterious land's central mystery.

The white walls of the Potala (OPPOSITE PAGE) *dominate the city of Lhasa depicted on an 18th-century Tibetan* thang-ka, *or painted scroll. The structure seen today dates from the 17th century, though a palace was built on the same site as far back as the 7th century.*

The Dalai Lamas *were god-kings who ruled Tibet for more than 500 years until the country was annexed by the Chinese in 1951. In Tibetan Buddhist belief, the Dalai Lamas are reincarnations of the Bodhisattva Avalokitshvara, the Lord of Compassion. He is the 8-armed figure in the central mandala of the* thang-ka *(ABOVE). The present Dalai Lama fled his country in 1959.*

ASSISI

> *Let the tongue harmonize with the mind, and the mind accord with God.*

"A FERTILE HILLSIDE HANGING FROM A TALL mountain" is how the thirteenth-century Italian poet Dante, in his *Divine Comedy*, describes the hill of Assisi, which "hangs" from Mount Subasio in the Italian province of Umbria. Dante goes on to describe how on the Assisi side of the mountain "a sun is born to the world, as it sometimes is from the Ganges"—an allusion to St Francis, at once the Church's most lovable and its most austere saint.

No other town in Italy, perhaps no other town in the world, is quite like Assisi. At every step, the traveller is reminded of St Francis, *il Poverello*, the Poor Man of God. Yet Assisi does not look particularly striking from a distance. It is one among many such hilltop towns in this beautiful region. But the visitor only has to share for a few days the frugal life of one of Assisi's convents or monasteries, climb its narrow medieval streets, rest the eye on curly terracotta roof tiles, or light a candle in one of its churches to feel that it would be possible at any moment at the turn of a street to come face to face with the saint himself, *il Poverello*.

The wool merchant's son

According to a legend widespread in the Middle Ages, St Francis, like Christ, was born in a stable between an ox and a donkey. His birthplace was reputed to be the little cavelike Oratory of St Francis. The reality was far different: Francis was born in Assisi in 1182 to Pietro Bernardone, a wool merchant, and his wife, Pica. They lived in a large and comfortable house near the Piazza del Commune or marketplace, where the Roman temple of Minerva still stands.

The child was baptized in the Romanesque cathedral of San Rufino and he was christened Giovanni. It may have been because his mother was French or because of his father's business connections with France that he was always called Francesco—the little Frenchman—or Francis.

The Assisi of Francis's youth, according to all reports, was a "new Babylon" given over

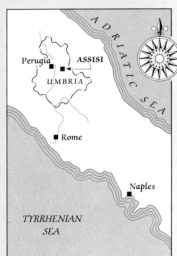

The hermitage of the Carceri, *built in the 15th century, nestles among thick woodland on the mountain above Assisi. The small oratory that stood here in St Francis's day, and the many quiet grottos nearby, were the young saint's favourite retreats.*

Reality and legend *walk hand in hand in Assisi, the home of St Francis—"the most saintly among saints". The enchanting hillside town in the Italian province of Umbria probably looks little different from when he knew it. To walk through Assisi is to walk in his footsteps.*

to all kinds of indulgence. Certainly Francis, never an outstanding student, became, with his father's money behind him, one of a group of high-living, somewhat dissolute youths, and, indeed, their leader in riotous behaviour.

The town probably looks little different from when the young Francis knew it. Certainly all the most notable buildings in the town are in some way connected with the saint. All roads lead to his basilica—a somewhat forbidding-looking structure— that dominates the town. Planned on two levels, it was built to honour and commemorate the saint on the Colle d'Inferno (Infernal Hill), where Francis had specifically requested to be buried. Though Francis's wish to be laid to rest in the place where condemned criminals had once been executed was eventually respected, the Pope ordered that its name be changed to Hill of Paradise.

Although the body of the saint was on view here until the fifteenth century, it was then sealed off in a secret vault, in order to protect it. Only in 1818 was the hiding place discovered and the coffin of St Francis can now be viewed in the crypt.

Red and white stone from Mount Subasio has been employed symbolically in the construction of the basilica, the red of the lower level representing the darkness of the tomb, the white of the upper church reflecting the purity and light of Christ's mission. Both upper and lower churches are artistic treasure houses.

Their interiors, however, offer sharply contrasting impressions. The tranquil obscurity of the lower church lends itself to meditative, inward reflection. The upper church, much higher and lighter, encourages a more expansive religious expression.

The aspiring knight

Francis appears to have had no real intention of following his father's profession. It was probably at his church school, dedicated to the dragon-slayer, St George, that he became devoted to the ideals of chivalry: heroism and endurance in a noble cause, fidelity, the longing for perfect love. It was a devotion

The Romanesque bell tower of the beautiful 12th-century church, now cathedral, of San Rufino is seen against the backdrop of Mount Subasio. St Francis and St Clare were baptized here. Apart from lively carvings on the west front, the exterior is stark and elegant.

161

that, translated into Christian terms, was to last all his life. But first it made him into a soldier.

In the year that he was 20, Assisi made war on its neighbour and bitter enemy, Perugia, and Francis rode with the cavalry. Along with others he was captured and thrown into jail. But even cooling his heels for a year in prison did not dampen his ardour. He wanted to be a knight.

Soon after he had returned from Perugia, he rode out of Assisi again—still in pursuit of the chivalrous dream—on an expedition to the south of Italy. But he only got as far as Spoleto. Something happened there to change his mind. According to legend, he heard a voice in his dreams, bidding him to return to Assisi.

Back in Assisi one day, when the ex-roisterer and knight was passing the little church of San Damiano he felt compelled to go inside. He prostrated himself before a crucifix that hung there and it seemed to him that the figure on the cross spoke, saying: "Go, Francis, and repair my house because it is falling into ruin."

Francis took these words literally and, having not only sold his horse but some cloth belonging to his father, tried to give the proceeds to the priest at San Damiano. Reluctant to become involved in what seemed certain to develop into a family crisis, the priest refused this bounty. Francis is then said to have placed the money anonymously on a windowsill of the chapel.

The incident culminated in his being hauled before a public tribunal. In the course of this his father disinherited him and, to show his disdain, Francis, in a symbolic act of total renunciation of worldly goods, removed all his clothes. Deeply moved at this gesture, Bishop Guido, who was presiding over the tribunal, covered the young man with his mantle. At the age of 24 Francis had renounced the world. From that day on he became a beggar and devoted his life to helping others, particularly lepers, and to the Order of Minor Brothers which he founded.

The Poor Clares

In the crowd that gathered at the tribunal to watch Francis's confrontation with his father was a young girl, one of three daughters of the noble family of Offreducci. So impressed was she with this gesture of rejection of the material world that she decided to follow Francis—a decision that ended in her running away from home one night to become the first Franciscan nun.

As the number of "Poor Clares" grew, the bishop of Assisi gave them shelter in San Damiano, where Francis had received his call, and where Clare spent the rest of her life.

Within walking distance of the town, San Damiano is today a small Franciscan monastery. But it has been preserved exactly as it was when Clare and her sisters lived there. The humble dormitory still has power to move, speaking as it does of the Franciscan ideals of humility, poverty and gladness. It is almost possible to see Clare and her nuns sitting in the little choir on the crude wooden stalls, listening to the scriptures read from a

lectern whose base is not much more than a roughly squared-off log.

The window through which St Francis placed the money intended for the repair of San Damiano is now blocked up. On the altar stands a copy of the crucifix that originally addressed the saint. The original is in the thirteenth-century basilica of St Clare, where her body, blackened by age, can still be seen.

In the thirteenth century San Damiano stood in the middle of fields outside Assisi. Not far away was another simple oratory, that of the Portiuncula. This tiny, long-neglected chapel in the woods below the town was given to Francis at the beginning of his mission by the brothers of the Benedictine

Francis receives the stigmata (OPPOSITE PAGE) *in a fresco by Giotto. Francis, who had withdrawn to meditate on Mount Verna, was visited by an angel. As the angel approached, the image of a crucified man appeared behind his 6 wings—2 hid the body, 2 rose above the head and 2 were outstretched. Then darts of flame were emitted which imprinted on Francis's body the 5 wounds of Christ.*

The radiance and richness of creation filled Francis with joy. He needed nothing more. He and his companions strictly observed their vows of absolute poverty. They begged for food and owned no worldly goods.

Franciscan brothers still wear the Umbrian peasant tunic with a rope belt tied with 3 knots.

A lay Franciscan order counted Dante, Leonardo and Michelangelo in its number.

A view over the surrounding countryside from the magnificent Basilica of St Francis. The Pope laid the foundation stone for the building on 17 July 1228—the day after Francis was canonized. There were many followers of the saint, however, who felt that the scale of the project was ostentatious and quite out of keeping with the saint's devotion to that "dearest Lady, Poverty".

Nor did it accord with St Francis's stipulation that friars' houses should be built of mud and wood and "even the Church should look poor".

monastery on Mount Subasio. The Portiuncula ("a little parcel of land") was the birthplace of the Franciscan Order and in its extreme simplicity the tiny oratory accorded precisely with Francis's ideas of what was appropriate.

Since the sixteenth century, this, one of the humblest spots linked with the saint, has been totally enclosed by the Church of Santa Maria degli Angeli, which took 100 years to build (1569–1679). It is not difficult to imagine what Francis would have thought of this ostentatious edifice—he who, when he returned after an absence and found that the friars had built a brick shelter at the Portiuncula, rather than their usual branch and twig dwelling, tore the tiles off the roof with his bare hands.

Triumph of the spiritual knight

In his later years, Francis increasingly withdrew to the haunts of early days, to the many caves that had served as hermitages for himself and his first followers in this landscape of wooded hills broken by ravines and gorges. They had often retired to the spartan rock-hewn hermitage of the Carceri above Assisi, in a great cleft in Mount Subasio. With San Damiano, the hermitage is today the place where the Franciscan message of simplicity and joy is most powerfully present. Though it was at Gubbio that he tamed the wolf and at Cannara that he preached his famous sermon to the birds, it is here, on the wooded rocky slopes around the Carceri, where green-flowering hellebores light the shade under ilex trees and the air is filled with birdsong, that these tales fire the soul.

At the age of 42, exhausted by fasts and almost blind, Francis received a new source of anguish: the stigmata, the replication on his body of the wounds of Christ. In May 1226, knowing he was dying, he asked to be carried from Assisi to the Portiuncula, "so that the life of the body should end where the life of the soul had begun". On the way he stopped to take leave of Clare, and it was at San Damiano that Francis, in great pain, composed his famous paean of praise to the creator, the *Canticle of the Sun*. At the Portiuncula on 3 October 1226 he died.

It is said that as Francis left Assisi for the last time on his short final journey to the Portiuncula he looked back at the city of his birth and said: "May thou be blessed by God, holy city, since through thee many souls will be saved. . . ."

The tiny chapel of the Portiuncula, now completely enclosed in the Church of Santa Maria degli Angeli, stood abandoned in the woods below Assisi when Francis took it over. A much simpler construction then, it was his base throughout his mission. He came back here to die, and at his death a flock of skylarks rose above the roof.

The Giotto fresco (LEFT) shows Francis preaching to the birds. On one occasion, when their song disturbed his prayers, he is said to have asked them to stop singing. They did so, resuming only when he had finished praying.

As creations of God, animals and the elements were for Francis his brothers and sisters. Thus Water was his sister, the Sun his brother.

MONT-ST-MICHEL

> ❛ *Mont-St-Michel is for France what the Great Pyramid is for Egypt.* ❜
>
> FRENCH WRITER VICTOR HUGO IN 1884.

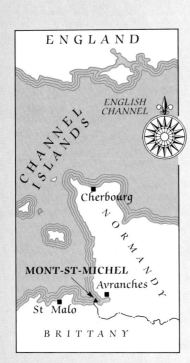

IN THE SOUTHWEST CORNER OF NORMANDY, France, pilgrims and travellers have been coming to a tiny island for more than 1,000 years. Connected to the mainland by a causeway, Mont-St-Michel rises dramatically from a flat expanse of sands washed smooth by the powerful tides that sweep into the bay. In fine weather, the conical rock, encrusted with monastic buildings, terraces, gardens, houses and fortifications, can be seen for miles around, its spire lifting a golden statue of the Archangel Michael toward the heavens. But in a mist, the dark outlines of roofs and pinnacles seem to float like those of a ghostly palace on a sea of grey vapour.

According to legend, at the start of the eighth century, St Aubert, bishop of Avranches, was visited in a dream by the Archangel Michael, who told him to build an oratory on a large isolated rock nearby. Upon waking, Aubert doubted the authenticity of the dream, prompting St Michael to appear to him again with the same command. But once more Aubert hesitated—so St Michael appeared for a third time, and rapped him on the head with his finger. This left Aubert in no doubt and, in 708, he set about building an oratory on the rock.

Aubert's rock was then known as Mont Tombe, perhaps reflecting a folk memory that the place had been used as a Celtic graveyard. At that time, the sea had not yet encroached upon this part of the Normandy coastline and Mont Tombe was surrounded by the marshy woodlands of the forest of Scissy. Legends relate that the local Celtic priests, known as Druids, used the rock as a centre for sun worship, a tradition continued during the Roman period with the cult of the sun god Mithras. With Aubert, the sun god's reign ended; he was replaced by St Michael, leader of heaven's armies.

Monks and pilgrims

From its beginnings as Aubert's oratory to the present day, Mont-St-Michel has withstood sieges, structural collapses and changes, and neglect to become, after Versailles, France's most popular national monument. The narrow cobbled *Grande Rue*, the rock's main street which leads up to the monastery, is lined with bars, cafés, and souvenir shops, continuing the commercial tradition that inevitably accompanied the Mont's increasing fame as a powerful spiritual centre during the Middle Ages.

The Archangel St Michael (ABOVE) *attacks a winged dragon, symbolic of evil, over the Mont-St-Michel in a miniature from the medieval* Très Riches Heures *by the Duc de Berry.*

Founded in the 8th century *by St Aubert of Avranches, Mont-St-Michel grew to become a powerful religious centre in the Middle Ages, drawing pilgrims from far and wide. It is said that the Mont's conical rock was surrounded by a forest until the sea turned it into an island, now connected to the mainland by a causeway.*

Situated on the north face of the rock are the Gothic buildings known as La Merveille *(The Marvel), seen here to the right of the spires of the abbey church. Begun in 1203 by Abbot Jourdain, the* Merveille *took only 25 years to complete and comprised the monks' living and working quarters.*

The 12th-century church was rebuilt after a collapse at the start of the 13th, and combines an austere Romanesque nave with an exuberant Gothic choir.

The pilgrims who have come here down the centuries have taken away vessels filled with the Mont's sand and cockleshells; modern visitors have a wider choice of souvenirs, but the impulse remains the same—to have a physical reminder of an extraordinary place.

By the time Richard I, Duke of Normandy, installed 50 Benedictine monks on the Mont in 966, there was already a small community of lay folk there, including refugees from marauding Viking pirates. In the middle of the eleventh century, the Romanesque abbey church crowning the top of the rock was finished, though such were the difficulties of construction that part of it collapsed at the start of the next century.

It was not until 1203, however, after the Mont had been damaged by fire, that a new building programme began. This produced what was called *La Merveille* (The Marvel), a set of magnificent Gothic buildings raised on the north side of the rock. These are now the highlight of a visit. Begun by Abbot Jourdain and completed only 25 years later under Abbot Raoul de Villedieu, the *Merveille* consists of two massive sections, towering three storeys high.

The ''Marvel'' of the rock
On the lowest level of the eastern part of the *Merveille* is the *Aumônerie*, where the monks dispensed charity and gave lodging to poor pilgrims; above it lies the *Salle des Hôtes*, the principal guest room; and, at the top of this section, the monks' own dining hall, the refectory, a place brilliantly lit by a series of tall, deeply set lancet windows.

The western part of the *Merveille* houses the *Cellier*, a storeroom, and, above it, the *Salle des Chevaliers*, a hall divided into four aisles by rows of stone columns with carved capitals. Originally used as a scriptorium, where the monks painstakingly copied manuscripts, the *Salle* became, after 1469, the assembly place for the Knights of St Michael, an order founded by King Louis XI (1461–83). Immediately above this imposing hall are the cloisters—a haven of tranquillity suspended between earth and heaven.

But tranquillity was often in short supply during the centuries of the Mont's turbulent history. It survived assaults from the English during the Hundred Years' War (1337–1453) and an attack by the Huguenots in 1591. In the late eighteenth century, during and after the French Revolution (1789–99), it was

Mont-St-Michel is notorious for the fast incoming tides which have claimed many lives over the centuries. A lady pilgrim (ABOVE), caught by a rising tide, calls upon the Virgin Mary and is miraculously saved.

St Aubert is visited in a dream by St Michael (LEFT) in an illustration from a medieval French manuscript. According to legend, St Michael appeared before Aubert 3 times with the command to build an oratory on a nearby rock. Only when the archangel rapped him on the head with his finger did Aubert set about his task.

turned into a prison, remaining one until 1863. Eleven years later it was officially recognized as a historic building, and restoration work on it began. In 1922, religious services were once again held in the abbey church. Today at least one monk is in permanent residence, maintaining a spiritual tradition more than 1,200 years old.

THE ALHAMBRA

> *Nothing in life is more cruel than to be blind in Granada.*

MOORISH INSCRIPTION ON ONE OF THE WALLS OF THE ALHAMBRA.

IN JANUARY 1492 THE LAST MUSLIM RULER IN Spain, Boabdil, surrendered to the Catholic sovereigns Ferdinand of Aragon and Isabella of Castile in Granada. To mark this great triumph, a silver cross and the banner of St James were raised on one of the towers of the city's palace fortress: the Alhambra. A new era had begun.

Built on a hill overlooking Granada, the Alhambra is the finest surviving example of the creative genius of the Moors, Muslims who invaded Spain from North Africa in the early eighth century. The palace is a maze of shady courtyards and halls, gracious arcades, marble columns, fountains and pools; its walls are decorated with patterns of a lacelike intricacy and with multicoloured *azulejos* or glazed tiles. Most spectacular are the "stalactite" decorations, which, on the ceilings, seem to explode like giant starbursts.

The Alhambra's exterior is austere. Against the shimmering silver-capped peaks of the Sierra Nevada, its formidable walls and towers follow the contours of the hill. But inside beckons a world of delicacy and femininity, in the curves of horseshoe arches,

the glittering channels and pools of water, and the endless geometric and flowing arabesque patterns that cover almost every surface. For almost 250 years the Alhambra served the Nasrid rulers of Granada as a palace and harem, and residence for court officials. Over the centuries since Boabdil's surrender in the year Columbus set off to circumnavigate the globe, the Alhambra has survived fire and earthquake and neglect. Yet despite additions and extensive restorations, it still enchants visitors with its vision of a Moorish paradise.

Kings of the Nasrid dynasty

The palace evolved from the ninth-century fortress known as the Alcazába—parts of which can still be seen. It remained a relatively insignificant fortification until the thirteenth century, when the Moorish population of Granada suddenly swelled with refugees from the city of Córdoba, taken by the Christians in 1236. The shrinking Moorish kingdom, under threat from the Spanish Catholic armies, was now centred on Granada. Here in 1238 Mohammed I, the first

The Alhambra, *fortress palace of the Moorish rulers of Granada, is framed against the snow-capped Sierra Nevada. Built principally during the 14th century A.D., the Alhambra's formidable walls conceal a world of delicate colonnades, shady courtyards, pools and fountains.*

The cupola *of the Hall of the Two Sisters seems to explode like a giant starburst. The impression of dynamic outward movement is created by the Alhambra's famous stalactite decoration, an art form unique to Islam.*

king of the Nasrid dynasty, came to the throne. He at once strengthened the neglected fortifications and improved the water supply by building new aqueducts. Towers and ramparts were added to the fortress by the king's son, Mohammed II, who also raised a wall around the edge of the hill.

The Alcazába was now a considerable bastion. But it was the next two kings, Yusuf I (1333–54) and Mohammed V (1354–91), who created the exquisite interiors of what is now called the Alhambra. It was during Yusuf's reign that the Court of Myrtles, one of the most delightful courtyards in the palace, was constructed. Situated near the modern entrance to the complex, the court is named after the two long myrtle hedges bordering the marble pathways on either side of the central rectangular pool. Fed by a low circular fountain at each end and ignited by the brilliant orange of goldfish, the pool is almost at the level of the paths; its still water, like a smooth glass carpet, reflects the slim columns of the elegant arcades.

A delight in fountains

The beauty of the court lies in its imaginative use of water, which the Moors, as descendants of a desert people, delighted to incorporate into their architecture. Pools, fountains and channels reflected sunlight and provided visual refreshment during the scorching heat of day. The plashing of fountains, echoing around the courts, also induced the tranquil meditative atmosphere for which these pleasing shady retreats were designed.

At the north end of the Court of Myrtles rise the battlements of the austere Tower of Comares. Below it is the Hall of Ambassadors, the largest room in the palace, with its ceiling rising 60 feet high. Here foreign dignitaries came to pay their respects to the king, who sat on a throne in a recess opposite the entrance. It was in this hall, in 1492, that Ferdinand was reputed to have discussed plans with Christopher Columbus for his forthcoming voyage.

The most famous court of the Alhambra is the Court of Lions, built by Mohammed V, and named after the 12 alabaster lions that support the central fountain. Out of the mouth of each lion a stream of water pours into the circular channel surrounding the fountain. The channel is also fed by four others, cut into the stone paving, which lead from the shallow basins of fountains situated

The Mirador de Daraxa (OPPOSITE PAGE) *leads off from the Hall of the Two Sisters. This exquisitely decorated belvedere resembles, in the words of Hans Christian Andersen, "a fantastic, petrified lace-bazaar". The two windows overlook the Daraxa garden, with its lemon trees, cypresses and fountain.*

The interior surfaces of the Alhambra testify to the Moorish genius for ornate decoration. Since Islam forbade representational art, the Moors created intricate abstract and geometric designs (LEFT) *in their plasterwork and on azulejos (tiles).*

Flowing Islamic script (BELOW) *also embellishes walls with texts from the Koran, eulogies of the buildings and their creators, and the frequently used: "God alone will conquer."*

THE ALHAMBRA

Intricate repetitive motifs *create a soft, feminine texture on the surfaces of the Court of Lions (*RIGHT*) and the Royal Baths (*BELOW*). Dating from the reign of Yusuf I, the baths consist of a number of chambers with cool marble floors and ceilings pierced by star-shaped windows, which may have once contained coloured glass.*

in adjacent rooms. The arcades around the court rest on 124 delicate columns, while on its western and eastern sides two pavilions provide vantage points from which to view the water spilling from the lions' mouths like strings of liquid diamonds.

The genius of Moorish art

The architects of the Alhambra were masters of proportion, decoration and lighting. The surfaces of marble floors and pools were designed to reflect the bright Andalusian sun and fill the courts with a golden radiance. Since, according to Islamic practice, representational art was forbidden, Moorish decoration was abstract in form. Geometric and floral patterns, as well as sayings from the Koran in elegant Kufic script, cover plaster and stone surfaces, and were originally painted in bright colours. The reds, blues and greens of *azulejos* adorn the walls of halls, galleries and the Royal Baths.

But the most dramatic architectural feature of the Alhambra is the stalactite ornamentation which creates the effect of a honeycomb composed of thousands of cells filled with natural light and shadow. In domes, niches and on arches, this unique Islamic decorative device seems to soak up light reflected from adjacent surfaces and

then, as in the ceiling of the Hall of the Two Sisters, explodes with vibrant energy.

Similar in conception is the ceiling of the Hall of Abencerrajes. Reached by a doorway from the Court of Lions, the hall is named after a noble family of Granada who were supposedly massacred here in the late fifteenth century. The eye is irresistibly drawn up to the profusion of stalactites whose endless detailed intricacies create a sense of the cosmic.

The genius of the Alhambra and Moorish art is particularly evident when compared with the unfinished palace of Charles v, the

The Court of Myrtles (ABOVE) by the British painter David Roberts. He was one of a number of artists and writers who visited the Alhambra in the 19th century.

The Catholic sovereigns
Ferdinand of Aragon and Isabella of Castile accept the surrender of Granada by the Moorish ruler Boabdil in a 19th-century representation.

Holy Roman Emperor and King of Spain. Begun in 1526, the palace was built within the Alhambra, part of which had to be demolished to make room for it. With its circular courtyard bordered by solid marble columns, Charles's Renaissance palace seems simple, strong and majestic compared with the Alhambra's fairy-world of filigree.

The "Last Sigh of the Moor"

In the centuries following the Christian takeover of Granada, the Alhambra suffered not only from fire and earthquake, but from general neglect; it also became the lair of criminals, and the home of gypsies. In the nineteenth century, the palace was visited by Romantically inclined writers and artists such as Washington Irving, Richard Ford, George Borrow, Gustave Doré, and David Roberts. Irving was fortunate enough to live in one of the palace's chambers for three

The American writer Washington Irving stayed in the Alhambra for 3 months during 1829; and published his famous The Alhambra 3 years later.

months during 1829. Three years later the American writer published his famous *The Alhambra*, which wove together historical facts and legends, and conjured up a world of oriental mystery and magic.

Amid the murmuring of fountains the ghosts of the Moorish rulers still linger in the courtyards and halls so lovingly embellished. The palace was enshrined in their hearts. According to tradition, after the keys of the Alhambra had been handed over to the Christians in 1492, Boabdil and his entourage left Granada for ever.

Several miles from the city, Boabdil turned to look at the palace for the last time. Overcome with emotion, he gazed at the familiar walls; and his mother, Ayxa, rounded on him, saying: "You weep as a woman for what you could not defend as a man." This spot is still known as the *Ultimo Suspiro del Moro*, the "Last Sigh of the Moor".

Stillness and tranquillity pervade the Court of Myrtles (LEFT), also called Court of the Pond, where motionless water mirrors elegant arcades and the battlemented Tower of Comares. Of the numerous inscriptions around the court, one proclaims its beauty: "I am the nuptial bride, endowed with every beauty and perfection."

The Court of Lions (RIGHT) is the most famous of the Alhambra's courts, and is named after the 12 alabaster lions that support the central fountain. Built under Mohammed V, the court, with its arcade supported by 124 slim columns, was reserved for the use of the royal family only.

Washington Irving was captivated by its beauty "with sunshine gleaming along its colonnades and sparkling in its fountains. . . . It needs but a slight exertion of fancy to picture some pensive beauty of the harem, loitering in these secluded haunts of Oriental luxury."

THE FORBIDDEN CITY

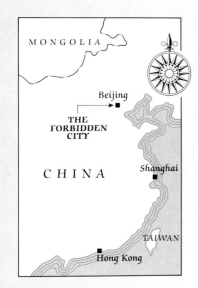

AT THE HEART OF BEIJING, CAPITAL OF CHINA, lies the Forbidden City, probably the greatest palace complex in the world and the most potent symbol of China's dynastic past. Its very name speaks of mystery and intrigue, of the opulent courtlife of emperors, surrounded by their ministers, concubines and eunuchs, and shut off from the world by formidable gates and walls.

Through these gates, visitors now come to marvel at the scale, splendour, elegance and craftsmanship of this labyrinth of tiled-roofed buildings adorned with mythological creatures. There are audience halls, pavilions, marble steps and balustrades, bronze lions and incense burners, as well as gracious formal gardens.

But the symmetry and harmony of the buildings and their courtyards, beautifully proportioned and filled with light and air, belie the rich, dark interiors, redolent of the emperors of the past and their sinister glamour. As the British writer Osbert Sitwell (1892–1969) observed: "And in each hall, with its tall red columns and gold ceiling and coloured walls, broods a painted, gilded and shimmering-eyed beauty, like that of a peacock's tail, in which the Manchu Emperors seem still angrily to live and move, as might a wasp in the heart of a ripe nectarine."

Like intricately carved Chinese ivory boxes, nesting one inside the other, the rectangle of the Forbidden City lies enclosed within the Imperial City, which in turn lies within the North or Inner City, itself part of the old walled capital of Beijing. The heart of this complex, the walled and moated inner sanctum of the Forbidden City or Imperial Palace, expresses the seclusion and absolutism of China's rulers. From here, 24 emperors of the Ming and Qing dynasties reigned, aloof from the rest of the world, from the fifteenth century until 1911, when the Republican Revolution began.

The siting of the city

The beauty of the Forbidden City lies not so much in any one building as in the ordered rectilinear layout of its temples, palaces and gardens. This Chinese tradition of city-building can be traced back as far as the ancient city of Chang'an, built between 200 B.C. and A.D. 200. A surviving plan of Chang'an from the seventh century A.D. is strikingly similar to that of the Forbidden City as it is today. Both are symbolic of an ordered universe.

The Forbidden City *in Beijing was the palace residence of the Chinese emperors from the early 15th century to 1911, when the Republican Revolution brought an end to the imperial era. Entrance to the complex is by the Meridian Gate (ABOVE), seen beyond the frozen waters of the Golden Stream canal.*

Ferocious-looking bronze lions, such as this one, guard the palaces, halls and gateways of the Forbidden City. Other bronze animals that ornament the precincts include tortoises and storks.

THE FORBIDDEN CITY

Since its original construction in the early 15th century, the Forbidden City has been added to, repaired and renovated, so that it reflects different periods of Chinese history. The two engravings (RIGHT and BELOW), probably dating from the 18th and 19th centuries respectively, show the inner court of the emperors and a view of the city looking north toward Coal Hill.

The first westerner to enter the city was a Jesuit missionary named Matthew Ricci, at the end of the 16th century. Ricci lived in Beijing for several years and was eventually allowed to build a church and mission house there.

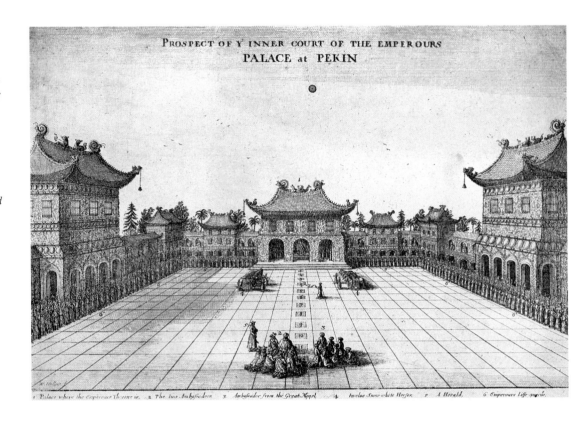

PROSPECT OF Y INNER COURT OF THE EMPEROURS PALACE at PEKIN

1. Palace where the Emperour Throne is. 2. The two Ambassadors. 3. Ambassador from the Great Mogol. 4. twelve Snow-white Horses. 5. A Herald. 6. Emperours Life-guards.

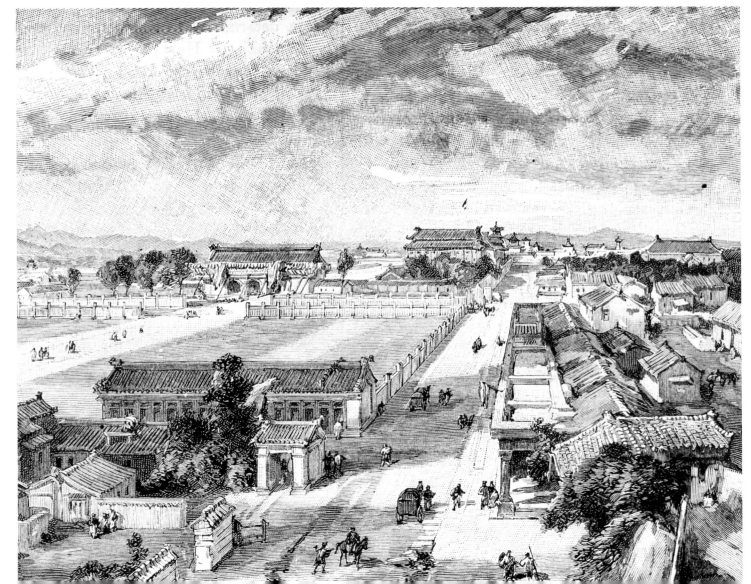

For, according to the Chinese world-view, every emperor was held to rule by the Mandate of Heaven—the consent of the gods. In the cosmic triad of Heaven, Earth and Man, the emperor as Son of Heaven was seen as the mediator responsible for bringing about order and harmony on Earth. The ideal state was characterized by balance and hierarchy, and the symmetry of the Forbidden City reflects this.

A central doctrine that played a fundamental role in the siting of early Chinese cities was *fengshui* ("wind-water") or geomancy: the traditional art of siting houses, public buildings and tombs in harmony with the earth's vital energy. *Fengshui*, which embraced practical, aesthetic and mystical considerations, underlies the planning of the Forbidden City. Buildings were aligned along north-south axes, with all major buildings facing south, the direction of the sun's beneficence and therefore of holiness.

The Forbidden City's central north-south axis was also the central axis of Beijing. In the early fifteenth century, just after it had been built, the approach to the Forbidden City ran along this axis for half a mile from the great central gate in Beijing's southern wall. From here the way led north through the Gate of Heavenly Peace (where officials had to leave their horses and carriages unless exempted); it then passed through the Gate of Uprightness and finally the Meridian Gate, the formal entrance to the Forbidden City.

At the heart of Beijing

On the far side of the Forbidden City, the axis continued through its northernmost gate, the Gate of Martial Spirit, and beyond the moat into the imperial pleasureground of Jingshan or "Scenic Mountain", commonly known as Coal Hill. This artificial hill was made from earth and rocks scooped up during the construction of the moat and the dredging of lakes on the west flank of the palaces. It was here in 1644, as the Manchus were attacking the city, that the last Ming emperor hanged himself, having first killed his family. The axis comes to an end at the site of the Bell Tower and Drum Tower, where a bell was rung to salute the morning, and a drum beaten to bid farewell to the day.

The Forbidden City was the heart of Beijing. It was the place where, as one Chinese classical writer proclaims, "earth and sky meet, where . . . wind and rain are gathered in, and where yin and yang are in harmony". Here lived the emperor, whose role, said the Confucian sage Mencius, was "to stand in the centre of the earth and stabilize the people within the four seas".

The full name of the emperor's imperial palace was the Purple Forbidden City, after the Purple Luminous Constellation which has the Pole Star at its centre. As the heavens revolved around the Pole Star, so the earth revolved around the emperor. His Dragon Throne was at the centre of not only the main hall, the Forbidden City, the Imperial City and the Inner City, but also, so the Chinese believed, of the world.

From Khubilai Khan to the last emperor

The earliest recorded city on the site of Beijing was built under the Zhou Dynasty (1122–221 B.C.). The river plain in which it lay was fertile, and the city was well sited to guard China's vulnerable northern border, repeatedly under threat from the uncivilized but vigorous nomads of the steppes.

Marco Polo, *the son of a Venetian merchant, was, in 1271, one of the first western visitors to China. Polo travelled to Beijing (then called Dadu, "Great Capital") where he witnessed the magnificent court life of the emperor Khubilai Khan.*

His descriptions of the emperor's palace—forerunner of the Forbidden City—evoke its grand scale and opulence: gold, silver and marble were evident everywhere in great abundance.

In the thirteenth century A.D., the Mongols, under the infamous Genghis Khan, invaded China, and it was the latter's grandson, Khubilai, who moved the Mongolian court to Beijing (then called Dadu, "Great Capital"). From here, the Mongol armies were able to complete their conquest of southern China. It was to Khubilai's court that Marco Polo, one of the earliest western visitors to China, came in 1274. His descriptions of the Khan's fabulous palace—forerunner of the Forbidden City—where magicians caused golden trays and goblets to float across the room, later earned him the nickname *Il Milione*, "teller of a million lies".

It was after the Mongol Dynasty had been driven out by the Ming that the Forbidden City as it is known today was created. Building began under the emperor Yongle (1403–24), possibly on the very site of Khubilai's old palace: it took 1,000,000 men 16 years to complete. Over the centuries, buildings were added, refurbished or renovated, so that the palace reflects different periods of Chinese history.

This vast complex, comprising more than 8,000 rooms and chambers with attendant courtyards and gardens, is spread over an area of about 250 acres. Following traditional palace design, government officials worked in the southern part of the city, the imperial family lived in the north, behind the beautiful Gate of Heavenly Purity, which divided the two areas. No adult male other than the emperor himself was allowed into this residential quarter, which was heavily guarded by eunuchs.

Entry to the grounds of the inner palaces was, and still is, by the massive Meridian Gate, from which the emperor would review the imperial army. The drum and bell that once were sounded when the emperor passed under the gate's central door are silent as today's visitors go through it. Beyond the gate lies Golden Stream, a canal shaped like a bow and spanned by five marble bridges.

Guests arrive at the Forbidden City (OPPOSITE PAGE) *in a Chinese painting dating from around the turn of the 15th century. Elegant golden roofs adorn the well-proportioned palaces and halls, which are aligned to face south and in this picture seem to float among the clouds.*

The boy emperor Pu Yi is shown (BELOW) *reviewing the imperial household in a scene from Bernardo Bertolucci's The Last Emperor (1988). After the revolution in 1911, Pu Yi was allowed to live in the Forbidden City* (BOTTOM) *until 1924. The last of the Qing emperors, he died in 1967.*

THE FORBIDDEN CITY

The Dragon Throne in the Hall of Supreme Harmony was the centre not only of the Imperial Palace, the Imperial City and Beijing, but also, according to Chinese thinking, of the world.

From here the Hall of Supreme Harmony, the most important of the ceremonial buildings, rises on its three-tiered terrace. Inside was the centre of the Chinese world, the Dragon Throne, where, surrounded by bronze incense-burners and gilt columns, the emperor presided as the Son of Heaven. In this hall grand ceremonies were held to celebrate occasions such as the winter solstice, the new year and the emperor's birthday.

Behind the Hall of Supreme Harmony lie the Hall of Middle Harmony, and the Hall of Preserving Harmony, where banquets were held for foreign dignitaries. North of these halls, and reflecting their layout, is a group of three palaces, the Palace of Heavenly Purity and the Palace of Earthly Tranquillity being used as residences for the emperor and empress respectively.

Between the two palaces lay the Hall of Mutual Ease, which symbolically united emperor and empress and therefore Heaven and Earth, yang and yin, male and female. Beyond the palaces lay the imperial gardens, where pools, rockeries, pavilions, and old pine and cypress trees made a welcome change from the processions of buildings.

Apart from its palaces and halls, the

After the expulsion of Pu Yi in 1924, the Forbidden City gradually fell into decay (BELOW). Now, as a public museum, the palaces and courtyards are slowly being restored to something like their former glory.

Forbidden City contains temples, gardens, libraries, theatres and living quarters for the thousands of resident servants, eunuchs and concubines. Concubines, who were protected and served by eunuchs, could improve their status by bearing the emperor a son. It is said that when the emperor summoned one of these ladies to his bed chamber, she was obliged to remove all her clothes (to prove she carried no weapon) and wrap herself in a yellow gown, before being carried off to the emperor on the back of a eunuch.

The end of an era

After nearly five centuries, rule from the Dragon Throne came to an end with the outbreak of the Chinese revolution in 1911. The four-year-old boy emperor Pu Yi was forced to abdicate by the leaders of the new republic, though he was permitted to live on in the Imperial Palace until 1924. During the following years, the palace buildings gradually fell into decay.

In 1949, Chinese Communist forces took over Beijing and the defeated Nationalists retreated to Taiwan, taking with them many treasures from the Forbidden City. Now, as a public museum, the city is in no sense ''Forbidden'': the doors of the sacrosanct recesses of imperial power have been swept open by the winds of the twentieth century.

One of the last acts of the empress dowager Cixi (1834–1908) (LEFT) was to appoint the 3-year-old Pu Yi (ABOVE) as emperor in 1908. The empress, a former concubine of the emperor Xianfeng (1850–61), was the power behind both the emperors Tongzhi (1862–74) and Guangxu (1875–1908).

Narrow-minded and autocratic, Cixi was virtual ruler of China for about 50 years, during which time she resisted attempts at modernizing the country. Funds which were originally allocated for the modernization of the Chinese Navy, for example, were used instead to build the empress a sumptuous summer palace.

DENMARK

ELSINORE

NORTH OF COPENHAGEN, ON A PROMONTORY overlooking the sea, stands a great fortress whose massive fortifications dramatically contrast with its elegant copper-roofed pinnacles. Down the centuries Kronborg Castle has been used as a royal residence, a garrison, a prison and, latterly, a museum. But the castle's fame chiefly rests on its connection with two great figures of legend. One is Hamlet, prince of Denmark, immortalized in the play by William Shakespeare. Although Shakespeare called the castle Elsinore, an Anglicized form of Helsingør, this name properly applies only to the town below the castle; but as Elsinore it is now known to all the world.

The other Danish hero who draws visitors to Kronborg is Holger the Dane, one of the 12 knights or Paladins of Charlemagne (742–814), Emperor of the West. Like the British King Arthur, Holger is a "sleeping hero"— one who is said to sleep underground until the hour of his country's greatest danger, when he will rise and fight to defend it.

The Hamlet of legend

The story of Hamlet—the prince who feigns madness while planning revenge on the king who murdered his father, married his mother and usurped his throne—seems to be an old Scandinavian, rather than specifically Danish, legend. In the earliest written version, the twelfth-century Danish historian Saxo Grammaticus treats it as history and sets it in Jutland. Saxo's "Amleth" wins back his kingdom and dies in battle in Jutland.

Saxo's story was known in Elizabethan England through a French version which set it vaguely in Denmark, and to Englishmen of Shakespeare's time the best-known place in Denmark was Elsinore. Here, in 1585, an impressive new castle had been completed. Not surprisingly, Shakespeare, who wrote *Hamlet* 15 years later, made Elsinore the setting for his play.

The castle's white sandstone walls rose from what had been in the Middle Ages a bleak and desolate spit of land running into the Sound at its narrowest point between Denmark and Sweden. Here, in the 1420s, Erik of Pomerania, king of Denmark, Sweden and Norway, had built the citadel of Krogen

The magnificent fortress of Kronborg, begun in 1574, overlooks the narrow Sound between Denmark and Sweden. To the Elizabethans it was the best-known place in Denmark and as "Elsinore" became the setting for Shakespeare's Hamlet.

Kronborg (ABOVE), *shown in an engraving of about 1696, was strengthened with massive fortifications on its landward side during the reign of Christian V (1670–99).*

Hamlet, the legendary prince of Denmark, is depicted in a 16th-century manuscript (RIGHT) and portrayed as Shakespeare's melancholy Dane (FAR RIGHT) by the great British actor John Gielgud at Kronborg in 1939. Hamlet was first performed at the "real" Elsinore in 1816.

to control shipping passing through the Sound on its way to or from the Baltic and to enforce the payment of Sound Dues. More than a century later, Frederick II, at war with the Swedes, needed to demonstrate his control of the Sound and in 1574 began to rebuild Krogen, which he renamed Kronborg (Crown Fortress).

Financed entirely from the Sound Dues, Kronborg was the finest Renaissance castle in the North. Partly a military bastion, with room for a garrison, it was also a princely residence with copper-clad towers and spires. Inside, there were richly furnished rooms with coffered ceilings and painted panels, and tapestries showing a hundred or more Danish kings, some real, others legendary. Here Frederick received a legation sent from Queen Elizabeth I to present him with the Order of the Garter; here his daughter Anna spent her honeymoon with James VI of Scotland, later James I of England.

But it was probably not so much the castle's magnificence that struck the Elizabethans as the great bronze cannons with which it continued to enforce the hated Sound Dues. Every ship had to stop at Elsinore to pay them, so it was a familiar, if unwelcome, sight to Elizabethan seamen.

Shakespeare's Elsinore

This at once formidable fortress and great Renaissance palace became Shakespeare's Elsinore, which he suggests (*Hamlet* Act I, Sc. iv) stood dramatically on a cliff-top. In fact Shakespeare must have known its true position because actors he worked with had performed at Kronborg for the court. However, the playwright's imagination recast the castle and Saxo's legend into a Renaissance world of political skulduggery played out in corridors, chambers, and on battlements.

From the end of the eighteenth century, many foreigners, especially English and Germans, began making their way to the Elsinore of Shakespeare's imagination. Some were disappointed to find a Kronborg restored by Christian IV after a fire in 1629 had almost gutted the original castle. Swedish occupation from 1658 to 1660 had also taken its toll. The new Kronborg looked almost like the old, but probably lacked the resonance of Hamlet's Elsinore.

At the end of the eighteenth century, the castle's Romantic deficiencies were partly redeemed by the creation of an "allegorical" garden. Here visitors could wander to the

Kingdom of Heaven via a Hermit's Hut and a makebelieve grave marked by a broken column. By 1805 the garden was being called "Hamlet's Garden", and the grave "Hamlet's Grave". Soon tourists took the grave to be Hamlet's actual burial place; and, in 1857, an enterprising Dane obtained permission "to arrange Hamlet's Grave in a manner corresponding to legend". He moved the broken column elsewhere and began charging 32 skillings to see it!

There is no longer a grave of Hamlet at Elsinore. Visitors now come to see the beautiful copper-roofed castle and a pleasant town with cobbled streets and old houses. But viewed from the sea, the castle can still evoke the Elsinore of Shakespeare, its grandeur concealing murder and intrigue.

Deep beneath Kronborg sits the statue of Holger the Dane, the Danish national hero. According to legend, he is sleeping under the castle until the hour of Denmark's greatest danger—a tradition enshrined in one of Hans Andersen's fairytales.

Known in French literature as Ogier le Danois, Holger was one of the Paladins or champions of the emperor Charlemagne, and lived for 200 years with the enchantress Morgan le Fay in Avalon. This powerful, brooding statue was commissioned in 1906 from the Danish sculptor Hans Peder Pedersen-Dan.

INDIA

THE TAJ MAHAL

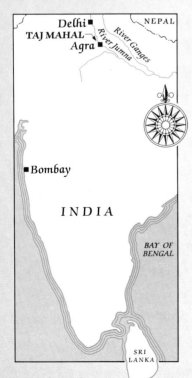

ON THE BANKS OF THE RIVER JUMNA AT AGRA, northern India, the Taj Mahal has inspired visitors with a sense of beauty and harmony for more than 300 years. The building was born of inspiration. For if emotions can be embodied in architecture, then surely the love that was inspired in one man by his beloved wife is frozen in the white marble of the Taj. The man was Shah Jahan, fifth Great Moghul emperor of India (1628–58), who built this unique mausoleum for his wife, Mumtaz Mahal, after she had tragically died in childbirth.

Shah Jahan, like his Moghul forebears, was both a man of action and a cultured patron of the arts, especially architecture. He was an able military commander: in his early twenties he gained the gratitude and admiration of his father, the emperor Jahangir, by successfully leading imperial troops against rebellious tribesmen.

According to legend, Shah Jahan first met his future wife—then named Arjumand Banu—while she was selling trinkets from a stall in a bazaar. This may seem a surprising occupation for a woman with noble Persian blood in her veins, but this was no ordinary bazaar. It was part of the traditional Muslim New Year's celebrations, during which ladies of the court were given the chance to sell knick-knacks to noblemen at exorbitant prices, and also engage in some light-hearted flirtation.

"Chosen One of the Palace"

Legend or not, there is no denying the romance and splendour of their marriage on 30 April 1612—a day favoured by astrologers. Agra buzzed with excitement. Processions filled the streets with colour during the day; at night, the dark cloth of sky was stitched with fireworks. The young bride, 19 years of age, was soon after given a new name, Mumtaz Mahal (Chosen One of the Palace), from which Taj Mahal is derived.

By all accounts, Shah Jahan and Mumtaz were truly devoted to each other. In his wife the emperor found a woman of natural charm, who was dignified, yet warmhearted, intelligent and discreet. Mumtaz was also without the scheming nature that tarnished the character of her powerful aunt Nur Jahan, wife of the emperor Jahangir. Shah Jahan was able to discuss state affairs with his queen, seek her advice, and generally treat her as a confidante. And when the emperor went off on military campaigns,

"A most perfect pearl on an azure ground", the
Taj Mahal is a vision of delicacy and symmetry. It is
the most famous mausoleum in the world and was built
by the 17th-century Moghul emperor Shah Jahan
(RIGHT) for his wife Mumtaz Mahal (FAR RIGHT) after
she had died in childbirth. Some 20,000 men laboured
for 22 years to build this jewel of Moghul architecture.

Mumtaz would insist on accompanying him.

It was during one such campaign in the Deccan, some 500 miles south of Agra, that Mumtaz went into labour with her fourteenth child (of the others, only seven had survived). At dawn on 7 June 1631, she died after giving birth. An apocryphal story relates that just before her death she asked her distraught husband to build her a mausoleum that would be unrivalled for its beauty anywhere else in the world. The Taj Mahal, as it turned out, proved to be just such a monument.

Shah Jahan was stricken by the loss of his wife. Public appearances were cancelled; he refused to wear his regal clothes, eat rich food, or even listen to music; he would often suddenly burst into tears; his hair rapidly turned grey. He gave up leading military expeditions from the front, preferring to stay in his capital and let others take over the burden of field command. He was in mourning, it is said, for two years.

To the memory of Mumtaz

The emperor's one solace, it seems, was to throw himself, straightaway, into the building of his wife's mausoleum on the banks of the River Jumna. Shah Jahan had always been enthusiastic about architecture, and now seized this chance to divert his grief into something creative. He is said to have supervised proposals for the design, personally judging wooden models that were submitted for his approval.

It is not known whether there was any one architect who produced the final design, which casts doubt on the legend that the Taj's chief architect had his head cut off by the emperor to prevent him building a monument of equal splendour. However, the probability is that Shah Jahan himself had a decisive influence on the final plans.

The building of the mausoleum went on for 22 years. As many as 20,000 labourers and craftsmen were employed on the task. White marble was quarried at Jodhpur, some 100 miles away. It was then transported by

*The massive square-shaped gateway (*BELOW*) to the Taj Mahal opens onto a glorious vista of the mausoleum. It rises up to 100 feet and is topped with domed pavilions; its brass door replaced the original solid silver one, which was plundered by a local Hindu tribe after the collapse of the Moghul Empire.*

*Equally delightful is the view of the Taj from the River Jumna, shown (*RIGHT*) in another 19th-century engraving.*

elephant and, in the words of one European observer, by "powerful teams of oxen and of fierce-looking, big-horned buffaloes, which were dragging enormous, strongly made wagons. . . ." Precious stones were brought from home and abroad: lapis lazuli from Ceylon (Sri Lanka), malachite from Russia, carnelian from Baghdad, turquoise from Tibet.

No expense was spared. In 1632, an English traveller, Peter Mundy, witnessed the initial stages of the construction, which were "prosecuted with extraordinary dili-gence", and in which "Gold and silver [were] esteemed common Mettall, and Marble but as ordinarie stone". Smiths set to work on the silver doors of the grand entrance gate—though these were later stolen by a local Hindu tribe. Masons, carpenters, calli-graphers, inlay specialists and other crafts-men combined their skills to create an everlasting memorial to one woman.

A vision of symmetry
The Taj Mahal and its surrounding buildings were completed in 1653. Visitors now, as

they emerge from the gloom of the entrance gate arch, are faced with the same sudden vision of white marble that Shah Jahan would have seen over 300 years ago. What strikes the onlooker immediately is the symmetry of the building and the purity of its colour. The eye is naturally led by the straight lines of the long watercourse to the horizontal plane of the building's sandstone and marble base. On this, the domed octagonal structure soars upward in unison with arches, cupolas, and four minarets.

The beauty of the white marble is that it reflects the changing hues of sunlight. At dawn or dusk, its surface glows gently with shades of violet, rose pink, and muted gold. And in an early morning mist the building seems to float ethereally in the sky, almost as if the mist had shaped itself into the familiar curves of India's most famous monument. Even more ghostly is the Taj under a full moon—when light seems to emanate from the ice-coloured dome, mirrored in the rippled water of the oblong pool.

The visitor approaching the monument along the avenue of water lined with dark green cypresses gradually perceives that the pure marble surfaces of the Taj are in fact decorated. Inlaid floral and arabesque motifs intertwine; and verses from the Koran are inscribed above the doorways in flowing calligraphy. Above it all stands the great dome, rising some 230 feet above the ground, and bursting out into the sunshine like the bud of a giant flower.

The royal cenotaphs

The upward movement and sense of balance is emphasized by two sandstone mosques that flank the mausoleum. In fact, the mosque to the east, known as the "Reply", is there for only aesthetic reasons—it cannot be used for prayer because it does not face Mecca. And the symmetry lies not only in the buildings but also in the cool ornamental gardens, divided into four sections—a sacred number in Islam—by the two long pools whose reflections of the Taj create a further vertical symmetry.

Inside the mausoleum, in contrast to the glare outside, the light is soft, being filtered through lattice windows and the filigree mesh of an intricate marble screen surrounding the two cenotaphs of Mumtaz and Shah Jahan. In fact, the original screen was made of gold, encrusted with gems, but it was soon taken away before it could be stolen. The

Inside the tomb, surrounded by a pierced marble screen, the cenotaph of Mumtaz lies to the right of her devoted husband's. The Moghuls, it has been said, built like giants and finished their work like jewellers. Inlaid flowers (TOP) on the marble of the cenotaph were created from up to 60 different gemstones.

The timeless silhouette of the Taj (OPPOSITE PAGE) has inspired visitors for more than 300 years. For British writer Rudyard Kipling the monument seemed "the embodiment of all things pure, all things holy, and all things unhappy. That was the mystery of the building."

new screen, with its ivory colour and lacelike texture, creates a feminine softness that complements the cool solidity of the cenotaphs. The bodies of the royal couple were actually interred in the crypt below the cenotaphs: the latter are their symbolic and public resting places.

The inlay work—known as *pietra dura*—on the marble of the cenotaphs is rightly famous. Moghul craftsmen cut out of the marble the desired shape—usually floral or geometric—and then inserted precious and semi-precious stones, chosen for their colour and texture, which had been cut to fit flush into the marble. Great skill was needed to do this—a single inlaid flower can contain as many as 60 pieces of gemstone.

Decline and restoration

After its completion, the Taj retained its splendour until the decline of the Moghul Empire during the eighteenth century, when the entire complex fell into disrepair. Under British ascendancy in India in the nineteenth century, the place was sometimes used for open-air parties, and regimental bands filled the night air with music from the terraces. It was on one such occasion that the wife of a British army officer, on contemplating the Taj, remarked: "I would die tomorrow to have such another over me."

Two other Britons are often cited in connection with the Taj, for bad and good reasons. The first, Lord William Bentinck, governor-general of India (1828–35), intended to dismember the Taj and ship the pieces back to England for auction. Fortunately, the Victorian public were so unimpressed by a trial auction of marble from the Agra Fort that the scheme was abandoned. On the other hand, Lord Curzon, Viceroy of India (1898–1905), was a dedicated conservationist who did much to restore India's cultural monuments. This included renovating the Taj so that its glory could be enjoyed as much by posterity as by its creator.

There is a sad coda to the story of Shah Jahan. His reign came to an end in 1658, when his scheming son Aurangzeb took over the throne and had his father confined in Agra Fort. It was during these last years, until his death in 1666, that the old emperor would gaze across the River Jumna from the high walls of the fort at the outline of his wife's memorial. Eventually he would be reunited with her, lying by her side beneath the great dome of marble.

***Lord Curzon**, Viceroy of India (1898–1905), was instrumental in restoring Shah Jahan's great monument, photographed (ABOVE) in the late 19th century.*

The white dome of the Taj (RIGHT), a "soaring bubble of marble", as Mark Twain described it, seen from Agra Fort. It was from here that Shah Jahan, imprisoned by his son, would spend his last days gazing at the resting place of his beloved Mumtaz.

NEUSCHWANSTEIN

> *In a dream I conceived it; my will called it into being. Strong and fair it stands, a fortress proud and peerless.*
>
> WOTAN UPON BUILDING VALHALLA IN WAGNER'S OPERA *DAS RHEINGOLD*.

PERCHED ABOVE THE RUGGED GORGE OF THE River Pollat, amid the majestic scenery of the Bavarian Alps, is the most magical castle in the world. Its ivory white pinnacles, set against a backdrop of dark green firs, seem from afar to be as airy and delicate as spun sugar. The fairytale castle of Neuschwanstein was begun in 1869 by King Ludwig II of Bavaria (1845–86). More "medieval" than anything built in the Middles Ages, Neuschwanstein represents the realization of one man's dream.

The dream began in Ludwig's childhood. At about the age of six, he loved to play with bricks, from which, according to his grandfather, Ludwig I, he made "astonishingly good buildings". He also enjoyed acting and dressing up.

During the summer months, Ludwig's family—his father and mother, Ludwig himself and his younger brother Otto—would go to Hohenschwangau, the ancestral seat of the lords of Schwangau, which his father, King Maximilian II, had bought in 1833. When Maximilian "restored" the castle his romantic approach was reflected in his choice of a stage designer rather than an architect to draw up the plans. He loved old legends and had the walls painted with tales of medieval heroes, especially Lohengrin, the Swan Knight, who, according to tradition, had inhabited this very castle.

The Swan Knight

Lohengrin became an important figure in Ludwig's imagination. From the murals he knew how Lohengrin had arrived in Antwerp in a boat drawn by a swan on the River Schelde to be the champion of Else, the Princess of Brabant; how he had agreed to become her husband on condition that she never asked him his name or lineage; how on their wedding night she broke her promise and he answered her question, whereupon the swan reappeared and Lohengrin departed as mysteriously as he had come.

As a child, Ludwig made a sketch of Lohengrin's castle of Schwanstein—now his

The fairytale castle of Neuschwanstein was built in the Bavarian Alps by the romantic and eccentric King Ludwig II. He described its setting as "one of the nicest ever found". Ludwig's wish that his palaces, which he regarded as holy places, should be destroyed after his death to preserve their purity, was not observed. Thus Walt Disney, another maker of magic kingdoms, was able to model his Sleeping Beauty's castle on Neuschwanstein.

NEUSCHWANSTEIN

Ludwig's obsession with the Lohengrin saga first drew him to the composer Richard Wagner, whom he came to idolize. The king and Wagner (OPPOSITE PAGE) became artistic collaborators. Without Ludwig's support, Wagner would not have been able to produce Tristan, complete The Ring, or compose Parsifal.

Lohengrin's arrival at Antwerp is shown in this mural (BELOW) above the stove in the Living Room at Neuschwanstein. Ludwig's taste for the theatrical led him on one occasion to stage this scene on the Alpsee, a lake near the castle. His cousin, playing Lohengrin, glided across the water in a boat drawn by an artificial swan, while an orchestra played the appropriate Wagnerian accompaniment.

father's Hohenschwangau—and would often draw swans, his favourite bird. Later he would create his own Schwanstein (*Schwan* is German for swan).

Ludwig grew up a shy, sensitive boy with a rich, romantically inclined imagination. Before the age of 13, he had heard of the German composer Richard Wagner (1813–83) and become devoted to his work, but not until February 1861 did he hear his first Wagnerian opera—*Lohengrin*. Ludwig was overwhelmed by the music and spectacle and pestered his father to arrange another, special performance just for him.

In 1864 Maximilian died and Ludwig, at the age of 18, became king. Within five weeks he had sent for Wagner, thus initiating what would become a remarkable artistic collaboration. He and the composer saw themselves not simply as patron and artist, but as joint creators: as well as money, Ludwig provided Wagner with advice, criticism, and even inspiration. Although the king himself was not musical (his piano

teacher said he had "no talent whatever"), he worshipped Wagner because his operas gave a physical reality to his own internal dream-world.

The impulse that attracted the king to Wagner's operas also lay behind his desire to build fabulous castles. As a result of this, government was neglected, the Privy Purse drained. To curtail Ludwig's activities, his ministers eventually hatched a plot to have him declared insane. In 1886 they took him from Neuschwanstein and imprisoned him in the little castle of Berg. There, two days later, his body and that of his keeper, Dr Gudden, were found in the waters of Lake Starnberg.

Ludwig's death was almost certainly suicide—the last desperate act of a man whose life had been robbed of its purpose. When his cousin, the Empress Elisabeth of Austria, who knew him better than anyone else, was told of his death, she said: "The king was not mad; he was just an eccentric living in a world of dreams." Those dreams were his gift to posterity.

The castle of Lohengrin

The first of Ludwig's new palaces was Neuschwanstein. In the spring of 1867 he had visited the famous Gothic castle of Wartburg, clinging to a crag above the Wartburg Valley near Eisenach in Thuringia. The castle appealed to his love of the theatrical and romantic, and he wanted one like it. A suitable site was found on a crag about a mile from Hohenschwangau—the original Schwanstein. Here lay the ruins of an old watchtower which Ludwig decided to rebuild as a New Schwanstein (Neuschwanstein). On 5 September 1869 the foundation stone of the *Palas* or main block was laid.

Following in his father's footsteps, Ludwig employed Christian Jank, the scenic artist of the Court Theatre, to design the exterior. He provided the king with sketches of fantastic edifices, and from these a host of painters and craftsmen built what is essentially a series of sets for Wagner's operas *Lohengrin, Tannhäuser* and *Parsifal*.

Neuschwanstein was first and foremost Lohengrin's castle. The five-storeyed *Palas* is Romanesque, the style Ludwig deemed historically appropriate to the legend. Since his childhood, the king seems to have identified himself with this knight. Certainly, as an adult, he enjoyed dressing up in the role and, after his death, his Lohengrin costume was found among his effects.

Scenes from *Tannhäuser*

The courtyard at Neuschwanstein is based on the décor of the castle courtyard at Antwerp in Act II of an actual production of *Lohengrin*. The idea for the Singers' Hall came from *Tannhäuser*. Tannhäuser was a German poet of the thirteenth century. According to legend, he found his way into the subterranean land of love and delight presided over by the goddess Venus inside the Venusberg—identified with the Hörselberg between Eisenach and Gotha. Wagner had set one scene of his *Tannhäuser* in the Singers' Hall of the Wartburg, so Ludwig asked Jank to design a version of this for Neuschwanstein.

The king also wanted to re-create the scene inside the Venusberg, in the form of a "Grotto of Venus". A spectacular grotto was planned, but, for want of a site, it was transferred to the grounds of Ludwig's palace of Linderhof. At Neuschwanstein he made do with a smaller, indoor version. Paintings in his study showing the Tannhäuser legend set

the scene for the little grotto that leads off from it. Containing a cascade and an artificial moon, this improbable indoor grotto has its own special enchantment.

As the king grew older, the castle of Lohengrin and Tannhäuser became the Grail Castle of *Parsifal*. Parsifal (English Perceval) was a knight of the Round Table who won a sight of the Holy Grail. Ludwig knew the story as a child, and it was a letter from the king in 1865 that inspired the first draft of Wagner's opera.

The setting for *Parsifal* was in Ludwig's mind for years before it was first performed. His designs for a Hall of the Grail eventually took shape as the throne room at Neuschwan-

stein, and, in 1883–84, the Singers' Hall was painted with scenes from the Parsifal story. Parsifal was the father of Lohengrin, so that Neuschwanstein begins and ends in the legend of the Swan Knight.

Neuschwanstein was still unfinished when Ludwig was taken to Berg. For him it was a shrine, a holy place. No one but Wagner, perhaps, could ever have shared his lofty vision of Neuschwanstein as the mysterious Grail Castle. It belonged to that heroic and high-souled world, illusory but enduring, which they had created between them. "When we two are long dead," Ludwig wrote to Wagner, "our work will still be a shining example to distant posterity. . . ."

The Singers' Hall, *where Wagner concerts are given every September, gives some indication of the exuberance and richness of decoration evident throughout the castle. Outstanding works by master craftsmen, sculptors, painters and woodcarvers greet the eye at every turn. It took 14 sculptors 4½ years to complete the king's bedroom. A similar extravagance is evident in the 2 million stones used in the exquisite tessellated pavement of the throne room. Yet Ludwig was also ahead of his time when it came to practical detail: the castle had a well-designed kitchen, central heating and an elevator.*

In his youth Ludwig—*who cut a dashing figure as a romantic young dandy—loved to explore this countryside (*RIGHT*) on foot or on horseback. In later life, much changed physically and a virtual recluse, he ventured forth into his beloved Alps only at night.*

The views from inside the castle were spectacular. From the balcony of the throne room, Ludwig would have gazed out beyond the Alpsee (the lake behind the castle) surrounded by wooded, gently rolling hills, to the rugged peaks of the Thannheim mountains.

TRIUMPH OF THE SPIRIT

"There are numerous wonders in the world,
but none more wonderful than man."

SOPHOCLES (495–406 B.C.)

"No man is an Island, entire of itself."

JOHN DONNE (1572–1631)

*T*he great shrines and monuments of the world bear concrete witness to man's creative and religious impulse. Other places have a special quality that is less tangible. It arises usually from a communual spirit—often one that has triumphed over extraordinary hardship and adversity. The people of Oberammergau, for example, have over the centuries kept their vow to perform their famous Passion Play, often against enormous odds. Cretan freedom fighters at the monastery of Arkadi preferred certain death to surrender, and became an inspiration for future generations.

In 1941 the people of Coventry witnessed the devastation of their city and their medieval cathedral. In the face of despair, they were able to build on a spirit of forgiveness and reconciliation, and eventually resurrected their place of worship. Also in World War II, Italian prisoners on one of the Orkney islands constructed a beautiful chapel from rudimentary scrap materials. The chapel still stands, a moving testimony to their response to adversity.

These places represent the triumph of man's determination to conquer the forces of darkness and to forge his own destiny. As such, they shine out like beacons of hope.

OBERAMMERGAU

> *One sees that the performance is not learned; it is lived....*
>
> GERMAN ACTOR-MANAGER EDUARD DEVRIENT, AFTER THE 1850 PLAY.

IN A PEACEFUL VALLEY HIGH IN THE BAVARIAN Alps lies the village of Oberammergau. Viewed from the craggy heights of the Kofel which dominates it, the town appears in no way spectacular. But of the cluster of buildings that hugs the banks of the River Ammer, two—because of their size—arrest the eye. The first is the church, the second, the theatre. Both, over the centuries, have played a major role in village life, but it is the theatre that, every ten years, becomes the magnet that draws thousands upon thousands of people from every corner of the globe. They come to view what has become perhaps the most celebrated dramatic presentation in history: the Passion Play that is now synonymous with Oberammergau.

This dramatic reenactment of the suffering and death of Jesus Christ had its origins in the Thirty Years' War, when strife between the Catholic League and the Protestant Union engulfed Europe in a war of almost unprecedented savagery. In the wake of war came famine and pestilence.

The coming of the plague

For Catholic Bavaria, the worst years of the plague began in 1627 and, as the dreaded disease crept closer, the elders of Oberammergau decided to close their village against all comers. Guards were posted along its outskirts and at night flares blazed to illumine anyone who might attempt to enter. But one man got past them: Kaspar Schissler, who had been working in nearby Eschenlohe, was desperate to return to his native village for the annual church festival. He brought the plague with him, to his own family, to the whole village.

By the end of October 1632, 84 adults and uncounted children had died. In 1633, the wretched survivors gathered in the parish church and made a solemn vow to perform a Passion Play every ten years—for ever—if only God would lift the plague from the village. Miraculously, it would seem, there were no more deaths and the people of Oberammergau have remained ever mindful of their bargain.

The play represents the triumph of a community spirit, for the people of the village have performed it almost every decade for over 350 years. They have defied bans, sustained hardships and criticisms of all kinds, and have stubbornly presented it even against a background of war. The Franco-Prussian War of 1870, the First and

The village of Oberammergau every 10 years attracts thousands of visitors who come to watch—and share in—its famous Passion Play. Despite bans and hardships, the play has been performed here for more than 350 years.

*Living tableaux, many based on famous paintings, punctuate the action of the play. The Last Supper (*RIGHT*) was based in every detail on the painting by Leonardo da Vinci.*

then the Second World Wars caused disruptions of varying lengths. Most serious was the outbreak of World War II, which put a stop to the 1940 performance and interrupted the play for a decade. When it reappeared in 1950—like a phoenix risen from the ashes—the astonishing number of more than half a million people came to see it.

Not only has Oberammergau had to fight to keep its play going, each performance can be an ordeal in itself. Though the first plays were staged in the tiny village church, by the seventeenth century they were given in the open air, against a dramatic mountain backdrop. When Hans Christian Andersen went in 1860 he had to sit in the pouring rain. Only since the 1930s have the actors not had to perform exposed to the elements. The chorus still suffers in the traditional way—wearing oilskins, if it is necessary, beneath their costumes.

The play begins with the triumphal entry into Jerusalem and ends with the Ascension of Christ. Interspersed with the scenes of the play are living "tableaux" of Biblical events, some based on famous paintings. The Last Supper, for example, is modelled—down to the details of the table setting—on the painting by Leonardo.

Children's parts have long been shared, and so too, since 1980, have leading adult roles. The season lasts six months, and the

The crown worn *by this actor playing Jesus in 1922 was made from local thorns; today they are imported from the Holy Land.*

The performance is particularly gruelling for the Christ, who has to hang on the cross for 28 minutes with the minimum of support.

performance is demanding. It lasts from 9 in the morning until 5.30 in the evening, with a three-hour break and is the culmination of long and demanding preparations.

As a Passion Play year approaches, the village appoints a committee which selects the actors in good time for the men to grow their hair and beards—the women may have been growing their hair for years.

A spiritual rite

The text for the first Passion Play performed at Oberammergau was borrowed from the monks at the monastery in nearby Augsburg. Over the years it has been cut, added to, revised and, twice, entirely rewritten. The present play is a version of one written in 1810 and revised by the local parish priest, Alois Daisenberger, for the 1850 season. In the 1960s and 1970s accusations of anti-semitism led to further revisions which were intended to show the Jews in a historically more accurate light.

Most significant is the fact that the play has retained from its medieval roots the virtue of speaking simply and directly to the emotions. Each new generation is born into the play. It is in every villager's blood. For it is not a mere spectacle, but a rite of deep spiritual significance which both shapes and nourishes the community. Oberammergau *is* the play.

Kreuzabnahme.

Kunstverlag Leo Schweyer

Anyone born in Oberammergau, or long in residence, is eligible for a part in the play. The scene here shows Christ being taken down from the cross in the 1900 production.

Acting ability is not so important as stamina and the right appearance. Under the regulations governing the play, the only make-up used is that simulating the blood of Christ. Anyone who has become unsuitable for a part, perhaps by going grey, will be passed over.

Pressure from the women of Oberammergau has resulted in the relaxation of the rule prohibiting married women, or indeed any woman over 35, from taking part in the play. In the past girls have postponed their weddings in order not to forfeit the opportunity. For the 1990 play, in a complete break with tradition, a married woman has been cast as the Virgin Mary.

The theatre at Oberammergau in 1860 (OPPOSITE PAGE) offered no shelter for either audience or actors. Although by 1899 the auditorium had been covered, the stage remained open to the elements. For the 1930 and 1934 performances, when the theatre was enlarged, the main stage was roofed with glass to keep the actors dry but preserve the wonderful view of the Bavarian Alps beyond the proscenium.

ARKADI MONASTERY

> *The flame that was ignited in this crypt, and which lit up glorious Crete from end to end, was the fire of god—a holocaust in which the Cretans died for liberty.*

COMMEMORATIVE INSCRIPTION IN THE
MONASTERY'S GUNPOWDER ROOM.

IN ONE OF THE MOST HEROIC EPISODES IN recent Greek history, on 9 November 1866, Cretan men, women and children, besieged by the Turks at the monastery of Arkadi, crowded into an old wine cellar. The situation was desperate. Jubilant Turkish troops had burst through into the monastery compound and were gathering at the door of the cellar. The Cretan war cry was "Freedom or Death": it was about to be put to the test. For the barrels which they stood among were filled not with wine but gunpowder.

A lithograph depicting this tragic moment evokes the gloom of the cellar—men, women and children huddled together with their leader Constantine Giaboudakis standing astride the gunpowder barrels, gripping the pistol that would send them all to eternity. But, for the Cretans, then as now, that single gunshot transformed Arkadi into a symbol of heroism, sacrifice and freedom.

In 1866 the monastery of Arkadi had become the centre for an insurrection against the Turks, who had been ruling Crete for some 200 years. The local Turkish commis-

sioner Mustapha Pasha had threatened to raze the building if the leading Cretan revolutionaries did not leave it. In defiance of his threat, 960 monks, resistance fighters, women and children, who had gathered in the monastery for protection, prepared themselves for the inevitable onslaught.

A sacrifice for freedom

The outnumbered defenders fought bravely, but on 9 November the Turks broke through into the monastery. As had been prearranged, those Cretans who were able rushed to the gunpowder room. There, as unsuspecting Turks gathered at the cellar door, Giaboudakis aimed his pistol at the gunpowder barrels and fired. A later folk ballad relates that the almighty explosion caused the earth to tremble and the mountains of Crete to echo. The carnage was horrific—more than 800 Cretans died; Turkish losses were considerably higher.

This supreme act of courage and sacrifice had profound reverberations beyond the island and its people, who still mark the

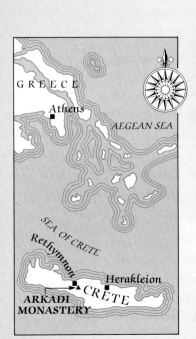

Arkadi monastery, near Rethymnon, on the north coast of Crete, is the most sacred monastery on the island. In 1866 it became the centre for a Cretan insurrection against the ruling Turks. Heavily outnumbered, the Cretans chose to blow themselves up rather than surrender to the enemy. Their action, however, was an inspiration to their fellow countrymen and attracted support for Crete from the major western powers. The monastery's chapel (ABOVE and RIGHT), a hybrid of different styles, dates from the 16th century.

event with a public holiday. For the first time the world powers took notice of what became known as "the Cretan question". Supplies and donations for the Cretans came from mainland Greece, Russia, and the British—who commissioned a ship, the *Arkadi*, to transport goods and volunteers. In the U.S.A., the Senate publicly gave its support to the Cretans.

Sympathy also came from leading world figures such as Garibaldi and Victor Hugo. The British poet Algernon Swinburne wrote a poem about it. Although it would be another 30 years before the Turks finally left the island for good, Arkadi had put Crete and its struggle for liberty on the political map.

A haven of tranquillity

Amid the silence and serenity that emanates from the monastery and its idyllic setting in the hills, it is now difficult to imagine the events of 1866. The scars, though, can still be seen: bullet holes in the refectory door; a Turkish shell embedded in a grand old Cypress tree in the monastery compound; walls crumbled by intensive gunfire. The most overt reminder of the tragedy is the windmill outside the main western gate: it has been converted into an "ossuary", preserving the skulls of the Cretans who died in the holocaust.

But despite the signs of warfare, the spirituality of the monastery prevails. Traditionally founded in the fifth century A.D. by the Byzantine Emperor Arcadius, most of the monastery's buildings date from the sixteenth century. The site the monks chose for this retreat would be hard to better. Set on a tableland among gently rising hills, the monastery is surrounded by shimmering olive groves, oaks and orange trees.

The first impression of Arkadi is that of a long sandy-coloured wall punctuated by small dark windows. Entry is by the rebuilt western gate through which the ornate amber-coloured façade of the church looms into view like a sunrise.

The layout of the monastery is simple. Framing the courtyard is the main, roughly square-shaped structure, a honeycomb of small dark austere rooms—monks' cells, storerooms, cellars. These, with the cloisters and pergolas canopied with green vine leaves, provide welcome shade for the few monks who still reside here.

Cats, hens, beehives, an old wine press are reminders that the monastery's concern with

the spiritual has always been tempered by its domestic needs and hospitality to visitors. The British writer Edward Lear experienced the latter first hand when he visited Arkadi in 1864. He was warmly welcomed and served a sumptuous supper of stewed pigeon and salads, cherries, beans, cheese, and honey; there was wine and, afterward, coffee to drink.

Arkadi is many things: first it is a place for spiritual contemplation and learning, a living monastery of the Greek Orthodox Church. For visitors it is an oasis of tranquillity and a place steeped in history. For Cretans Arkadi is all these things and also a symbol of an unquenchable determination to govern their own destiny.

Two years before the Arkadi tragedy, the British writer Edward Lear came to the monastery, shown (RIGHT) in a watercolour based on a drawing Lear made at the time. He met Abbot Gabriel, the hero of the siege, whom he found "a very jolly man and hearty". The two men got on well with each other, having in common the fact that they had both travelled in the Holy Land.

Amid the smoke of gunfire, *Turkish soldiers launch an assault on Arkadi monastery in an engraving from* The Illustrated London News *(LEFT), published on 26 January 1867, nearly 3 months after the siege. Monks, resistance fighters, women and children withstood a powerful force of 15,000 Turkish regular troops for nearly two days.*

Despite their valiant efforts, the defenders could not stop the Turks from storming the walls. The tragic and heroic conclusion came when those Cretans who were able made their way to the gunpowder room: there, true to their battle cry "Freedom or Death", they blew themselves up rather than surrender.

A monk of the Greek Orthodox Church *stands impassively at the entrance of the monastery church (ABOVE). It was inside the church that the soldier priest Abbot Gabriel, at dawn on the first day of the battle, is said to have inspired his countrymen with the words: "There is no death, my children. Let us fight heroically and then appear before our God with clean hands. Long live the struggle! Long live freedom!" Gabriel was also, tradition relates, the moving force behind the final holocaust. He himself, however, was shot while recklessly firing at the enemy from a second-storey terrace.*

213

THE ITALIAN CHAPEL

> ❛ *Nowhere in Britain have the two wars left a more eloquent residue than in Orkney.* ❜
>
> BRITISH WRITER RONALD BLYTHE, 1988.

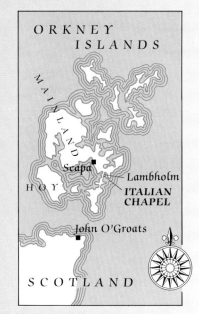

ON THE SMALL WINDSWEPT ISLAND OF Lambholm, connected to the Orkney mainland by a causeway, there is a corner of a field that is forever Italy. The Italian Chapel, with its simple concrete façade, two-pillared porch and barrel-shaped nave, is a curious little building which represents the triumph of human creativity and resourcefulness over adversity. For it was built during World War II by Italian prisoners of war, who, incarcerated thousands of miles from home in a bleak, cold climate, felt the need to create a place of warmth and beauty in which to worship God in their own way.

The unique result can still be seen today: a chapel dedicated to the Madonna, Queen of Peace, under whose guiding light the Italians worked and whose portrait shines out of the wall behind the altar. Built during a time of terrible discord between nations, the chapel has survived to become a much-loved Orkney landmark, and a symbol of hope and reconciliation.

The Italian prisoners had been sent to Orkney in 1942 to help build the Churchill Barriers, concrete causeways designed to prevent German U-boats from attacking British warships anchored at Scapa on the mainland. For the men of Camp 60 on Lambholm the habitual wind, rain and mud provided a sharp contrast with the heat of North Africa, where they had been captured.

However, with energy and imagination, they began to transform their cheerless camp. Concrete paths were made, flowers planted, and a theatre, which included painted scenery, was set up. To satisfy their spiritual needs, plans for a chapel were made under the initiative of a sympathetic camp commandant, Major T.P. Buckland, the camp padre, Father P. Giacobazzi, and an artistic prisoner named Domenico Chiocchetti.

A work of art and ingenuity

First two prefabricated (Nissen) huts were obtained and placed together end to end. Then Chiocchetti recruited a skilled working party from among his fellow prisoners, including a smith, a cement worker and electricians, to help him beautify the soulless interior. Raw materials were scarce, so the workers cleverly made use of odd bits of scrap which they gleaned from wherever they could, including the seashore and wrecked ships.

Soon the inside of the hut was almost unrecognizable. Plasterboard, fitted around

Built by Italian prisoners *of war during World War II, the Italian Chapel, on Lambholm, Orkney, embodies the creative spirit of men living in adversity. The chapel was constructed from two prefabricated huts placed end to end. The ugly exterior was partly disguised by the ornate concrete façade, while the inside (*RIGHT*) was transformed into a work of beauty, principally by an artistic prisoner named Domenico Chiocchetti.*

*After the war, Chiocchetti's home town of Moena donated a carved figure of Christ crucified (*ABOVE, LEFT FOREGROUND*) to the people of Orkney as a token of friendship.*

215

THE ITALIAN CHAPEL

Views of the altar and the
entrance (BELOW) show the skill
and ingenuity with which
Chiocchetti and his team turned
two soulless huts into a place fit
for worship. The striking arabesque
iron screen frames a vista of the
altar, on either side of which are
coloured windows depicting St
Francis of Assisi and St Catherine
of Siena.

The painting on the wall behind
the altar is the Madonna and
Child, surrounded by cherubs
holding a scroll inscribed with the
words: Regina pacis ora pro nobis
(Queen of peace pray for us).
Chiocchetti based the painting on
the Madonna of the Olives by
Nicolo Barabino (1832–91), a
reproduction of which he carried
with him throughout the war.

the walls and ceiling, was painted to resemble brickwork and, at the base of the walls, carved stone. The altar and altar rail were made from clay, cast in chalk and moulded in cement. A smith named Palumbo made two candelabra and the delightful arabesque rood-screen from wrought iron. Brass for another two candelabra, and wood and stones for the tabernacle and floor, were taken from a sunken ship, as were the tiles (from the toilets of the *Ilsenstein*!) placed around the altar.

Chiocchetti himself, using brushes Major Buckland had procured for him with some difficulty, painted the two windows flanking the altar with images of St Francis of Assisi and St Catherine of Siena, and outlined the panes to imitate lead. He also decorated the vault of the sanctuary with frescoes of the four evangelists and cherubim and seraphim.

Nor did the work stop with the inside of the hut. For, to disguise the ugly exterior, Chiocchetti and a helper built a façade with a pillared porch from cement, and decorated it with Gothic pinnacles, glass windows, and a circular-framed clay head of Christ set above the entrance. In the empty belfry Chiocchetti, showing typical flair, placed a cardboard bell until a real one from a ship could later be installed. In this way, using scant material resources but a great deal of ingenuity, the Italians created their unique sanctuary. When the chapel was virtually finished, the men celebrated their achievement by holding a service, complete with a recording of the bells and choir of St Peter's Rome.

Chiocchetti returns

At the end of the war, the Italians were repatriated, and the huts of Camp 60 disappeared; but the Italian Chapel, as it became known, remained standing, a reminder of the spirit of cooperation that had informed its creation. That spirit was perpetuated by the Orcadians, who, in 1958, formed a committee to ensure the chapel would be preserved.

Two years later, the committee invited Chiocchetti to return to Orkney from his Italian home town of Moena. The visit gave the Italian a chance to see his beloved chapel again, and, with the help of a local man, to repair and repaint it. The two men worked away for three weeks, during which time articles and photographs of it appeared in the national newspapers of both Britain and Italy. The highlight of the visit was the Dedication Service on Palm Sunday, 10 April, parts of which were broadcast on Italian radio.

More than 40 years later, the chapel still stands strong against the Orkney weather. For some visitors it is simply a historical curio. But for others, the chapel is a living symbol of the spiritual resilience of men living in adversity.

Proud members of Camp 60 line up in front of their beloved chapel. Chiocchetti, who provided the artistic inspiration, can be seen standing on the extreme left of the group.

The prisoners also erected nearby a concrete statue of St George slaying the dragon, an apt symbol of the victory of hope over darkness and despair. Italian coins, and a roll bearing the prisoners' names, were placed inside the statue's base.

Chiocchetti carries out repair work to the chapel porch 15 years after the end of the war. He had returned to Orkney at the invitation of a local committee set up to ensure the chapel's preservation and upkeep. At the end of his visit, a special service of dedication was held, parts of which were broadcast on Italian radio.

217

COVENTRY CATHEDRAL

> **' To the glory of God this cathedral burnt November 14 AD 1940 is now rebuilt 1962. '**
>
> INSCRIPTION ON THE FLOOR OF THE CATHEDRAL'S NAVE.

IN A NIGHT OF DEVASTATION IN LATE 1940, AT the beginning of World War II, the city and medieval cathedral of Coventry was engulfed in the flames of 40,000 German fire bombs and 500 tons of high explosives. It was the blackest moment in the city's history; but from it was born a new cathedral, forged from the fires of the old, a symbol of triumph over destruction and despair.

To preserve the sense of continuity between the two cathedrals, the modern one was physically joined, via a great open porch, to the ruins of the old. The two buildings present a dramatic contrast: the new cathedral powerfully sturdy with its flat roof and massive stone walls; its predecessor an empty burnt-out shell. The old ornate Gothic spire still soars upward, but little else of the building remains.

On the evening of 14 November 1940, the buildings and spires of Coventry rose innocently into the frosty moonlit night. But the silence that had descended on the city was ominously broken at about 7 p.m. by air-raid sirens and the steady sinister drone of aircraft engines. Within ten minutes, the unprecedented horror of "total war" rained down on the people of Coventry. Amid the sirens' wail and frantic beams of searchlights, German Heinkels dropped flares to help the main force of Junkers 88s. The city was soon turned into an inferno, with walls and roofs blasted to rubble. In a matter of hours, centuries of undisturbed English history had been wiped out.

The aftermath

Coventry, an important arms-manufacturing centre, was the first city to be targeted for systematic destruction from the air. The Germans deemed their mission—codenamed "Moonlight Sonata"—successful, and afterward coined a sinister new verb: "to Coventrate", meaning "to destroy utterly".

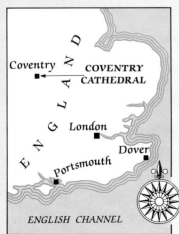

The new cathedral of Coventry rose from the ashes of the medieval cathedral of St Michael, destroyed during a bombing raid at the start of World War II. The new building is connected to the ruins of its predecessor via an open porch, and is thus symbolically linked with the past.

Symbolizing the triumph of hope over darkness, a blaze of golden light pours through the stained glass of the Baptistery window, designed by the artist John Piper and made by Patrick Reyntiens. Below the window is the font, fashioned from a boulder brought from a hillside near Bethlehem.

218

COVENTRY CATHEDRAL

The church of St Michael
(BELOW) was built in the mid-12th century near the site of Coventry's first cathedral, which had been the glory of the city's monastic community. This first cathedral fell into ruins after the closing down of Coventry's monastery by King Henry VIII in 1538.

Almost 400 years later the ancient church of St Michael became the city's second cathedral, when the diocese of Coventry was created in 1918. But little more than 20 years then passed before it was destroyed by bombing.

The medieval cathedral of St Michael, for so long a source of inspiration to the people of Coventry, was set ablaze by incendiary bombs. Attempts to extinguish the fire failed, and it was left to run its course.

Next morning, after the "all clear" had sounded at 6.15 a.m., the city held its breath. People emerged to find whole buildings had been levelled; familiar landmarks had vanished; streets were unrecognizable. St Michael's was now just a shell. The tower and spire had survived, but not much else.

As black smoke wreathed its way upward from the smouldering rubble, a small group of people arrived to inspect the remains of the cathedral. Among them was Provost Richard Howard and the stonemason and caretaker of the grounds, Jock Forbes.

In an atmosphere of overwhelming grief, bitterness and despair, Jock Forbes did something which was, in the circumstances, extraordinary: he found two charred beams from the now non-existent medieval roof and tied them together to form a cross. He then planted this cross among the rubble. Thus, in an impromptu act of inspiration, he transformed two tangible reminders of man's destructiveness into a cross of forgiveness, and of hope.

Then, in a similar vein, the Reverend A.P. Wale picked up three of the many nails that had fallen from the roof beams as they had burnt, and fastened them together into the shape of a cross. These two simple, but symbolically charged, acts provided an immediate focus through which the people of Coventry could overcome their anger. Two months later, the charred cross was given a more permanent place behind a stone altar, built by Jock Forbes from the rubble, in the apse of the cathedral shell. On the altar was placed the cross of nails. And, on the wall behind the altar, Forbes inscribed, at the request of Provost Howard, the words "Father Forgive". Coventry had taken a significant step toward healing its wounds.

Rising from the ashes

The decision to build a new cathedral was taken the very morning after the bombing. But the foundation stone was laid 16 years later, in 1956. During the following years, the new building, designed by the eminent British architect Basil Spence, grew in size and stature. By 1961 the roof was put on. A year later the completed cathedral echoed with the singing of seven choirs at the consecration service in the presence of Queen Elizabeth II. The phoenix had risen from the ashes.

The external appearance of Coventry's new cathedral, with its solidity and unadorned simplicity, at first caused much controversy. The genius of the cathedral's design, however, lies in the way it is connected, literally—and therefore symbolically—to the remains of St Michael's. In this way, hundreds of years of Christian history are preserved by their link with the new building. Equally, the latter is given a profound and solemn foundation from its junction with St Michael's.

The open-air ruins of St Michael's have their own sense of peace, tinged with an air of melancholy. The focal point is still the altar

The bombing of Coventry was a traumatic shock for the British people. Newspapers, such as the Daily Mail *and* The Illustrated London News, *conveyed the full horror of the raid, in which more than 550 people died.*

On 16 November, two days after the bombing, King George VI visited the city, and was shown around the ruins of St Michael's (LEFT).

The Cross of Nails, the Charred Cross and the words "Father Forgive" in the old cathedral's sanctuary (OPPOSITE PAGE) are poignant symbols of the city's determination to overcome its anger and grief after the bombing raid.

The powerful bronze sculpture (RIGHT) by Jacob Epstein shows St Michael, leader of Heaven's armies, triumphant over the bound Devil. The sculpture is one of several superb works of art with which the cathedral is endowed. The most spectacular of these is Graham Sutherland's tapestry (BELOW), which is 79 feet high and 38 feet wide. The seated figure of Christ is surrounded by four symbolic Biblical figures—a lion, a bull, an eagle and man.

with a replica of Jock Forbes' now-famous Charred Cross, and the Cross of Nails. From the steps that lead under the porch to the new cathedral, the first impression is of the great south window with panes of glass engraved with the ethereal forms of angels, saints and prophets.

Inside the cathedral, the nave's grey marble floor stretches away and slim girder-like columns rise up to the ceiling canopy. Here they spread outward into a network of diamond shapes that enclose slats of wood arranged in a herringbone pattern. At the far end of the cathedral, the artist Graham Sutherland's tapestry, the largest in the world, depicts Christ enthroned in glory.

But before focusing on this, the eye is naturally drawn to the blaze of blue, red, green and gold streaming from the Baptistery window to the right of the entrance. Designed by the painter John Piper, the window stretches from floor to ceiling and has at its heart a honeycomb of yellow and gold glass brilliantly illumined by even the weakest of sunlight. Standing in front of, and in stark contrast to, this great panel of resonant colour is the font—a roughly hewn boulder brought especially from a hillside near Bethlehem.

Behind the High Altar hangs the spectacular Sutherland tapestry—79 feet high and 38 feet wide. Here, against a background of green with yellow bordering the images, Christ, in a white robe, sits on a throne. The expression on his face blends compassion with the enigmatic. Surrounding this majestic Christ are four symbolic Biblical figures: the lion, bull, eagle, and man, all stylishly depicted with a dynamic energy that emphasizes their cosmic status.

Treasures of the cathedral

The Sutherland tapestry and the Piper window are giant creations. But there are other works of art—some less prominent—which are equally compelling and moving: the ten stained glass windows which, angled into the west and east walls to catch the maximum amount of sunlight, cast their exotic colours into the floor's grey pools of marble; the satin-finish bronze lectern on which stands the sculptor Elizabeth Frink's powerful cast-bronze eagle; Jacob Epstein's triumphant sculpture of St Michael, fixed to the outside of the cathedral near the Baptistery window, the saint's arms spread in a gesture of victory as he stands over a

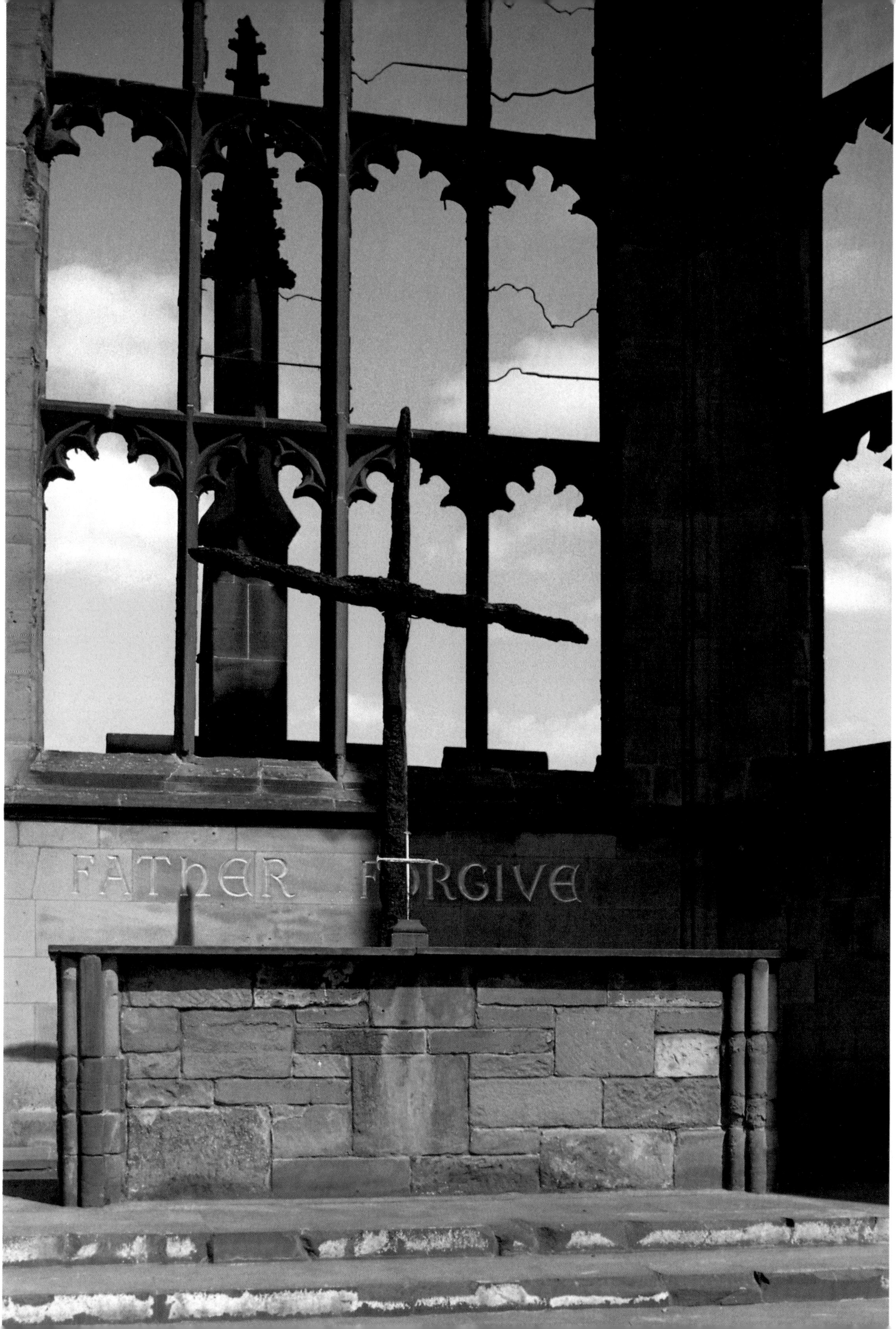
FATHER FORGIVE

Before the consecration of the new cathedral in 1962, the shell of St Michael's was still used for services, such as the funeral (RIGHT) of Dr Neville Gorton, Bishop of Coventry. Gorton died in November 1955 and is buried close to the spot where, in 1943, he was enthroned in the ruins of the old cathedral as Coventry's fourth bishop. It was Gorton who had started the appeal fund for the new cathedral, the building of which he declared at the time to be "the noblest use of the noblest site in the city".

A wrought-iron screen representing the crown of thorns separates the Chapel of Christ in Gethsemane (OPPOSITE PAGE) from the rest of the cathedral. It was in the garden of Gethsemane that Jesus Christ, in a moment of great suffering, prayed to God, and was strengthened by the appearance of an angel, depicted on the back wall of the chapel.

vanquished and bound Devil; the elegant Chapel of Unity, designed to resemble a Crusader's tent; and the stark simplicity of the High Altar, made from concrete.

In the south aisle stands the Czech Crucifix, begun by its maker in a prisoner of war camp during World War II, and presented to the cathedral in 1968. In the north aisle is a poignant sculpture depicting the Head of Christ. It was made by an American who used material from a crashed car in which three people died.

One of the less evident jewels in the cathedral is the Chapel of Christ in Gethsemane. At the front, a spiky wrought-iron screen represents the crown of thorns; the back wall of the chapel is dominated by a dark, kneeling angel, with a halo studded with sparkles of glass, looming out of the muted gold mosaic. To the right of the angel are the apostles who fell asleep in the garden, though Jesus had asked them to stay awake and keep watch with him during his dark night of the soul.

A symbol of forgiveness

Coventry Cathedral is more than a collection of beautiful works of art informed by a religious spirit. The building is imbued with the sense of having been created in an atmosphere of goodwill. During its construction, gifts and donations were sent from many different countries, including China, Canada, Denmark, Sweden and the U.S.S.R.

But perhaps the most poignant act of support and friendship came in 1961–62, when a group of young German Christians gave up their jobs for six months and, with money they had raised in Germany, converted the old vestries into the International Centre—a place for people of all nationalities to meet and discuss ways of promoting world peace.

The cathedral is the physical symbol of the triumph of forgiveness. This spirit is expressed in the Coventry-based Community of the Cross of Nails, which operates worldwide. Among the practical services rendered by the community has been the building of a hospital wing in the German city of Dresden, devastated by Allied bombers in 1945. This spirit of reconciliation is the same that inspired the building of Coventry Cathedral, and which made Jock Forbes, at a time of deep crisis, create from two charred, black beams a shining cross of hope.

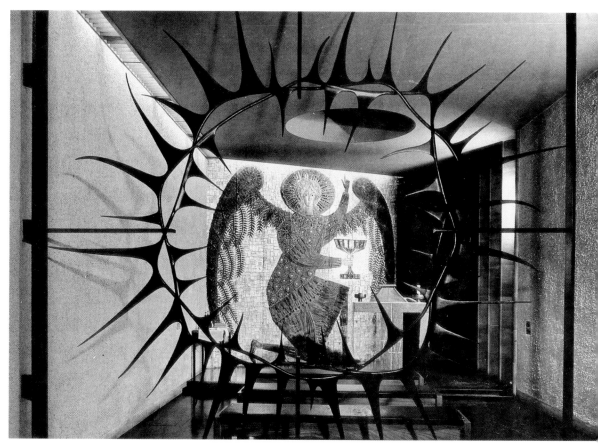

GAZETTEER

Practical information regarding travel and accommodation, and what to see and do at the places described in the book is given below where appropriate. Local opening and closing times, however, should be checked before a visit.

ETERNAL REALMS

THERA (ATLANTIS?)
Aegean Sea
36°23'N 25°27'E

AS WELL AS A REGULAR BOAT SERVICE TO and from Athens, there are daily flights (1½ hrs) from the Greek capital to Thera, also known as Santorini.

Although it is not a typical "holiday" island, large numbers of people have been drawn to Thera in recent years, for not only does it have some of the most important excavation sites of the Minoan culture in Greece, it is also extremely interesting and unusual geologically.

The remains of the classical city of Thera, on a rocky promontory on the east of the island, can still be visited. The modern town of Thera is on the west coast.

Important archeological excavations began at Akrotiri in the south of the island in 1967. The superb Minoan frescoes unearthed then are now on display in the National Archeological Museum in Athens.

The last serious volcanic eruption was in 1956, but hot springs are an indication of continuing volcanic activity.

CADBURY CASTLE (CAMELOT?)
nr Yeovil, Somerset, Great Britain
50°57'N 2°38'W

THE SUPPOSED SITE OF CAMELOT IS NOT A castle at all, but a massive Iron Age earthwork on a hill to the west of the village of South Cadbury. Cadbury Castle

has been described as the finest prehistoric camp in Somerset, if not in England, and from the top there are superb views over the surrounding countryside.

The area is redolent of history. At Athelney (the -ey ending comes from the Saxon *ea*, meaning island), King Alfred's vigil before a battle against the Danes in A.D. 878 is commemorated by an obelisk.

The nearest large town, Yeovil, is accessible by both road and rail from most major cities in the United Kingdom.

GLASTONBURY (AVALON?)
Somerset, Great Britain
51°9'N 2°42'W

THE TOWN OF GLASTONBURY IN mid-Somerset is accessible by road from London and other major cities in the United Kingdom. According to legend, Joseph of Arimathea brought to Glastonbury the Holy Grail, the cup which Jesus Christ drank from at the Last Supper. The Grail is said to be buried beneath Chalice Spring on Glastonbury Tor, the hill that dominates the town.

Because of its Arthurian and spiritual associations, the town has become the goal of many pilgrims.

Only a mile from the Tor are the remains of prehistoric lake villages. Objects excavated from these sites—weapons, ornaments and pottery—are displayed at the City Museum housed in the Tribunal, which is open daily.

The Abbey—where King Arthur's grave was reputedly discovered in 1191—remains impressive and evocative, though it is little more than a ruin. Next to the abbey can be seen a descendant of the original Glastonbury Thorn, which, according to legend, sprang from the staff of Joseph of Arimathea.

TIMELESS LANDSCAPES

MOUNT ARARAT (AĞRI DAĞI)
Turkey
39°50'N 44°15'E

THE MAIN ROAD COMES NEAREST TO THE mountain at the town of Doğubayazıt, which can be reached by bus from Kars or Van.

Doğubayazıt provides the best base for people intending to climb the mountain, as well as for those who simply wish to stay a while to contemplate its splendours from a distance. It is well provisioned with accommodation and eating places.

Climbing the mountain—and certainly attempting the summit—is a business for experienced mountaineers. Horses and guides can be hired at the towns of Iğdir, Aralık and at Doğubayazıt; and camping expeditions to the lower slopes may be arranged for the amateur.

Serious climbers should inform the Turkish Mountaineering Club in Ankara of their intention to climb.

Just to the east of Doğubayazıt is an extraordinary fairytale palace—the Ishak Pasha Saray—built in the 18th century.

THE NILE
Egypt (Africa)

EGYPT HAS THREE INTERNATIONAL airports, at Cairo, Alexandria and Luxor, which are also interconnected by internal flights.

An enjoyable way of getting a feel for this great river is to hire a felucca—a traditional Nile sailing boat. These are not, however, recommended for long trips.

Specialist tour operators offer a number of different Nile cruises, especially between Luxor and Aswan. Facilities aboard the cruise steamers, which carry between 50 and 100 passengers, vary, as do the lengths of trips. Shorter cruises usually last between 5 and 7 days; the longer Aswan–Cairo cruise may last 15 days and include several nights in Cairo; this allows time for visits to the Giza pyramids and the Sphinx, as well as to the Egyptian Museum in Cairo.

Both Luxor and Aswan have much to offer in the way of magnificent historical remains. At Aswan there are interesting temples. Nearby is Elephantine Island and one of the three largest dams in the world. Farther south is Abu Simbel, with the two magnificent temples of Rameses II.

AYERS ROCK (ULURU)
Northern Territory, Australia
25°23'S 131°5'E

THE CLOSEST TOWN TO AYERS ROCK IS Alice Springs—about 280 miles and a 6- or 7-hour drive away. Now that there is an airstrip at the tourist resort near the rock, it is possible to fly there not only from Alice Springs, but from Sydney, Perth and Adelaide.

Ayers Rock itself is in Uluru National Park, for which an entrance fee is charged. As well as the ascent of the rock—an exhausting climb of 1,142 feet, though helped by a handrail—there is much to absorb the attention. It is advisable to allow several days to explore the area, taking advantage of ranger-conducted tours, which provide insights into plant and animal life, geological features and, of course, the local Aboriginal history and mythology.

A walk around the base of the rock takes about 5 hours, allowing time to view the caves and paintings around its 5½-mile circumference. The magical colour of the rock at sunset can best be appreciated from special viewing areas.

To the west of the rock, about 18 miles away, is a boulder formation called the Olgas, which are held by some to be even more enchanting than Ayers Rock itself.

Just outside the National Park, Yulara Tourist Resort provides first class accommodation and facilities.

Before venturing to the rock, 14 miles from the resort, it is worth spending some time at the Visitor Centre. This not only has a museum of local geology, flora and fauna, but also offers information on the park and its walks as well as slide shows. Also worth visiting is the Aboriginal Gallery next to the centre.

MOUNT FUJI
Honshu, Japan
35°22′N 138°44′E

THE MOUNTAIN DOMINATES THE Fuji-Hakone-Izu National Park and is visible from Tokyo skyscrapers. Some of the best views, however, are from the Fuji Five Lakes area, on the northern side of the mountain. Here, on a clear day, Mount Fuji is reflected in the waters of Lake Kawaguchi.

The lakes and the mountain region can be reached by train or bus from the capital city. Though it is possible to visit Fuji all year round, the summer months, when the slopes are open to climbers, are hot and crowded. The best seasons are spring, when plum and cherry blossom provide stupendous displays, or autumn, when nature again works miracles with her colour palette.

The snowcapped mountain is only open to climbers for two months of the year. The beginning of the climbing season is marked with a special ceremony at Fuji-Yoshida on 1 July; the end of the season is marked by a festival at the end of August. In the course of the season thousands of people, young and old, make their way to the summit.

The ascent must be taken seriously. Warm clothing, stout walking shoes or boots and supplies of food and water will ensure that dramatic fluctuations of temperature do not cause distress.

The climb to the top takes between 7 and 9 hours, though the time is halved by starting from the 5th Station, halfway up the mountain. This point is accessible by car and bus—a 3-hour drive from Tokyo.

Climbers who leave the 5th Station in late afternoon may climb through the night in order to catch the sunrise from the summit. Other approaches are also possible. Having explored the crater at the summit, the descent takes about 5 hours, at most.

CAPPADOCIA
Turkey

THE PROVINCIAL CAPITAL, KAYSERI (ROMAN Caesarea) can be reached by air from Istanbul or Ankara.

Although the best seasons for visiting Cappadocia are probably spring or autumn, even in the height of summer the daytime temperatures are tolerable and nights are cool.

The extraordinary Open Air Museum of Göreme, the highlight of a visit to the region, lies about 55 miles to the southwest of Kayseri. Most visitors stay at Ürgüp, which is geographically central.

The Göreme Valley lies about 4 miles to the northwest of Ürgüp and the museum is open from 8 a.m. until early evening. Parking is available outside the site. A pleasant way to visit Göreme, however, is on muleback; these animals can be hired at the nearby village of Avcılar. Guides may be hired at Ürgüp, where help is also available in planning itineraries.

About 30 miles from Ürgüp, there is evidence of amazing engineering and architectural skills in the underground cities of Derinkuyu and Kaymaklı. Extending 400 ft below the surface of the earth, the subterranean city of Derinkuyu is an extraordinary complex of corridors and steps on 8 levels, leading to living quarters, chapels, storerooms and even cemeteries.

THE GANGES
India

UNLIKE THE NILE, INDIA'S SACRED RIVER has not become a highway for luxury cruise boats. However, probably the best place to experience Ganga's holy waters is Benares (Varanasi), one of the oldest cities in the world.

The capital of Hinduism, Benares is one of several particularly holy bathing places along the river. It is accessible by air, road and rail from Delhi and accommodation is available in the city.

The best time of year to visit is between October and March. The Indian summer—which is exceptionally hot—lasts from April to June and the monsoon season lasts from mid-June to the end of September.

All of the city's 2,000 temples are dedicated to Lord Shiva, who is said to live there. And thousands of pilgrims visit the city every year to bathe in the sacred waters. The ultimate goal of every Hindu is to die in Benares and be cremated on the burning ghats; only then is the soul liberated from the endless wheel of karma.

Of the city's 64 ghats, 5 are exceptionally sacred and must be visited by pilgrims in a particular order on the same day. One of these is the Dasaswamedh Ghat, on which almost every street in Benares converges. Another is the Manikarnika Ghat—the so-called "burning ghat" which is not recommended for the unprepared or faint-hearted visitor.

It is suggested that an initial visit to the ghats in the late afternoon should be followed up with an early morning trip. Pilgrims begin to arrive well before dawn and are there in their thousands by the time the sun is up.

HALEAKALA CRATER
Maui, Hawaiian Islands
20°43′N 156°12′W

ONE OF THE BEST ROADS ON MAUI LEADS from the town of Kahului, where most visitors arrive, up to the crater about 40 miles away.

Haleakala Crater lies within the National Park of the same name. Information about walks within the park and its flora and fauna is available from the Visitor Center at the entrance. Even more magnificent than the view from the center is that from the Red Hill Visitor Building on the mountain-top, overlooking the crater.

The best way to get to know Haleakala is on foot or on horseback. For a serious trek it would be sensible to allow 3 or 4 days. Shorter ranger-conducted hikes are also available. There are a number of camp sites, as well as a limited number of campers' cabins. The latter are allocated, by lottery, three months in advance, and applications should be made to: Haleakala National Park Service, PO Box 537, Makawao, Maui, Hi 96768.

It is possible to make short tours around the rim, or to go on a conducted hike into the crater itself; one of these follows the Sliding Sands Trail and takes about 4 hours.

Sunrise and sunset are the best times to appreciate the awesome grandeur of Haleakala.

An unforgettable experience can be rounded off by freewheeling back down the mountain on a hired bicycle—a journey that takes some 7 hours.

SHENANDOAH VALLEY
Virginia/West Virginia, U.S.A.

FROM WASHINGTON D.C. IT IS A 2-HOUR drive to New Market in the heart of the Shenandoah Valley. And only half an hour's drive from here is the famous Skyline Drive that stretches 105 miles along the crest of the Blue Ridge Mountains in Shenandoah National Park. As the road ascends, it offers splendid views both of the Shenandoah River and of the valley itself. The park is a birdwatcher's paradise and it also supports an abundance of wild flowers. Nature has indeed made a miraculous recovery in this region once devastated by the Civil War.

Shenandoah is the valley of Stonewall Jackson's famous Valley Campaign, and the area is peppered with reminders of the Civil War. At New Market, the Hall of Valor commemorates the battle fought there on 15 May 1864, one of the last Confederate victories. It contains a magnificent panoramic survey of the entire Civil War and a walking tour of the park, which covers 160 acres, traces the steps of the teenage V.M.I. cadets, whose courage inspired the victory.

The Visitor Center in Lexington has a permanent exhibition that provides an introduction to the area and its heritage. Both Robert E. Lee and Stonewall Jackson had their homes, colleges and churches— as well as their final resting places—in the town. Robert E. Lee's office at the Washington and Lee University has been preserved exactly as he left it the day he died. The general is buried in the crypt on the Museum Level of the Lee Chapel and Museum within the university campus.

Stonewall Jackson's house contains many of its owner's personal possessions and a slide show introduces visitors to the enormous contribution he made as a civilian during the decade in which he taught at the Virginia Military Institute.

THE HIMALAYAS
Asia

WHILE CLIMBING THE GREAT HIMALAYAN peaks is reserved for only a few, trekking in the region, an exhilarating and satisfying experience, is open to anyone.

It is not necessary to have special climbing skills or experience, but it is clearly important to prepare physically and mentally for an expedition into the mountains.

Trekking is dictated by season. In Kashmir, for example, the season lasts from May to October. A trek can be organized by a reputable adventure travel company or advice sought from an Indian Tourist Office before departing. Alternatively, writing to the State Trek Office in the area to be visited is a way of getting the names of local agents.

It is recommended that would-be trekkers arm themselves with as much information as possible from the start. Useful books on the subject are: *Trekking in the Indian Himalaya* by Garry Weare (1986) and *Trekking in the Himalayas (Nepal)* by Stan Armington (1979), both published by Lonely Planet Publications.

SACRED WONDERS

ALTAMIRA
nr Santander, Spain
43°20′N 4°5′W

THE NORTHERN SPANISH TOWN OF Santander in the province of Cantabria is the nearest large town to Altamira. From Santander buses run to Santillana del Mar (about 20 miles away) and from there it is a short, well-signposted walk to the caves.

At the time of writing the caves are open to the public, although admittance is restricted to 30 visitors per day. Written application must be made, at least six months in advance, stating the date required to: Centro de Investigación y Museo de Altamira, Santillana del Mar, 39330, Cantabria, Spain. The caves are open from 10 a.m. to 2 p.m. in winter; from 10 a.m. to 1 p.m. in summer.

If it is not possible to visit the caves, there is free entry to the nearby museum of prehistory and the photographic reproduction of the caves at Santillana.

Since the caves are clearly the principal objective of most visitors, disappointment at Altamira may be offset by making a short (15-mile) trip to Puente Viesgo. The prehistoric cave paintings here, though not as well known as those at Altamira, are almost as well preserved.

STONEHENGE
Wiltshire, Great Britain
51°11′N 1°51′W

THE NEAREST LARGE TOWN TO STONEHENGE is Salisbury, where there is plentiful accommodation. It is accessible by road and rail (a 1¾-hr journey) from London. Buses run from Salisbury to the site, where parking facilities and refreshments are available.

It is at present not possible to wander freely among the standing stones. Access to the site is via a tunnel under the road, and visitors are directed around a path, separated from the stones by a fence.

The site is open year round (except over Christmas and on New Year's Day) from 10 a.m. to 6 p.m. in summer and from 10 a.m. to 4 p.m. in winter.

Particularly dramatic impressions of the stones and their shadows may be had at dawn and dusk.

The world-famous Bronze Age site is only one of many prehistoric sites on Salisbury Plain; nearby there is a Neolithic earthwork at Woodhenge, and a circular earthwork at Durrington Walls. It has been suggested that these two comprised a religious centre that was later moved to Stonehenge.

In the north of the county of Wiltshire, at Avebury, is another very important prehistoric monument: the Avebury Stone Circle. The circle is about 450 yards in diameter and is composed of about 100 huge standing stones.

THE TOMB OF TUTANKHAMUN

nr Luxor, Egypt
25°41′N 32°38′E

FROM CAIRO THERE ARE ROAD AND RAIL links with Luxor, the base for visitors not only to the Valley of the Kings on the west bank of the Nile, but also to the temples of Luxor and Karnak on the east bank.

Although winters in this area are pleasant, the summer heat, for those who are unused to it, may be overwhelming. Visitors should allow at least three days to see the major sights, and not venture out between midday and 4 p.m.

The Nile is crossed by ferry and it is important to have decided in advance which sites are to be visited. Tickets for individual sites have to be purchased on disembarking. Taxis, bicycles and horses are available for the 6-mile journey to the Valley of the Kings. Licensed guides can be hired through hotels by the half-day, and their assistance is invaluable.

Tutankhamun's Tomb is in the middle of the Valley of the Kings opposite the resthouse, where refreshments are available. While it is not permitted to take photographs in the tombs, pocket lamps and binoculars will help scrutiny of certain interiors.

Comfortable shoes with a good grip are recommended; and people with respiratory problems should beware of the dust.

The Luxor Museum houses some of the objects from Tutankhamun's tomb as well as a small collection of Egyptian art. In order to see the bulk of the treasures that once filled the tomb it is necessary to travel to Cairo, to the Museum of Antiquities, where they are on display. It is open daily throughout the year, though it closes at lunchtime during the summer months.

DELPHI
Greece
38°28′N 22°30′E

THERE ARE FIVE BUSES A DAY FROM ATHENS to Delphi, which is just over 100 miles from the capital. In ancient times pilgrims on their way to Delphi would stop en route at Levadia, for preliminary consultations with the oracle there. The modern pilgrim may take a train to Levadia, and make the rest of the journey to Delphi by bus. From Delphi itself there are several buses a day returning to Athens.

The entrance to the sanctuary is only about 10 minutes' walk from the modern village of Delphi, where accommodation, including a Youth Hostel and camp site, is available.

At least two days should be allowed to visit the site and the museum. It is possible to fit a quick tour of the ruins into one day, but the terrain is precipitous and occasionally difficult, and may prove tiring.

The Archeological Museum is best known for its Bronze Charioteer statue and the magnificent frieze of the Siphnian Treasury. It is sensible to visit the museum in the heat of the day, and preferably after having walked round the site itself. Then it is possible to begin to visualize the many treasures on display in their original settings.

GOTLAND
Sweden
57°30′N 18°33′E

THE CAPITAL, VISBY, IS A 40-MINUTE FLIGHT from Stockholm—a flight that is particularly memorable in a November sunset, when the skies in this part of the world are uniquely splendid. The island is also, of course, accessible by ferry from mainland Sweden; these leave from Nynäshamn—an hour's drive from Stockholm. Information can be obtained in advance from the Gotland Tourist Office, Norrmalmstorg, Stockholm.

The northeast corner of Gotland, and the island of Fårö, are out of bounds to foreigners. The rest of the island can, however, be explored by bus, car or bicycle. The last is a particularly pleasant means of transport, and complete bike packages are available through tourist offices.

Viking treasures—coins, weapons, jewellery—as well as picture stones and a priceless collection of medieval works of art are housed in the Historical Museum, the Fornsalen, at Visby.

SERPENT MOUND
Ohio, U.S.A.
38°59′N 83°21′W

THE MOUND IS SITUATED OFF STATE ROUTE 73 in Bratton Township in Adams County, near the village of Locust Grove.

It is possible to visit the site, which has a Visitor Center, every day from 9.30 a.m. to 5 p.m. from the end of May until Labor Day. At offpeak periods it is open on weekends only. Ranger-conducted tours may also be arranged in advance.

PETRA
Jordan
30°20′N 35°22′E

FROM AMMAN, WHERE MOST VISITORS enter Jordan, Petra is a 3-hour drive on the Desert Highway, or an 8-hour drive on the older Kings' Highway. The journey may be made by hired car, taxi or bus. The JETT bus company organize daily round trips leaving Amman at 7 a.m. Help in arranging transport as well as with planning an itinerary is available from good travel agents in Amman.

The most equable times of year to visit Petra are from March to May or from September to November. From December to March the desert nights can be extremely cold.

There is a Visitor Centre at Petra itself; here information, advice and guides are available.

A donkey or mule may be hired for the 2-mile trek through the Siq into Petra canyon. Hotel accommodation and a camp site are available for those who wish to stay overnight; it is forbidden to sleep in the canyon itself without written permission from the Department of Antiquities in Amman. Refreshments are available in the canyon from the Government Antiquities Department centre there.

At different times of day, sunlight produces quite spectacular colour changes on the magnificent façades. The Treasury, for example, glows a wonderful deep pink in the afternoon light around 4 p.m. Sunset and sunrise are good times to capture the city to east and west on film.

TIKAL
Guatemala
17°13′N 89°24′W

FLORES IS THE NEAREST LARGE TOWN AND base for visitors to Tikal. Accommodation is available at Tikal itself, and should be booked immediately on arrival at the ruins, though many prefer to return to Flores for the night.

The thousands of ruined monuments are within Tikal National Park, which is also notable for the abundance of its wildlife. Extended passes are available for those who wish to take advantage of the quieter times at dawn and dusk for observing the animal and bird life.

At least two days should be allowed simply in order to visit the most important structures—and to watch the sun rise from the top of a pyramid. In order to ensure best use of the time available, it is essential to employ a guide. It is possible to drive from plaza to plaza and organized tours are available.

The Tikal Museum houses a fascinating miscellany of objects, some of which were excavated from the North Acropolis.

All the usual strictures and precautions to be borne in mind when visiting the Tropics clearly apply here. Insect repellent, mosquito nets, water supplies and a pocket lamp are all essential baggage items.

MACHU PICCHU
nr Cuzco, Peru
13°32'S 72°0'W

THERE ARE DAILY FLIGHTS FROM LIMA TO Cuzco, the nearest large settlement to the ruins. Combined tour tickets to Machu Picchu are available from agencies in Cuzco, many of which will also provide an English-speaking guide. The ticket includes the round-trip to Machu Picchu (by train and bus), entry to the site and lunch at the Machu Picchu Hotel. Trains leave Cuzco at 7 a.m. and complete the 70-mile journey in about 3½ hours. The train back to Cuzco leaves at 3 p.m.

On the way up to Machu Picchu, the best views are to be had from seats on the left facing the engine (the reverse on the way down).

People who wish to stay overnight should book in advance for the Machu Picchu Hotel—the only one on the site. Accommodation is also available at the nearby village of Aguas Calientes. Booking is advisable for all hotels within reach of the ruins in the month of June, particularly at the feast of Inti Raymi.

For those with stamina and more time to spare, the most exciting approach to the ruins is on foot along the Inca Trail. This 65-mile trek, departing from Cuzco, takes between 3 and 5 days. Guides and bearers are provided and the journey should not be made without them.

Machu Picchu is open to visitors from 7.30 a.m. to 5 p.m. each day. Visitors at full moon may find a guard who is

agreeable to accompanying them into the site at that time.

During the dry season, June to September, there may be as many as 1,000 visitors a day. However, the ruins are much less crowded and just as impressive in the rainy season—from December to March. It is prohibited to take any bags or food onto the site.

As a precaution against the unpleasant effects of altitude sickness, it is strongly advised that visitors rest for at least a day in Cuzco on arrival, in order to allow their bodies to adjust to the high altitude.

TINTERN ABBEY
nr Monmouth, Great Britain
51°48'N 2°43'W

ACCORDING TO ONE AMERICAN VISITOR TO Britain, "he who visits England without seeing Monmouth and the River Wye does not know what beauty there is in Old England".

On the west bank of the Wye, 11 miles south of Monmouth and 5 miles north of Chepstow, the abbey is situated at the southern end of the village of Tintern Parva. It is accessible from London and major cities in England and Wales by road.

Though the abbey is no longer romantically swathed with ivy and boats no longer ply the river on the Wye Tour, the ruin and its setting still retain a special character. It is open daily from 9.30 a.m. (2 p.m. on Sundays) until 7 p.m. (May to September) or 4 p.m. (November to February). Within the abbey complex there is a Visitor Centre with exhibits related to the history of Tintern's development, demise and Romantic revival.

Accommodation is available at Tintern Village as well as in the environs. Visitors may establish a base here for excursions to the many other historical sites nearby.

Today the Wye Valley is best explored either on foot or by canoe. Downstream from Glasbury the river is open to the public for 100 miles; would-be canoeists must buy a river guidebook. The tidal effects on the river become increasingly marked below Tintern, however, and it is recommended that canoeists follow the rest of the route on foot.

There are two suggested walks: the Upper Wye Walk starting at Rhayader, and the better known Lower Wye Walk that follows the last 35 miles of the river from Ross down to Chepstow.

THE CREATIVE VISION

SHWEDAGON PAGODA
Rangoon, Burma
16°45'N 96°20'E

IT IS NOT POSSIBLE TO VISIT BURMA EXCEPT as a member of a guided group tour. Tourist visas are issued for 7 days only and can only be applied for in Bangkok, Thailand. Applications to participate in a tour should be made in advance to: Skyline Travel Service Company, Skyline Building, 23/13–14 Saladaeng Soi 1 Rama 4 Road, Bangkok 10500 Thailand. Phone Bangkok 2359780-1 or 2366582-4.

At least one day is needed to fully appreciate the pagoda and in order to capture its different moods in different lights. The most pleasant time to visit is between November and February; from February until the beginning of the rainy season (mid-May to mid-October) it is extremely hot.

Visits usually begin at the southern staircase, off Pagoda Road, and shoes and socks must be removed at the entrance. At the top of the staircase visitors must turn left, to walk in a clockwise direction in keeping with Buddhist custom. There is a lift service for those who do not wish to climb the stairs.

The best time of day to visit the pagoda is the evening, when the marble terraces are still pleasantly warm to bare feet. Dawn, too, is an agreeable time to visit.

Before leaving the pagoda it is worth visiting the museum, which houses a collection of objects presented by devotees.

HAGHIA SOPHIA
Istanbul, Turkey
41°2'N 28°57'E

THERE ARE DAILY FLIGHTS FROM MOST parts of the world into Istanbul's international airport. Travellers proposing to arrive by road or rail from continental Europe should ascertain in advance whether or not they will need transit visas for Yugoslavia and Bulgaria.

The climate in Istanbul is Mediterranean, and spring (April to June) and autumn (September to November) are ideal times to visit. Three or four days at least should be allowed in order to take in not only Haghia Sophia but some of the city's other outstanding attractions—including the Topkapi Palace and the Archeological Museum.

The best way to get around the city is by bus or taxi; ferries ply the Bosporus and are an integral part of the city's transport system. Probably the best way to see the Bosporus is on a tourist cruise, which takes about 2½ hours (from Istanbul to the Black Sea) and is very reasonably priced.

Haghia Sophia is right next to both the Topkapi Palace and the Blue Mosque with its textile and mosaic museums. The church is open every day except Monday from 9.30 a.m. to 5.30 p.m. (7 p.m. in July and August).

A memorable impression of the interior is to be had by approaching it from the main entrance (near the ruins of the church built by Theodosius) and entering it very slowly. There is one entrance fee to the floor of the church and an additional charge to see the mosaics in the galleries.

THE POTALA
Lhasa, Tibet, China
29°41'N 91°10'E

THE MOST USUAL AND QUICKEST ROUTE TO Lhasa in Tibet is by air from Chengdu, which is the capital of the Chinese province of Sichuan. The Chinese airline CAAC operates daily flights and the journey takes about 2 hours. Once in Tibet it is possible to hire a car with driver; vehicles are provided as a matter of course for visitors travelling with the Tibet/China International Travel Service.

The best time of year to visit the Potala is between April and October. Tibet is cool but dry in the summer, and very cold in the winter.

Only a relatively small part of the Potala is open to the public—but even in this part it is possible to get lost. It is closed on Sundays, but open every other day of the week from 9 a.m. until 4 p.m.

The Potala is a State Museum which is administered by 35 "caretaker" monks; visitors should always bear in mind, however, that for many Tibetans it is also a holy place. The Buddhist custom of walking clockwise around holy places should be observed when entering the rooms.

In order to avoid ill effects that might occur because of the altitude, visitors are advised to rest for the first day or so on arrival.

ASSISI
Italy
43°4'N 12°36'E

SPRING AND AUTUMN ARE THE BEST seasons to visit Assisi, which is about 10 miles east of Perugia and 120 miles northeast of Rome. Since it attracts thousands of visitors, it is advisable to book accommodation in advance for the summer high season as well as for the first 10 days of May, when the medieval pageant known as the Celendimaggio takes place. It is sometimes possible to stay in one of the convents, which provide simple but comfortable accommodation. The Festival of St Francis is on 3–4 October.

It would be sensible to allow at least two days at Assisi; not only are there many buildings in the town which have strong associations with the saint, there are numerous sites outside with similar connections.

Just down the hill outside the town, within walking distance, is the convent of San Damiano, where the tables and chairs used by St Clare and the sisters can still be seen in the refectory.

Hardly a mile above the town is the wood where Francis and his companions lived in caves as hermits. Here too is the saint's favourite retreat, the hermitage, Eremo delli Carceri, from which the road leads to the top of Mount Subasio.

MONT-ST-MICHEL
France
48°40'N 1°30'W

VISITS TO FRANCE'S SECOND BIGGEST tourist attraction after Versailles are not recommended during the summer months when there may be as many as 7,000 visitors a day. At such peak times guided tours conducted in most major European languages leave every 15 minutes and tend to be somewhat rushed, lasting about 1 hour.

At least two days are needed to begin to appreciate the site and its wealth of architectural detail; many people make Pontorsons (about 5 miles away) the base for a visit. An acceptable, less commercialized, alternative is Avranches—a little farther away.

The Mont can only be seen as an island—that is, almost completely surrounded by water—twice a month (about 36 hours after the new and full moons). A visit planned to coincide with

the full moon could be particularly memorable.

It is possible to walk around the base of the Mont—but it is essential to check the tides first. The sand and mud flats should never be crossed without a guide. They are extremely dangerous: not only are there quicksands but the incoming tide moves so rapidly that people can be taken unawares with disastrous consequences.

The Abbey opens every day at 9 a.m. and closes for lunch between 11.30 a.m. and 1.30 p.m.; it then reopens until 4 or 6 p.m. depending on the season.

THE ALHAMBRA
Granada, Spain
37°10'N 3°35'W

THE CLOSEST INTERNATIONAL AIRPORT TO Granada is at Malaga; from here it is a 2-hour drive to the old Moorish city. Alternatively visitors may arrive by car or train via France or Portugal.

The palace is open all year round, though hours of opening vary slightly with the season. From June to September it is open daily from 9.30 a.m. to 8 p.m.; from October to April, from 10 a.m. to 5 p.m; in May, from 9.30 a.m. to 6 p.m.

The palace complex is reached by the Granada Gate, off the Cuesta de Gomerez. This involves a walk or drive uphill; there is plenty of parking space at the top. In order to appreciate the palace and gardens to the full it would be sensible to allow two or three days. There are fine views of the Sierra Nevada from the Torre de la Vela (the Watchtower).

Accommodation should pose no problems for visitors, except over the busy Easter period.

Within the Alhambra complex itself is the romantic, but expensive, Parador Nacional San Francisco—a converted 15th-century convent.

THE FORBIDDEN CITY
Beijing, China
39°55'N 116°20'E

THE FORBIDDEN CITY HAS BEEN DESCRIBED as a "fascinating but daunting" tourist challenge. Certainly one can do very little more than simply identify the main halls in the course of one day; it would take several to explore it in anything like a more thorough fashion.

231

In order to get the most out of any visit, it is advisable to arrive early in the day and plan to eat inside the city. It is open daily from 8.30 a.m. to 4.30 p.m., with last tickets at 3.30 p.m.

While it is possible to fly to mainland China, it costs far less to fly to Hong Kong than it does to Beijing or Shanghai. From Hong Kong it is a 2½-hour flight to the capital of China. Trains from the U.S.S.R. and Hong Kong also go to Beijing, though train travellers should check, in summer, that the train is air-conditioned.

An interesting way of travelling would be to book a one-way ticket to Hong Kong, returning to Europe on the Trans-Siberian Railway.

The best season for visiting is the autumn, though spring is also pleasant. Early spring, however, is not advised for it is then that the air is filled with fine dust blown in by winds from the Gobi Desert.

Hotel accommodation should be booked in advance. If this has not been done, the China International Travel Service (CITS) or one of the Hotel Reservation Centres will be able to assist.

ELSINORE
(Kronborg Castle) Helsingør, Denmark
56°2′N 12°35′E

HELSINGØR, ON THE NORTHEAST COAST OF Zealand, is a 50-minute drive from Copenhagen. There are also frequent ferry connections with the Swedish town of Helsingborg, just across the Sound.

Cycling is a particularly pleasant way of exploring the countryside in Denmark, and is made safer generally by the abundance of cycle tracks.

Agents and hotels in Copenhagen can supply information about guided tours to Hamlet's Castle. One seven-hour excursion takes in the royal residences at Fredensborg and Frederiksborg as well as Kronborg Castle. A shorter ''Afternoon Hamlet Tour'' is available daily from May to September and lasts about 5 hours.

It is suggested that a visit might begin with the central courtyard and progress to the ramparts. Also of particular interest are the Danish Maritime Museum, housed within the castle, and the statue of Holger the Dane.

Helsingør itself is one of the oldest towns in the country and is close to several pleasant resorts. Accommodation is readily available.

THE TAJ MAHAL
Agra, India
27°17′N 77°58′E

THE TOWN OF AGRA IS A 30-MINUTE flight from Delhi and 1½ hours by air from Benares (Varanasi). It also has rail links with Bombay, Delhi and Madras and a road link with Delhi (123 miles).

It is possible to travel to Agra on the luxury air-conditioned Taj Express train that leaves New Delhi at 7 a.m., arriving in Agra at about 10.15 a.m. The return journey starts at 7 p.m. and takes about 3 hours. The U.P. State Tourism Development Corporation organizes air-conditioned coach trips to the Taj.

Winter—mid-October to March—is the high season and the most pleasant time for a visit as far as the climate is concerned. From mid-June to the end of September is the rainy season. From March to May the heat may mean visits are best limited to the early morning or evening.

Accommodation at Agra is plentiful, but should be reserved in advance in the high season.

Agra Fort, open from sunrise to sunset, is often visited first, as an introduction to Agra; it is sensible, therefore, to allow more than one day, if possible. The Taj itself is open from sunrise until 7.30 p.m.; it is not seen in its best light between 10 a.m. and 3 p.m. Within the Taj complex there is a museum with a collection of Moghul artefacts and a history of the mausoleum.

NEUSCHWANSTEIN
nr Füssen, West Germany
47°35′N 10°43′E

THERE ARE VARIOUS WAYS OF APPROACHING Neuschwanstein, which is in the Bavarian Alps, close to the border with Austria. One is by car down the so-called Romantic Road, which winds along to Füssen from Würzburg. The road is now too busy to merit the description ''Romantic'', though there are plenty of digressions along the route that deserve that appellation.

From Munich or Garmisch Partenkirchen there are organized trips to the castle.

Both Hohenschwangau and Neuschwanstein are open year round from 9 a.m. to 5.30 p.m. April to September; from 10 a.m. to 4 p.m. October to March. After first visiting Hohenschwangau, visitors may walk up to Neuschwanstein (½ hour), take a bus or, more romantic, a horse-drawn carriage.

Buses go up to the Marienbrücke, a bridge across the Pollat Gorge, from which there is a magnificent view of the castle and its setting.

In September there are Wagnerian concerts in the castle's Singers' Hall.

TRIUMPH OF THE SPIRIT

OBERAMMERGAU
West Germany
47°35′N 11°3′E

CLOSE TO NEUSCHWANSTEIN IN THE Bavarian Alps, Oberammergau is 10 miles from Garmisch and 50 miles from Munich. Rail services to Murnau link with local buses and trains for Oberammergau.

The Passion Plays are performed every decade, in years ending in zero, from late May until late September. The performance itself takes place between 9 a.m. and 5 p.m., with a break for lunch.

In order to be sure of accommodation in the town in a Passion Play year, it is necessary to book well in advance—a year, or even two years, would not be too early.

Even when there is no play, Oberammergau is still worth a visit. The 5,200-seater theatre, with its open stage, is an impressive structure. And there are guided tours of the backstage area, wardrobe, props, and scenery. In the foyer of the theatre there is a permanent woodcarving exhibition.

On 24 August, Mountain Hiking Day, an organized mountain walk finishes with a spectacular bonfire display on the mountainside.

COVENTRY CATHEDRAL
Coventry, Great Britain
52°25′N 1°31′W

THE CITY OF COVENTRY IS ACCESSIBLE BY road and rail from London and major cities in the United Kingdom. The cathedral is open every day from 9 a.m. to 5.30 p.m. in winter and until 7.30 p.m. in summer except when services are being held. Inside the cathedral there are guides who will answer questions.

A Visitor Centre with interesting

exhibits and an audio-visual presentation as well as a restaurant is attached to the cathedral.

The countryside to the south of Coventry is varied and extremely interesting historically. The ruins of Kenilworth Castle, Warwick Castle and Leamington Spa, with its gracious Georgian terraces, are all worth seeing.

ARKADI MONASTERY
nr Rethymnon, Crete, Greece
35°18'N 24°30'E

THE MONASTERY IS ACCESSIBLE BY BUS FROM the coastal resort of Rethymnon, which can be reached by bus from Herakleion, the island's largest city. The latter has an international airport, and there is a regular boat service to it from Athens. Arkadi is open every day from 7 a.m. to 8 p.m., and its historical museum houses an interesting collection of mementoes from the uprising of 1866.

On 7–9 November there are solemn commemorations of the sacrifice at Arkadi in the monastery itself and at Rethymnon.

THE ITALIAN CHAPEL
nr Kirkwall, Orkney, Great Britain
58°59'N 2°59'W

THE ITALIAN CHAPEL IS ON THE LITTLE island of Lambholm, near Scapa Flow. There are regular flights to Kirkwall on Mainland from Aberdeen, Edinburgh, Glasgow, Birmingham and Manchester, as well as regular inter-island flights. There are ferry crossings every day except Sunday to Stromness from Scrabster. Public transport on the islands is infrequent.

It is possible to drive across the Churchill Barriers causeway from Mainland to Lambholm, and the Italian Chapel, which is never closed, is on the itinerary of most organized tours to the islands.

The Orkneys are a birdwatcher's paradise, and, in the summer, when twilight lasts all night, vast numbers of seabirds arrive to nest here.

Summers are relatively mild and winters harsh. Accommodation should be booked in advance. Information is available from the Orkney Tourist Organization, Broad St, Kirkwall.

Kirkwall itself is one of the best preserved medieval towns in Scotland.

BIBLIOGRAPHY

Alcock, L. *"By South Cadbury is that Camelot . . ." The Excavation of Cadbury Castle* 1966–1970 Thames & Hudson, London, 1972

Andersen, H.C. *A Visit to Spain and North Africa 1862* (Trans. Thornton, G.), Peter Owen, London, 1975

Anderson, W. *Holy Places of the British Isles: A Guide to the Legendary and Sacred Sites* Ebury Press, London, 1983

Ashe, G. *Camelot and the Vision of Albion* Heinemann, London, 1971; *The Landscape of King Arthur* Webb & Bower/Michael Joseph, London, 1987; *The Quest for Arthur's Britain* Paladin, London, 1971

Atkinson, R.J.C. *Stonehenge and Neighbouring Monuments* HMSO, London, 1978; *Stonehenge* Penguin, Harmondsworth, UK, 1979

Baines, J., and Málek, J. *Atlas of Ancient Egypt* Phaidon, Oxford, UK, 1984

Balfour, M. *Stonehenge and Its Mysteries* Macdonald & Jane's, London, 1979

Barber, R.W. *Arthur of Albion* Barrie & Rockliff/Pall Mall Press, London, 1961

Batchelor, S. *The Tibet Guide* Wisdom Publications, London, 1987

Beckwith, M. *Hawaiian Mythology* Yale University Press, USA, 1940

Bedoyere, M. de la *Francis: A Biography of the Saint of Assisi* Fontana/Collins, London, 1976

Bentley, J. *Oberammergau and the Passion Play: A Guide to Mark the 350th Anniversary* Penguin, Harmondsworth, UK, 1984

Berenguer, Professor Magín *Prehistoric Man and His Art: The Caves of Ribadesella* (Trans. Heron, M.), Souvenir Press, London, 1973

Bingham, H. *Lost City of the Incas: The Story of Machu Picchu and Its Builders* Phoenix House, London, 1951

Bird, I.L. *The Hawaiian Archipelago. Six Months Among the Palm Groves, Coral Reefs, & Volcanoes of the Sandwich Islands* John Murray, London, 1875

Blunt, W. *The Dream King. Ludwig II of Bavaria* Hamish Hamilton, London, 1970

Bonnington, C. "In the Yeti's Footsteps" *Radio Times* 15–21 October, London, 1988

Booth, A. *Collins Illustrated Guide to Japan* Collins, London, 1988

Booz, E.B. *A Guide to Tibet* Collins, London, 1986

Bradley, A.G. *The Wye* Adam and Charles Black, London, 1910

Branigan, Professor K. (Ed.) *The Atlas of Archaeology* Macdonald, London, 1982

Breuil, A.H., and Obermaier, Dr H. *The Cave of Altamira at Santillana Del Mar, Spain* Tipografía De Archivos, Madrid, 1935

Brewster, R. *The Island of Zeus: Wanderings in Crete* Duckworth, London, 1939

Brodrick, A.H. *The Abbé Breuil Prehistorian: A Biography* Hutchinson, London, 1983

Burckhardt, J.L. *Travels in Syria and the Holy Land* John Murray, London, 1822

Bryce, J. *Transcaucasia and Ararat* Macmillan, London, 1877

Byron, R. *The Station. Athos: Treasures and Men* Century, London, UK; Hippocrene Books, New York, USA, 1984

Canby, C. *Archaeology of the World* Chancellor Press, London, 1980

Carter, H. *The Tomb of Tut-Ankh-Amen* (3 vols), Cassell & Company, London, 1927–33

Cavendish, R. (Ed.) *Man, Myth and Magic Parts 1–112* Purnell, London, 1970–71; *Mythology: An Illustrated Encyclopaedia* Orbis, London, 1980

Ceram, C.W. *Gods, Graves and Scholars: The Story of Archaeology* Book Club Associates, London, 1971; *A Pictorial History of Archaeology* Thames & Hudson, London, 1958

Chapman, R.S. *Lhasa: The Holy City* Chatto & Windus, London, 1938

Childs, W.J. *Across Asia Minor on Foot* William Blackwood, London, 1917

Chippindale, C. *Stonehenge Complete* Thames & Hudson, London, 1983

Cleare, J. *Collins Guide to Mountains and Mountaineering* Collins, London, 1979

Cooper, J.C. *An Illustrated Encyclopaedia of Traditional Symbols* Thames & Hudson, London, 1984

Courtauld, C. *In Search of Burma* Frederick Muller, London, 1984

Cumming, E.D. *In the Shadow of the Pagoda: Sketches of Burmese Life and Character* W.H. Allen, London, 1893

BIBLIOGRAPHY

David-Neel, A. *My Journey to Lhasa* Virago, London, 1986; *With Mystics and Magicians in Tibet* Bodley Head, London, 1931

Davidson, H.E. *Scandinavian Mythology* Hamlyn, London, 1969; *Myths and Symbols in Pagan Europe: Early Scandinavian and Celtic Religions* Manchester University Press, UK, 1988

Donnison, F.S.V. *Burma* Ernest Benn, London, 1970

Duncan, J.E. *Milton's Earthly Paradise: A Historical Study of Eden* University of Minnesota Press, 1972

Elisofon, E. *The Nile* Viking, New York, 1964

Elstob, E. *Sweden* Boydell Press/Rowman & Littlefield, New Jersey, 1979

Evans, I.H. *Brewer's Dictionary of Phrase and Fable* (2nd Ed.) Cassell, London, 1981

Farmer, D.H. (Ed.) *Oxford Dictionary of Saints* Oxford University Press, 1982

Ferrars, M. and B. *Burma* Sampson Low, London, 1900

Finucane, R.C. *Miracles and Pilgrims: Popular Beliefs in Medieval England* J.M. Dent, London, 1977

Fitzgerald, P. *Ancient China* Elsevier/Phaidon, Oxford, UK, 1978

Flaceliere, R. *Greek Oracles* (Trans. Garman, D.), Paul Elek, London, 1976

Fosbroke, Rev. T.D. *The Wye Tour, or Gilpin on the Wye* London, 1826

Frater, A. (Ed.) *Great Rivers of the World* Hodder & Stoughton, London, 1984

Gascoigne, B. *The Great Moghuls* Jonathan Cape, London, 1971

Geoffrey of Monmouth *The History of the Kings of Britain* (Trans. Thorpe, L.), Penguin, Harmondsworth, UK, 1966

Gerald of Wales *The Journey Through Wales and The Description of Wales* (Trans. Thorpe, L.), Penguin, Harmondsworth, UK, 1978

Ghilardi, A. *The Life and Times of St Francis* (Trans. Athanasio, S.), Hamlyn, London, 1967

Giamatti, A.B. *The Earthly Paradise and the Renaissance Epic* Princeton University Press, New Jersey, 1966

Grabar, L. *The Alhambra* Allen Lane, London, 1978

Graves, R., and Patai, R. *Hebrew Myths: The Book of Genesis* Cassell, London, 1964

Graziosi, P. *Palaeolithic Art* Faber & Faber, London, 1960

Gunn, P. *Normandy: Landscape with Figures* Gollancz, London, 1975

Hambley, G. *Cities of Mughul India* Elek Books, London, 1968

Hansen, W.F. *Saxo Grammaticus and the Life of Hamlet* University of Nebraska Press, USA and UK, 1983

Harpers Ferry National Historical Park, West Virginia National Park Service, US Department of the Interior, 1986

Harrer, H. *Seven Years in Tibet* (Trans. Graves, R.), Paladin, London, 1988

Hawes, L. *Constable's Stonehenge* HMSO, London, 1975

Hawkes, J. *Atlas of Ancient Archaeology* Heinemann, London, 1974

Hearn, L. *Writings from Japan* (Ed. King, F.), Penguin, Harmondsworth, UK, 1984

Heatwole, H. *A Guide to Skyline Drive and Shenandoah National Park* (Bulletin No. 9) Shenandoah Natural History Association, USA, 1978

Henry, F. *Irish Art in the Early Christian Period to AD 800* Methuen, London, 1965

Highwater, J. *Arts of the Indian Americans* Harper & Row, New York, 1983

Hill, C.E. *The Danish Sound Dues and the Command of the Baltic* Duke University Press, North Carolina, 1926

Hillary, E. *From the Ocean to the Sky* Hodder & Stoughton, London, 1979

Hitching, F. *The World Atlas of Mysteries* Pan Books, London, 1979

Hobson, C. *Exploring the World of the Pharaohs* Thames & Hudson, London, 1987

Howey, M.O. *The Encircled Serpent: A Study of Serpent Symbolism in all Countries and Ages* Rider & Co, London

Huxley, E. *A Journey Through Australia* Chatto & Windus, London, 1967

Irving, W. *The Alhambra* Macmillan & Co, London and New York, 1921

Jacobson, H. *In the Land of Oz* Hamish Hamilton, London, 1987

Jenkins, E. *The Mystery of King Arthur* Michael Joseph, London, 1975

Jones, G. *A History of the Vikings* Oxford University Press, London and New York, 1968

Joy, W. *The Explorers* Shakespeare Head Press, Sydney, 1971

Keay, J. *When Men and Mountains Meet. The Explorers of the Western Himalayas 1820–75* Century, London, 1983

Kelly, L. *Istanbul: A Travellers' Companion* Constable, London, 1987

Kelly, R.T. *Burma: Painted and Described* Adam & Charles Black, London, 1905

Keneally, T. *Outback* Hodder & Stoughton, London, 1983

Khouri, R. *Petra: A Guide to the Capital of the Nabataeans* Longman, London, 1986

Kidder, E. *Ancient Japan* Elsevier/Phaidon, Oxford, UK, 1977

Kinross, Lord *Within the Taurus: A Journey in Asiatic Turkey* John Murray, London, 1970

Kipling, R. *From Sea to Sea and Other Sketches* (Vol. 1), Macmillan & Co, London, 1900

Kirke, W. *Central Australia: Handbook to Adventure* Alice Springs Regional Tourist Association Inc, Australia, 1980

Kissack, K. *The River Wye* Terence Dalton Ltd, Lavenham, UK, 1978

Klein, W. *Burma* Apa Productions, Hong Kong, 1981

Kuhn, H. *The Rock Pictures of Europe* (Trans. Brodrick, A.H.), Sidgwick & Jackson, London, 1966

Lear, E. *The Cretan Journal* Denise Harvey & Co, Athens, Greece, and Dedham, UK, 1984

Lacy, N.J. (Ed.) *The Arthurian Encyclopedia* Garland, New York, 1986

Lebeau, J. & C., "*Gotland: l'îsle aux cent clochers*", *Connaissance du Monde* (Vol. 23), Paris, 1960

Lehrman, J. *Earthly Paradise: Garden and Courtyard in Islam* Thames & Hudson, London, 1980

Lindsay, J. *Men and Gods on the Roman Nile* Frederick Muller, London, 1968

London, J. *The Cruise of the Snark* Seafarer Books/The Merlin Press, London, 1971

Luce, J.V. *The End of Atlantis* Paladin, London, 1970

Macaulay, R. *Fabled Shore: From the Pyrenees to Portugal* Hamish Hamilton, London, 1949; *Pleasure of Ruins* Thames & Hudson, London, 1977

McCann, P. *Celtic Mythology* Hamlyn, London, 1970

Maitland, D. *The Insider's Guide to China* Merehurst Press, London, 1987

Malory, Sir Thomas *The Works of Thomas Malory* Oxford University Press, London, 1954 (repr. 1959)

Manthorpe, V. (Ed.) *The Japan Diaries of Richard Gordon Smith* Viking/Rainbird, Harmondsworth, UK, 1986

Marinatos, S. "On the Atlantis legend", *Critica Chronica IV*, 1950

Mason, K. *Abode of Snow* Rupert Hart-Davis, London, 1955

Maugham, W.S. *The Gentleman in the Parlour: A Record of A Journey from Rangoon to Haiphong* William Heinemann, London, 1930

Mazonowicz, D. *Voices from the Stone Age* Allen & Unwin, London, 1974

Mehling, F.N. (Ed.) *Spain: A Phaidon Cultural Guide* Phaidon, Oxford, 1986

Metford, J.C.J. *Dictionary of Christian Lore and Legend* Thames & Hudson, London, 1983

Meyer, K.E. *The Pleasures of Archaelogy: A Vista to Yesterday* Andre Deutsch, London, 1971

Michell, J. *The Earth Spirit: Its Ways, Shrines and Mysteries* Avon Books, New York; Thames & Hudson, London, 1975

Moffitt, I. *The Australian Outback* Time-Life Books, Amsterdam, 1976

Morier, J. *A Second Journey Through Persia, Armenia, and Asia Minor, to Constantinople, Between the Years 1810 and 1816* Longman, Hurst, Rees, Orme and Brown, London, 1818

Morrit, J.B.S. *A Grand Tour: Letters and Journey 1794–96* Century, London, 1985

Mountford, C.P. *Brown Men and Red Sand* Phoenix House, London, 1950

Murnane, W.J. *The Penguin Guide to Ancient Egypt* Penguin/Allen Lane, Harmondsworth, UK, 1983

Myatt, C. *The Insider's Guide to Hawaii* Merehurst Press, London, 1987

Newby, E. *A Short Walk in the Hindu Kush* Picador, London, 1982; *Slowly Down the Ganges* Hodder & Stoughton, London, 1966

Nigg, W. *Francis of Assisi* (Trans. Neil, W.), Mowbrays, London, 1975

Norman, B. *Footsteps: Nine Archaeological Journeys of Romance and Discovery* BBC Books, London, 1987

O'Connor, V.C.S. *The Silken East: A Record of Life and Travel in Burma* Hutchinson, London, 1928

O'Flaherty, Doniger, W. (Trans.) *Hindu Myths* Penguin, Harmondsworth, UK, 1975

Orkney's Italian Chapel P.O.W. Chapel Preservation Committee, Orkney

Pashley, R. *Travels in Crete* (Vol. 1), John Murray, London, 1937

Perowne, S. *Holy Places of Christendom* Mowbrays, London, 1976

Parrot, Dr F. *Journey to Ararat* (Trans. Cooley, W.D.), Longman, Brown, Green, and Longmans, London, 1845

Popham, P. *The Insider's Guide to Japan* Merehurst Press, London, 1987

Powell, T.G.E. *Prehistoric Art* Thames & Hudson, London, 1966; *The Celts* Thames & Hudson, London, 1980

Prescott, W.H. *History of the Conquest of Peru; With a Preliminary View of the Civilization of the Incas* (2 Vols.), George Routledge & Sons, London and New York, 1882

Prest, J. *The Garden of Eden: The Botanic Garden and the Re-Creation of Paradise* Yale University Press, New Haven and London, 1981

Pritchard, J.B. (Ed.) *The Ancient Near East: An Anthology of Texts and Pictures* (Vol. 1), Princeton University Press, New Jersey, 1973

Provatakis, Theocharis M. *Monastery of Arkadi* Athens, 1980

Quest for the Past Reader's Digest, New York, 1984

Roberts, N. *The Companion Guide to Normandy* Collins, London, 1980

Romain, William F., "The Serpent Mound Solar Eclipse Hypothesis: Ethnohistoric Considerations" *Ohio Archaeologist* Vol. 38 No. 2, Spring 1988

Ryley, J.H. *Ralph Fitch: England's Pioneer to India and Burma* T. Fisher Unwin, London, 1899

Schnieper, X. *Saint Francis of Assisi* Frederick Muller, London, 1981

Shearer, A. *Northern India: A Guide to the Sacred Places of Northern India* Harrap Columbus, London, 1987

Shenandoah National Park, Virginia National Park Service, US Department of the Interior, 1986

Shetrone, H.C. *The Mound-Builders* D. Appleton, New York and London, 1930

Sieveking, A. *The Cave Artists* Thames & Hudson, London, 1979

Simpson, C. *The New Australia* Hodder & Stoughton, London, 1971

Simpson, J. *Touching the Void* Jonathan Cape, London, 1988

Sitwell, S. *Golden Wall and Mirador: From England to Peru* Weidenfeld & Nicolson, London, 1961

Smart, W.J. *Where Wye and Severn Flow* R.H. Johns, Newport, UK, 1949

Snailham, R. *Normandy and Brittany: From Le Tréport to St-Nazaire* Weidenfeld & Nicolson, London, 1986

Snow, D. *The American Indians: Their Archaeology and Prehistory* Thames & Hudson, London, 1976

Sorrell, A. *Reconstructing the Past* Batsford, London, 1981

Spencer, B., and Gillen, F.J. *Across Australia* (Vol. 1), Macmillan, London, 1912

Squier, E., and Davis, E. *Ancient Monuments of the Mississippi Valley*, 1848

Stark, F. *Turkey: A Sketch of Turkish History* Thames & Hudson, London, 1971

Suyin, H. *Lhasa, The Open City: A Journey to Tibet* Jonathan Cape, London, 1977

Through the Moon Gate: A Guide to China's Historic Monuments Oxford University Press, London and New York, 1986

Tichy, H. *Himalaya* Robert Hale, London, 1971

Tomlin, E.W.F. *The Last Country: My Years in Japan* Faber & Faber, London, 1974

Trevelyan, R. *Shades of the Alhambra* The Folio Society, London, 1984

Tugorès, M. "Gotland trop peu connue", *Connaissance du Monde* (Vol. 117), Paris, 1968

Twain, M. *Roughing It* American Publishing Co, US, 1875

van der Post, L. *A Portrait of Japan* The Hogarth Press, London, 1968

Vitaliano, D.B. *Legends of the Earth* Indiana University Press, Bloomington/London, 1973

Waldman, C. *Atlas of the North American Indian* Facts on File Publications, New York and Oxford, 1985

Wallace, R., and the Editors of Time-Life Books *Hawaii* Time-Life Books, Amsterdam, 1978

Wan-go Weng and Yang Boda *The Palace Museum: Peking, Treasures of the Forbidden City* Orbis, London, 1982

Westwood, J. *Albion: A Guide to Legendary Britain* Paladin, London, 1987

Willey, G.R., and Sabloff, J.A. *A History of American Archaeology* Thames & Hudson, London, 1974

Williams, H.C.N. *The Latter Glory: The Story of Coventry Cathedral* The Whitehorn Press, Manchester, UK, 1985

Yasuda, K. *The Japanese Haiku* Charles E. Tuttle, Vermont, 1957

Yule, H. *A Narrative of the Mission to the Court of Ava in 1855* Oxford University Press, Oxford, 1968

INDEX

ACKNOWLEDGEMENTS

Picture Credits

l = left; *r* = right; *c* = centre; *t* = top; *b* = bottom

Front cover: Picturepoint; *inset* J. Allan Cash;

Back cover: *tl* Robert Harding Picture Library; *tr* Simon McBride; *cl* Shostal Associates; *cr* David Paterson; *b* Bavaria-Verlag;

2/3 Cotton Coulson/Susan Griggs Agency; 10 Museo del Prado/Aldus Archive; 11/12 Aldus Archive; 13*t* Sherard 446, Department of Plant Sciences, University of Oxford; 13*b* Aldus Archive; 14*t* Richard Ashworth/Robert Harding Picture Library; 14*b* Timothy Walker/Oxford Botanic Garden; 15 Bodleian Library, MS. Pers. d.29. fol. 21_R; 16*t* Fitzwilliam Museum, Cambridge; 16*br* Hope Collection Portrait/Ashmolean Museum, Oxford; 16*bl* Bodleian Library, Oxford, K.3.6.Art; 17 Bodleian Library, Oxford, Oxonia Illustrata, 1675; 18 Dr. Harold Edgerton, MIT; 19 J. Allan Cash; 20*t* Sir Gerald Hargreaves' ''Atalanta''/Mary Evans Picture Library; 20*b* Hulton-Deutsch Collection; 21*t*/21*b* Aldus Archive; 22/23 Aspect Picture Library; 23 Bibliothèque Nationale, Paris/Robert Harding Picture Library; 24 Picturepoint; 25*t*/25*b* Mary Evans Picture Library; 26 The Metropolitan Museum of Art, The Cloisters Collection, Munsey Fund, 1932 and Gift of John D. Rockefeller, Jr., 1947; 27 Bodleian Library, Oxford, MS Douce 383, fol. 12v.; 28 Koningklijke Nederlands Akadamie van Wetenschappen/Robert Harding Picture Library; 28/29 Paul Broadhurst/Janet & Colin Bord; 29*t* British Library, Ms. 10294.94.90246/Robert Harding Picture Library; 29*b* Simon McBride; 30/31 Simon McBride; 32 Adam Woolfitt/Susan Griggs Agency; 33*l* Aldus Archive; 33*r* Simon McBride; 34/35 City of Manchester Art Galleries/Aldus Archive; 35 Heidelberg University Library, Cod.Pal.Germ.60, fol.179v.; 38/39 Robert Harding Picture Library; 40 The Mansell Collection; 41 Mary Evans Picture Library; 42/43 Sonia Halliday Photographs; 44 Carol Matheson/Tony Stone Associates; 44/45 Richard Ashworth/British Library/Robert Harding Picture Library; 45 Tor Eigeland/Susan Griggs Agency; 46*t* Ancient Art & Architecture; 46*b* British Museum/Michael Holford; 46/47 Tony Stone Associates; 48/49 Spectrum Colour Library; 50/51 Weldon Trannies; 52 Mary Evans Picture Library; 52/53 Picturepoint; 53*t* J. Allan Cash; 53*b* B. Norman/Ancient Art & Architecture; 54/55 Tony Stone Associates; 55 Bridgeman Art Library; 56*t* The Mansell Collection; 56*b* Yukio Ohyama/Q Photo International/Motovun Tokyo; 56/57 Popperfoto; 58/59 H.J. Burkard/Image Bank; 59*l* Gerold Jung/Image Bank; 59*r* Sassoon/Robert Harding Picture Library; 60 Anthony Huxley; 61 Robert Harding Picture Library; 62/63 Colin Jones; 64 Shostal Associates; 64/65 Colin Jones; 65 Raghubir Singh/The John Hillelson Agency; 66/67 Dario Perla/International Stock Photography; 67*l* W.E. Townsend/Bruce Coleman; 67*r* Wilson North/International Stock Photography; 68 Hulton-Deutsch Collection; 69*t* Mary Evans Picture Library; 69*b* Pacific Marianist Archives; photograph by Brother Bertram; 70/71 Colorific!; 71 Virginia Division of Tourism; 72*l* Library of Congress; 72*r* Cook Collection, Valentine Museum, Richmond; 73 Kent & Donna Dannen; 74/75 David Paterson; 76*l*/76*r* Royal Geographical Society; 77 Zefa Picture Library; 78 Aldus Archive; 78/79 Chad Elders/International Stock Photography; 83*r* Michael Holford; 84*t* Instituto Amatller de Arte Hispanico/Arxiu Mas; 85*t* Jean Vertut; 86/87 International Stock Photography; 88*l* British Library, Egerton MS 3028 f.30; 88*r* Janet & Colin Bord; 89*t* Hulton-Deutsch Collection; 89*b* Mary Evans Picture Library; 90/91 William MacQuitty; 92 Photograph by Harry Brown/Griffith Institute, Ashmolean Museum, Oxford; 93*l* Times Newspapers; 93*r* John Frost Historical Newspaper Service; 93*b* Photograph by Harry Brown/Griffith Institute, Ashmolean Museum, Oxford; 94*t* William MacQuitty; 94*b* J. Allan Cash; 94/95 William MacQuitty; 95 William MacQuitty; 96/97*t*/97*b* Photograph by Harry Brown/Griffith Institute, Ashmolean Museum, Oxford; 98 Ancient Art & Architecture; 98/99 Zefa Picture Library; 100*t* Bildarchiv Preussischer Kulturbesitz; 100*b* British Museum; 101*t* Popperfoto; 101*b*/102 Zefa Picture Library; 103 Ancient Art & Architecture; 104 Ecole Française d'Archéologie, Athens; 105*t*/105*b* The Mansell Collection; 106/107 Axel Poignant Archive; 108 Antikvarisk-Topografiska Arkivet; 109*l* Aldus Archive; 109*r* Antikvarisk-Topografiska Arkivet; 110/111 Shostal Associates; 112*t* Ohio Historical Society; 112*r* National Anthropological Archives, Smithsonian Institution; 113 Ohio Historical Society; 114 John Lewis/Historisches Museum, Baasel/Aldus Archive; 114/115 K. Goebel/Zefa Picture Library; 116/117 J. Allan Cash; 117 J. Allan Cash; 118 Scottish National Portrait Gallery; 118/119 Peter Clayton; 119 James Swinson/Das Photo; 120 J. Allan Cash; 121*t* The Mansell Collection; 121*b* J. Allan Cash; 122/123 Susan Griggs Agency; 124*t*/124*b*/124/125 British Library; 126/127 Susan Griggs Agency; 127 Peabody Museum, Harvard University, Photograph by Hillel Burger; 128 Michael Freeman/Bruce Coleman; 129*t*/129*b* B. Norman/Ancient Art & Architecture; 130/131 John P. Stevens/Ancient Art & Architecture; 132 Photograph by E.C. Erdis, Peabody Museum, Yale University & 1913 National Geographic Society; 132/133 Photograph by Hiram Bingham, Peabody Museum, Yale University & 1913 National Geographic Society; 133 Photograph by Hiram Bingham, Peabody Museum, Yale University & 1913 National Geographic Society; 134/135 Landscape Only; 136 The Tate Gallery, London; 136/137 Mary Evans Picture Library; 137*t* National Portrait Gallery; 137*b* Mary Evans Picture Library; 138/139 Roy Miles Fine Paintings, London/Bridgeman Art Library; 142/143 Mark Godfrey/The John Hillelson Agency; 144*t* Robert Harding Picture Library; 144*b* Popperfoto; 145 Popperfoto; 146/147 Tony Stone Associates; 147 Robert Harding Picture Library; 148/149 Robert Harding Picture Library; 149*t* ''British Romantic View of the First Anglo-Burmese War''/Richard M. Cooler; 149*b* Popperfoto; 150 Shirley Heaney/Horizon; 151 Erich Lessing/The John Hillelson Agency; 152*t* Farrell Grehan/Susan Griggs Agency; 152*b* The Mansell Collection; 154/155 Hutchison Library; 155 Paul Ricketts/Horizon; 156 Musée Guimet, Paris/Michael Holford; 157 Musée Guimet, Paris/Michael Holford; 158 Scala; 159 Ed Rooney/Tony Stone Associates; 160/161 Popperfoto; 162 Scala; 163 Dennis Stock/Magnum; 164 Scala; 165*t* The Mansell Collection 165*b* Hulton-Deutsch Collection; 166 Musée Condé de Chantilly/Giraudon; 166/167 Shostal Associates; 168 Dr. Georg Gerster/The John Hillelson Agency; 169*t* Mary Evans Picture Library; 169*b* Bibliothèque Municipal Edouard le Héricher, Avranches; 170 R. Everts/Zefa Picture Library; 171 Adam Woolfitt/Susan Griggs Agency/ 172 Popperfoto; 173*t*/173*b*/174*l*/174*r* Adam Woolfitt/Susan Griggs Agency; 175*t* reproduced by permission of the Provost and Fellows of Eton College; 175*b* Arxiu Mas; 176 Popperfoto; 177*t* The Mansell Collection; 177*b* Popperfoto; 178/179 Marc Riboud/The John Hillelson Agency; 179 Anthony Huxley; 180*t*/180*b*/181 Hulton-Deutsch Collection; 182 British Museum; 183*t* Angelo Novi/Recorded Releasing; 183*b* Zefa Picture Library/ 184*t* Popperfoto; 184*b* Hulton-Deutsch Collection; 185*t* The Mansell Collection; 185*b* Michael Durazzo/The John Hillelson Agency; 186/187 Kotoh/Zefa Picture Library; 188*t* National Museum, Copenhagen; 188*b* Royal Library, Stockholm; 188*r* Theatre Museum, Victoria & Albert Museum; 189 Arne Magnussen/Nordisk Pressefoto; 190/191/191*l*/191*r* Roland & Sabrina Michaud/John Hillelson Agency; 192 Mary Evans Picture Library; 192/193 Hulton-Deutsch Collection; 194*t*/194*b* Picturepoint; 195 Adam Woolfitt/Susan Griggs Agency; 196 Hulton-Deutsch Collection; 196/197 British Library; 197 Picturepoint; 198 APA Photoagency; 199 Rainer Binder/Bavaria-Verlag; 200 Bildarchiv Huber; 201*t* Josef Albert/Bavaria-Verlag; 201*b* The Mansell Collection; 202 Tony Stone Associates; 202/203 Shostal Associates; 206/207 Bildarchiv Huber; 207 Bavaria-Verlag; 208*t* The Mansell Collection; 208*b* Mary Evans Picture Library; 209 The Mansell Collection; 210 J.H. Lelievre/Explorer; 211 Robert Harding Picture Library; 212/213 Illustrated London News; 213*t* Carlos Navajas; 213*b* Ashmolean Museum, Oxford; 214/215/215/216*t*/216*b* Charles Tait; 217*l* By courtesy of the Orkney Library – Photographic Archive; 217*r* Charles Tait; 217*b* By courtesy of the Orkney Library – Photographic Archive; 218 R. Bond/Zefa Picture Library; 219 Sonia Halliday Photographs; 220 Coventry Cathedral; 221*b*/221*c* Illustrated London News; 221*t* John Frost Historical Newspaper Service; 222*t* Northern Picture Library; 222*b* Sefton Photo Library; 223 Woodmansterne Picture Library; 224/225 Coventry Telegraph; 225 Coventry Cathedral;

The publishers and authors would like to thank the following individuals and organizations from whom they received invaluable help in the compilation of this book:

Judith Beadle
Faye Carney
Katie Fischel
William F. Romain
Royal Geographical Society
Dr Chris Scarre
Zilda Tandy

University of Oklahoma for permission to reproduce on pages 122 and 129 extracts from *The Rise and Fall of Maya Civilization*, by J. Eric Thompson. Copyright © 1954, 1966 by the University of Oklahoma.

Map artwork Brian Mayor, Technical Art Services

240